WHO I AM IN CHRIST MEDITATIONS

Dr Michael H Yeager

ISBN: 9798717527729
Imprint: Independently published

DEDICATION

We dedicate this book to those who also face the dilemma of being human, to those who know what it's like to fall short of the glory and yet keep getting back up and striving by faith. We dedicate this to those who keep pressing towards the mark for the prize of the high calling of God in Christ Jesus; fellow believers who are on the journey of life, who stumble but never quit. They just keep getting back up and pressing on. It is only by the supernatural touch of God, the life of Christ, by which we are able to accomplish His will.

THE WORDS OF JESUS

Matthew 28: 19 Go ye therefore, and teach all nations, baptizing them in the name of the Father, and of the Son, and of the Holy Ghost: 20 teaching them to observe all things whatsoever I have commanded you: and, lo, I am with you alway, even unto the end of the world. Amen.

CONTENTS

ACKNOWLEDGMENTS

All of the Scriptures used in this **meditation book** is from the original 1611 version of the King James Bible. I give thanks to **God the Father , Jesus Christ and the Holy Ghost** for the powerful impact the word has had upon my life. Without the word Quickened in my heart by the **Holy Ghost** I would have been lost and undone. To the **Lord** of Heaven and Earth I am eternally indebted for **His** great love and his mercy, **His** protections and **His** provisions, **His** divine guidance and overwhelming goodness. To **Him** be all of the glory, honor and praise for ever and ever: Amen .

***FAITH IS NOT GIVEN FOR US TO TELL GOD WHAT TO DO, BUT FOR US TO HEAR AND TO OBEY GOD IN WHAT HE TELLS US TO DO!**

CHAPTER ONE

THERE WILL MUCH REPITITION IN THIS MEDIATAION BOOK!

THIS MEDITATION BOOK COVERS:

Who I Am in Christ
What I Have in Christ
What I Can Do in Christ
What Is My Purpose in Christ
Where I am Positioned in Christ
What Is My Responsibility In Christ
What Is My Destiny in Christ

IN CHRIST

Foundational Scriptures

Romans 3:24 Being justified freely by his grace through the redemption that is in Christ Jesus.

Romans 8:1There is therefore now no condemnation to them which are in Christ Jesus, who walk not after the flesh, but after the Spirit.

Romans 8:2 For the law of the Spirit of life in Christ Jesus hath made me free from the law of sin and death.

Romans 12:5 So we, being many, are one body in Christ, and every one members one of another.

1 Corinthians 1:2 Unto the church of God which is at Corinth, to them that are sanctified in Christ Jesus, called to be saints, with all that in every place call upon the name of Jesus Christ our Lord, both their's and our's:

1 Corinthians 1:30 But of him are ye in Christ Jesus, who of God is made unto us wisdom, and righteousness, and sanctification, and redemption:

1 Corinthians 15:22 For as in Adam all die, even so in Christ shall all be made alive.

---

2 Corinthians 1:21 Now he which established us with you in Christ, and hath anointed us, is God

---

2 Corinthians 2:14 Now thanks be unto God, which always causes us to triumph in Christ, and makes' manifest the savour of his knowledge by us in every place.

---

2 Corinthians 3:14 But their minds were blinded: for until this day remaines the same vail untaken away in the reading of the old testament; which vail is done away in Christ.

---

2 Corinthians 5:17 Therefore if any man be in Christ, he is a new creature: old things are passed away; behold, all things are become new.

---

2 Corinthians 5:19 To wit, that God was in Christ, reconciling the world unto himself, not imputing their trespasses unto them; and hath committed unto us the word of reconciliation.

Galatians 2:4 And that because of false brethren unawares brought in, who came in privily to spy out our liberty which we have in Christ Jesus, that they might bring us into bondage:

Galatians 3:26 For ye are all the children of God by faith in Christ Jesus.

Galatians 3:28 There is neither Jew nor Greek, there is neither bond nor free, there is neither male nor female: for ye are all one in Christ Jesus.

Galatians 5:6 For in Jesus Christ neither circumcision avails any thing, nor uncircumcision; but faith which works by love.

Galatians 6:15 For in Christ Jesus neither circumcision avails any thing, nor uncircumcision, but a new creature.

Ephesians 1:3 Blessed be the God and Father of our Lord Jesus Christ, who hath blessed us with all spiritual blessings in heavenly places in Christ:

Ephesians 1:10 That in the dispensation of the fullness of times he might gather together in one all things in Christ, both which are in heaven, and which are on earth; even in him:

Ephesians 2:6 And hath raised us up together, and made us sit together in heavenly places in Christ Jesus:

Ephesians 2:10 For we are his workmanship, created in Christ Jesus unto good works, which God hath before ordained that we should walk in them.

Ephesians 3:13 But now in Christ Jesus ye who sometimes were far off are made nigh by the blood of Christ.

Ephesians 3:6 That the Gentiles should be fellow heirs, and of the same body, and partakers of his promise in Christ by the gospel:

Philippians 3:13-14 Brethren, I count not myself to have apprehended: but this one thing I do, forgetting those things which are behind, and reaching forth unto those things which are before, I press toward the mark for the prize of the high calling of God in Christ Jesus.

Colossians 1:28 Whom we preach, warning every man, and teaching every man in all wisdom; that we may present every man perfect in Christ Jesus:

1Thessalonians 4:16 For the Lord himself shall descend from heaven with a shout, with the voice of the archangel, and with the trump of God: and the dead in Christ shall rise first:

---

1 Thessalonians 5:18 In every thing give thanks: for this is the will of God in Christ Jesus concerning you.

---

1 Timothy 1:14 And the grace of our Lord was exceeding abundant with faith and love which is in Christ Jesus.

---

2 Timothy 1:9 Who hath saved us, and called us with an holy calling, not according to our works, but according to his own purpose and grace, which was given us in Christ Jesus before the world began,

---

2 Timothy 1:13 Hold fast the form of sound words, which thou hast heard of me, in faith and love which is in Christ Jesus.

---

2 Timothy 2:1 Thou therefore, my son, be strong in the grace that is in Christ Jesus.

---

2 Timothy 2:10 Therefore I endure all things for the elect's sakes, that they may also obtain the salvation which is in Christ Jesus with eternal glory.

---

2 Timothy 3:15 And that from a child thou hast known the holy scriptures, which are able to make thee wise unto salvation through faith which is in Christ Jesus.

Philemon 1:6 That the communication of thy faith may become effectual by the acknowledging of every good thing which is in you in Christ Jesus.

---

2 Peter 1:8 For if these things be in you, and abound, they make you that ye shall neither be barren nor unfruitful in the knowledge of our Lord Jesus Christ.

---

2 John 1:9 Whosoever transgresses, and abides not in the doctrine of Christ, hath not God. He that abides in the doctrine of Christ, he hath both the Father and the Son.

Christ the Perfect Will of God

God is diligently searching for those who will simply be in agreement with him. What happened is that when man partook of sin he was put out of harmony with God. Jesus Christ was one with the Father, in word, deed and action. He boldly declared that if you hear me you hear the Father. The words he spoke he declared were not his but the Fathers. Even the works that he did were not of him but from the Father. The last words we hear Christ pray before he went to the garden of Gethsemane were: ***Father make them one with us even as we are one!***

IN HIM

John 1:4 In him was life; and the life was the light of men.

John 3:15-16 That whosoever believeth in him should not perish, but have eternal life. For God so loved the world, that he gave his only begotten Son, that whosoever believeth in him should not perish, but have everlasting life.

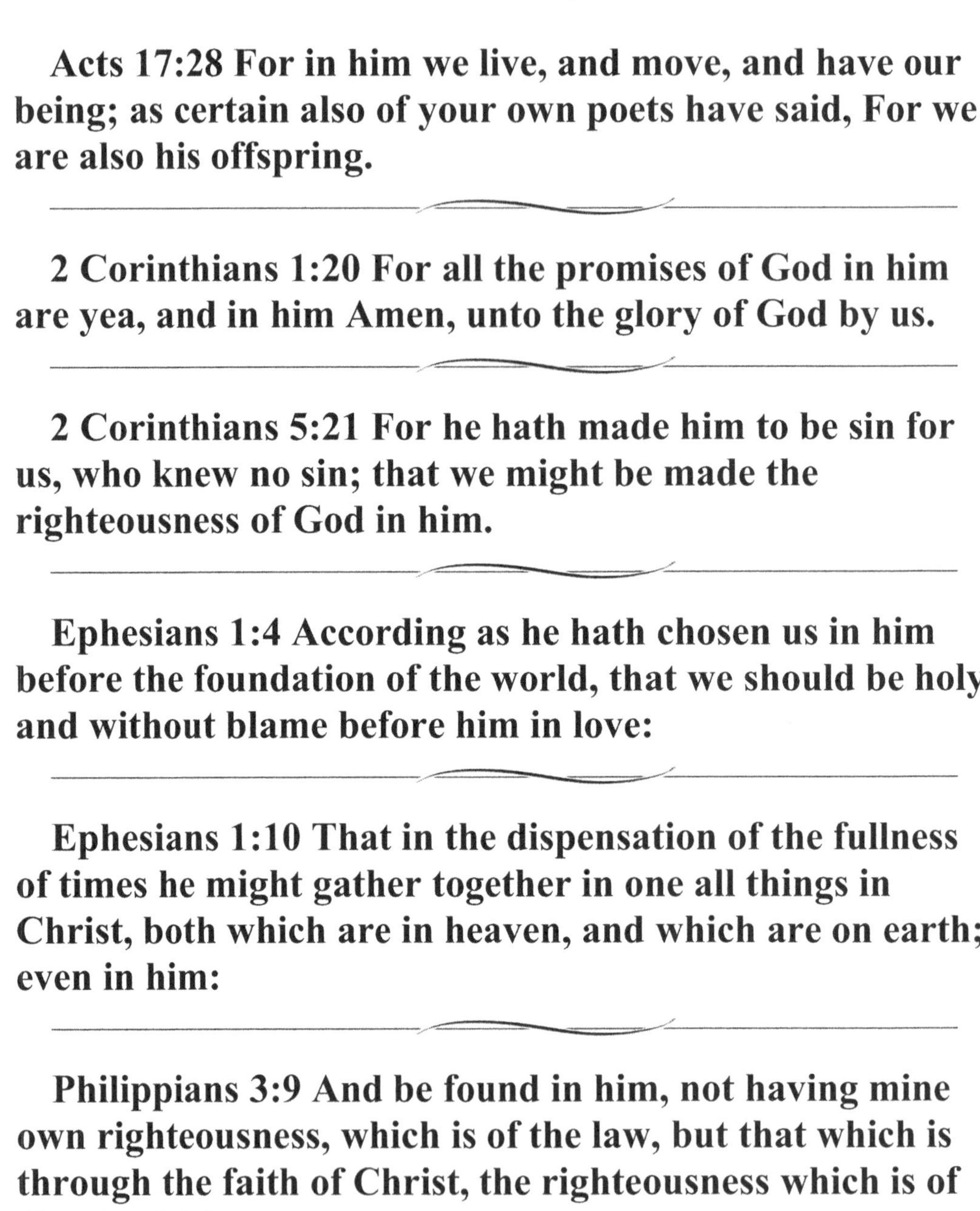

Acts 17:28 For in him we live, and move, and have our being; as certain also of your own poets have said, For we are also his offspring.

2 Corinthians 1:20 For all the promises of God in him are yea, and in him Amen, unto the glory of God by us.

2 Corinthians 5:21 For he hath made him to be sin for us, who knew no sin; that we might be made the righteousness of God in him.

Ephesians 1:4 According as he hath chosen us in him before the foundation of the world, that we should be holy and without blame before him in love:

Ephesians 1:10 That in the dispensation of the fullness of times he might gather together in one all things in Christ, both which are in heaven, and which are on earth; even in him:

Philippians 3:9 And be found in him, not having mine own righteousness, which is of the law, but that which is through the faith of Christ, the righteousness which is of God by faith:

Colossians 2:6-7 As ye have therefore received Christ Jesus the Lord, so walk ye in him: Rooted and built up in him, and established in the faith, as ye have been taught, abounding therein with thanksgiving.

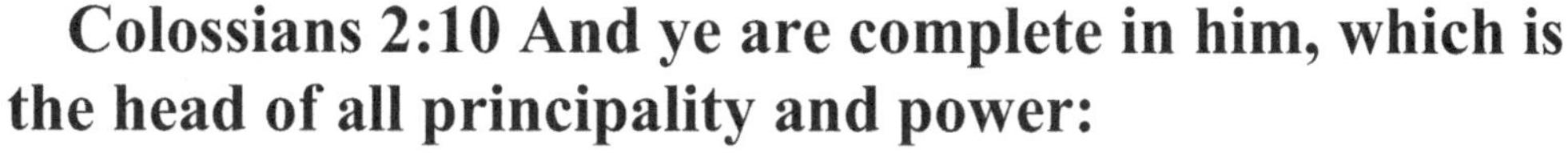

Colossians 2:10 And ye are complete in him, which is the head of all principality and power:

---

1 John 2:5-6 But whoso keeps his word, in him verily is the love of God perfected: hereby know we that we are in him. He that says he abides in him ought himself also so to walk, even as he walked.

---

1 John 2:8 Again, a new commandment I write unto you, which thing is true in him and in you: because the darkness is past, and the true light now shines.

---

1 John 2:27-28 But the anointing which ye have received of him abides in you, and ye need not that any man teach you: but as the same anointing teaches you of all things, and is truth, and is no lie, and even as it hath taught you, ye shall abide in him. And now, little children, abide in him; that, when he shall appear, we may have confidence, and not be ashamed before him at his coming.

---

1 John 3:3 And every man that hath this hope in him purifies himself, even as he is pure.

---

1 John 3:5-6 And ye know that he was manifested to take away our sins; and in him is no sin. Whosoever abides in him sins not: whosoever sins hath not seen him, neither known him.

---

1 John 3:24 And he that keeps his commandments dwells in him, and he in him. And hereby we know that he abides in us, by the Spirit which he hath given us.

1 John 4:13 Hereby know we that we dwell in him, and he in us, because he hath given us of his Spirit.

1 John 5:14-15 And this is the confidence that we have in him, that, if we ask any thing according to his will, he hears us: And if we know that he hear us, whatsoever we ask, we know that we have the petitions that we desired of him.

1 John 5:20 And we know that the Son of God is come, and hath given us an understanding, that we may know him that is true, and we are in him that is true, even in his Son Jesus Christ. This is the true God, and eternal life.

IN THE BELOVED

Ephesians 1:6 To the praise of the glory of his grace, wherein he hath made us accepted in the beloved.

1 Corinthians 15:58 Therefore, my beloved brethren, be ye stedfast, unmoveable, always abounding in the work of the Lord, forasmuch as ye know that your labour is not in vain in the Lord.

2 Corinthians 7:1 Having therefore these promises, dearly beloved, let us cleanse ourselves from all filthiness of the flesh and spirit, perfecting holiness in the fear of God.

Philippians 4:1 Therefore, my brethren dearly beloved and longed for, my joy and crown, so stand fast in the Lord, my dearly beloved.

James 2:5 Hearken, my beloved brethren, Hath not God chosen the poor of this world rich in faith, and heirs of the kingdom which he hath promised to them that love him?

Jude 1:20 But ye, beloved, building up yourselves on your most holy faith, praying in the Holy Ghost,

IN THE LORD

Ephesians 5:8 For ye were sometimes darkness, but now are ye light in the Lord: walk as children of light:

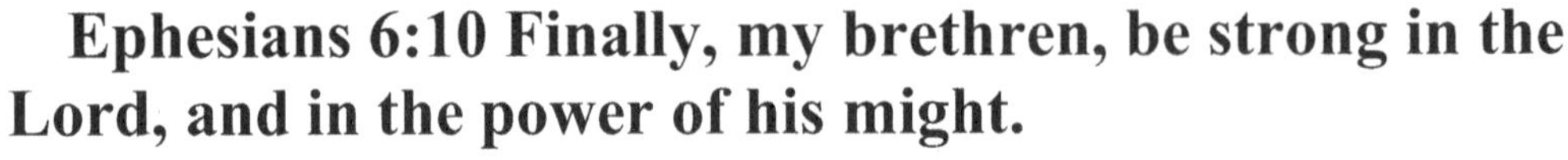

Ephesians 6:10 Finally, my brethren, be strong in the Lord, and in the power of his might.

---

1 Samuel 2:1 And Hannah prayed, and said, My heart rejoiceth in the Lord, mine horn is exalted in the Lord: my mouth is enlarged over mine enemies; because I rejoice in thy salvation.

---

2 Kings 18:5 He trusted in the Lord God of Israel; so that after him was none like him among all the kings of Judah, nor any that were before him.

---

2 Chronicles 20:20 ..... Jehoshaphat stood and said, Hear me, O Judah, and ye inhabitants of Jerusalem; Believe in the Lord your God, so shall ye be established; believe his prophets, so shall ye prosper.

Psalm 32:11Be glad in the Lord, and rejoice, ye righteous: and shout for joy, all ye that are upright in heart.

Psalm 33:1Rejoice in the Lord, O ye righteous: for praise is comely for the upright.

Psalm 37:3 Trust in the Lord, and do good; so shalt thou dwell in the land, and verily thou shalt be fed.

Psalm 37:4 Delight thyself also in the Lord: and he shall give thee the desires of thine heart.

Psalm 56:10 In God will I praise his word: in the Lord will I praise his word.

Psalm 118:8 It is better to trust in the Lord than to put confidence in man.

Proverbs 3:5 Trust in the Lord with all thine heart; and lean not unto thine own understanding.6 In all thy ways acknowledge him, and he shall direct thy paths.

Isaiah 26:4 Trust ye in the Lord for ever: for in the Lord Jehovah is everlasting strength:

2 Corinthians 10:17 But he that glorieth, let him glory in the Lord.

Ephesians 2:21 In whom all the building fitly framed together groweth unto an holy temple in the Lord:

Philippians 3:1 Finally, my brethren, rejoice in the Lord. To write the same things to you, to me indeed is not grievous, but for you it is safe.

Philippians 4:1 Therefore, my brethren dearly beloved and longed for, my joy and crown, so stand fast in the Lord, my dearly beloved.

Philippians 4:4 Rejoice in the Lord always: and again I say, Rejoice.

---

1 Thessalonians 3:8 For now we live, if ye stand fast in the Lord.

Revelation 14:13 And I heard a voice from heaven saying unto me, Write, Blessed are the dead which die in the Lord from henceforth: Yea, saith the Spirit, that they may rest from their labours; and their works do follow them.

IN WHOM

Romans 10:14How then shall they call on him in whom they have not believed? and how shall they believe in him of whom they have not heard? and how shall they hear without a preacher?

---

2 Corinthians 1:10Who delivered us from so great a death, and doth deliver: in whom we trust that he will yet deliver

---

Ephesians 1:7 In whom we have redemption through his blood, the forgiveness of sins, according to the riches of his grace;

Ephesians 1:11 In whom also we have obtained an inheritance, being predestinated according to the purpose of him who works all things after the counsel of his own will:

Ephesians 1:13 In whom ye also trusted, after that ye heard the word of truth, the gospel of your salvation: in whom also after that ye believed, ye were sealed with that holy Spirit of promise,

---

Ephesians 2:21-22 In whom all the building fitly framed together grows unto an holy temple in the Lord: In whom ye also are builds together for an habitation of God through the Spirit.

Ephesians 3:12 In whom we have boldness and access with confidence by the faith of him.

Colossians 1:14 In whom we have redemption through his blood, even the forgiveness of sins:

Colossians 2:3 In whom are hid all the treasures of wisdom and knowledge.

Colossians 2:11 In whom also ye are circumcised with the circumcision made without hands, in putting off the body of the sins of the flesh by the circumcision of Christ:

---

1 Peter 1:8 Whom having not seen, you love; in whom, though now ye see him not, yet believing, ye rejoice with joy unspeakable and full of glory:

JESUS CHRIST

All of our life as a believer is based upon the revelation of Jesus Christ. From Matthew chapter 1 to the end of the book of Revelation, Jesus Christ is spoken of in a personal way almost 10,000 times.

It is at the revelation of Jesus Christ in which faith will arise in your heart to accomplish the perfect will of the Father. Without this revelation of who Jesus Christ really is, we will not be to accomplish anything of eternal value.

Go over these Scriptures slowly as you meditate upon them, asking the Holy Spirit to quicken them to you in a profound way, in order to transform you into the likeness and the image of God. In order to become a partaker of all of God's wonderful nature and divine characteristics.

CHAPTER TWO

BY CHRIST

Romans 3:22 Even the righteousness of God which is by faith of Jesus Christ unto all and upon all them that believe: for there is no difference:

Romans 5:15 But not as the offence, so also is the free gift. For if through the offence of one many be dead,

much more the grace of God, and the gift by grace, which is by one man, Jesus Christ, hath abounded unto many.

Romans 5:17-19 For if by one man's offence death reigned by one; much more they which receive abundance of grace and of the gift of righteousness shall reign in life by one, Jesus Christ.) Therefore as by the offence of one judgment came upon all men to condemnation; even so by the righteousness of one the free gift came upon all men unto justification of life. For as by one man's disobedience many were made sinners, so by the obedience of one shall many be made righteous.

Romans 7:4 Wherefore, my brethren, ye also are become dead to the law by the body of Christ; that ye should be married to another, even to him who is raised from the dead, that we should bring forth fruit unto God.

---

1 Corinthians 1:4 I thank my God always on your behalf, for the grace of God which is given you by Jesus Christ;

---

2 Corinthians 1:5For as the sufferings of Christ abound in us, so our consolation also aboundeth by Christ.

Galatians 2:16 Knowing that a man is not justified by the works of the law, but by the faith of Jesus Christ, even we have believed in Jesus Christ, that we might be justified by the faith of Christ, and not by the works of the law: for by the works of the law shall no flesh be justified. 17But if, while we seek to be justified by Christ,

we ourselves also are found sinners, is therefore Christ the minister of sin? God forbid.

Ephesians 1:5 Having predestinated us unto the adoption of children by Jesus Christ to himself, according to the good pleasure of his will,

---

Ephesians 3:21 Unto him be glory in the church by Christ Jesus throughout all ages, world without end. Amen.

Philippians 1:11 Being filled with the fruits of righteousness, which are by Jesus Christ, unto the glory and praise of God.

Philippians 4:19 But my God shall supply all your need according to his riches in glory by Christ Jesus.

---

1 Peter 1:3 Blessed be the God and Father of our Lord Jesus Christ, which according to his abundant mercy hath begotten us again unto a lively hope by the resurrection of Jesus Christ from the dead,

---

1 Peter 2:5 Ye also, as lively stones, are built up a spiritual house, an holy priesthood, to offer up spiritual sacrifices, acceptable to God by Jesus Christ.

---

1 Peter 5:10 But the God of all grace, who hath called us unto his eternal glory by Christ Jesus, after that ye

have suffered a while, make you perfect, establish, strengthen, settle you.

In the Name of Jesus

The following scriptures are a declaration of the power and authority that we have in the name of Jesus. There is no other name that has been exalted above all else to bring in to subjection all of the powers and authorities that there is. As we submit to Jesus Christ, putting absolute faith and confidence in His name we will enter into a wonderful realm of victory. For us to be defeated, God would have to be defeated. Everything we do we do in the name of Jesus Christ is to be for the glory of the Father. Let us feast upon His wonderful Name drinking in its beauty, and eating of its substance.

BY HIM

1 Corinthians 1:5 That in every thing ye are enriched by him, in all utterance, and in all knowledge;

---

1 Corinthians 8:6 But to us there is but one God, the Father, of whom are all things, and we in him; and one Lord Jesus Christ, by whom are all things, and we by him.

Colossians 1:16-17 For by him were all things created, that are in heaven, and that are in earth, visible and invisible, whether they be thrones, or dominions, or principalities, or powers: all things were created by him,

and for him: And he is before all things, and by him all things consist.

Colossians 1:20 And, having made peace through the blood of his cross, by him to reconcile all things unto himself; by him, I say, whether they be things in earth, or things in heaven.

Colossians 3:17 And whatsoever ye do in word or deed, do all in the name of the Lord Jesus, giving thanks to God and the Father by him.

Hebrews 7:25 Wherefore he is able also to save them to the uttermost that come unto God by him, seeing he ever lives to make intercession for them.

Hebrews 13:15 By him therefore let us offer the sacrifice of praise to God continually, that is, the fruit of our lips giving thanks to his name.

---

1 Peter 1:21 Who by him do believe in God, that raised him up from the dead, and gave him glory; that your faith and hope might be in God.

BY HIMSELF

Jeremiah 51:14 The Lord of hosts hath sworn by himself, saying, Surely I will fill thee with men, as with caterpillers; and they shall lift up a shout against thee.

Hebrews 1:3 Who being the brightness of his glory, and the express image of his person, and upholding all things by the word of his power, when he had by himself purged our sins, sat down on the right hand of the Majesty on high:

Hebrews 6:13 For when God made promise to Abraham, because he could swear by no greater, he sware by himself,

---

Hebrews 9:26 For then must he often have suffered since the foundation of the world: but now once in the end of the world hath he appeared to put away sin by the sacrifice of himself.

BY HIS BLOOD

Romans 5:9 Much more then, being now justified by his blood, we shall be saved from wrath through him.

Ephesians 1:7 In whom we have redemption through his blood, the forgiveness of sins, according to the riches of his grace;

Colossians 1:14 In whom we have redemption through his blood, even the forgiveness of sins:

Hebrews 9:11-12 But Christ being come an high priest of good things to come, by a greater and more perfect tabernacle, not made with hands, that is to say, not of this building; Neither by the blood of goats and calves, but by his own blood he entered in once into the holy place, having obtained eternal redemption for us.

Hebrews 9:14-15 How much more shall the blood of Christ, who through the eternal Spirit offered himself without spot to God, purge your conscience from dead works to serve the living God? And for this cause he is the mediator of the new testament, that by means of death, for the redemption of the transgressions that were under the first testament, they which are called might receive the promise of eternal inheritance.

Hebrews 10:19-20 Having therefore, brethren, boldness to enter into the holiest by the blood of Jesus, By a new and living way, which he hath consecrated for us, through the veil, that is to say, his flesh;

1 John 1:7 But if we walk in the light, as he is in the light, we have fellowship one with another, and the blood of Jesus Christ his Son cleanses us from all sin.

Romans 3:24 Being justified freely by his grace through the redemption that is in Christ Jesus:25 Whom God hath set forth to be a propitiation through faith in his blood, to declare his righteousness for the remission of sins that are past, through the forbearance of God;

---

1 Peter 1:19 But with the precious blood of Christ, as of a lamb without blemish and without spot:20 Who verily was foreordained before the foundation of the world, but was manifest in these last times for you,

---

Hebrews 9:22 And almost all things are by the law purged with blood; and without shedding of blood is no remission.

Revelation 5:9 And they sung a new song, saying, Thou art worthy to take the book, and to open the seals thereof: for thou wast slain, and hast redeemed us to God by thy blood out of every kindred, and tongue, and people, and nation;

Revelation 1:5 And from Jesus Christ, who is the faithful witness, and the first begotten of the dead, and the prince of the kings of the earth. Unto him that loved us, and washed us from our sins in his own blood,

FROM WHOM

Ephesians 4:16 From whom the whole body fitly joined together and compacted by that which every joint supplies, according to the effectual working in the measure of every part, makes increase of the body unto the edifying of itself in love.

Colossians 2:19 And not holding the Head, from which all the body by joints and bands having nourishment ministered, and knit together, increases with the increase of God.

OF CHRIST

2 Corinthians 2:15 For we are unto God a sweet savor of Christ, in them that are saved, and in them that perish:

Philippians 3:12 Not as though I had already attained, either were already perfect: but I follow after, if that I may apprehend that for which also I am apprehended of Christ Jesus.

Colossians 2:17 Which are a shadow of things to come; but the body is of Christ.

Colossians 3:24 Knowing that of the Lord ye shall receive the reward of the inheritance: for ye serve the Lord Christ.

OF HIM

Romans 11:36For of him, and through him, and to him, are all things: to whom be glory for ever. Amen.

1 Corinthians 1:30 But of him are ye in Christ Jesus, who of God is made unto us wisdom, and righteousness, and sanctification, and redemption:

2 Corinthians 5:9Wherefore we labour, that, whether present or absent, we may be accepted of him.

Ephesians 1:17 That the God of our Lord Jesus Christ, the Father of glory, may give unto you the spirit of wisdom and revelation in the knowledge of him:

Ephesians 1:23 Which is his body, the fulness of him that filleth all in all.

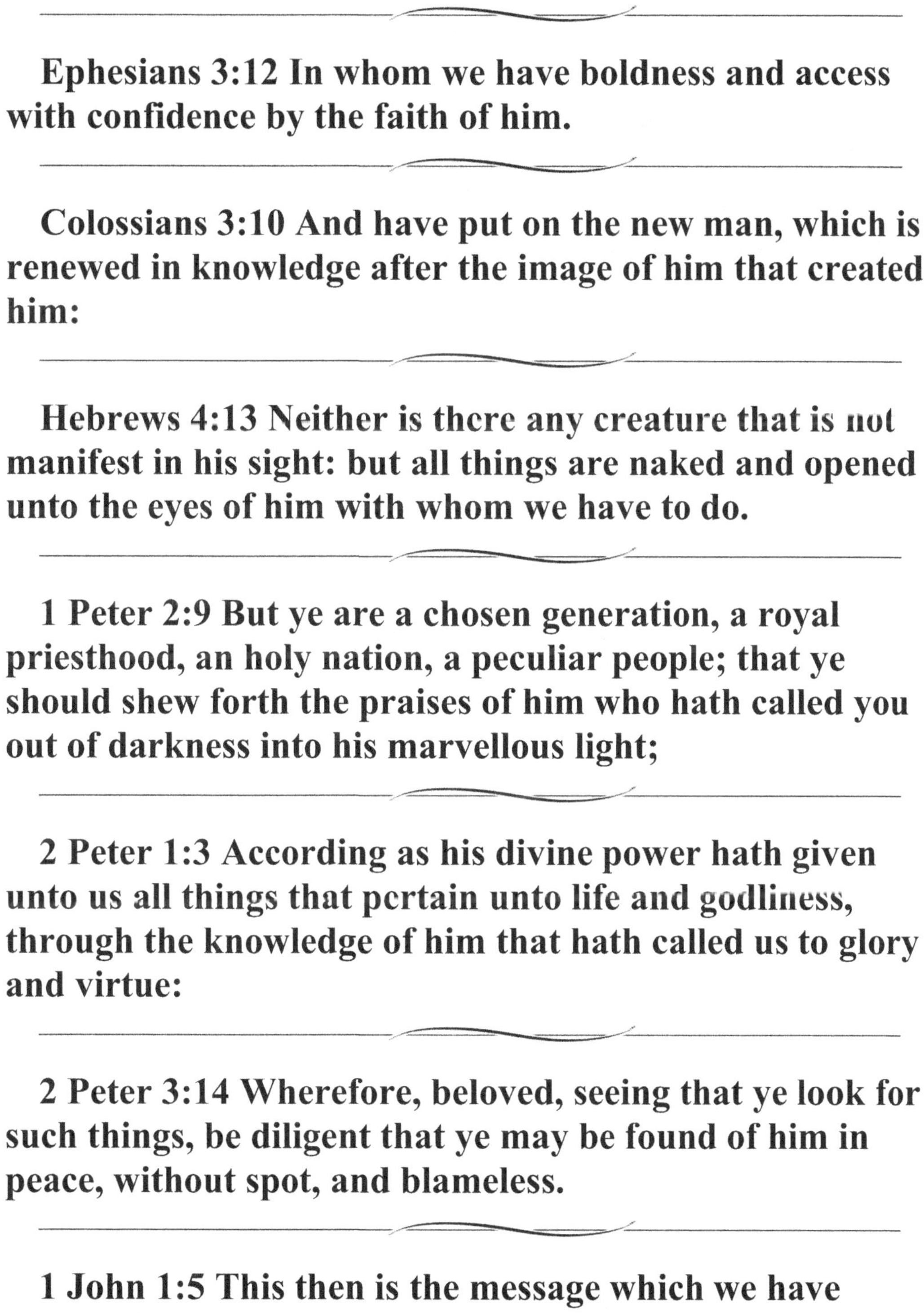

Ephesians 3:12 In whom we have boldness and access with confidence by the faith of him.

Colossians 3:10 And have put on the new man, which is renewed in knowledge after the image of him that created him:

Hebrews 4:13 Neither is there any creature that is not manifest in his sight: but all things are naked and opened unto the eyes of him with whom we have to do.

1 Peter 2:9 But ye are a chosen generation, a royal priesthood, an holy nation, a peculiar people; that ye should shew forth the praises of him who hath called you out of darkness into his marvellous light;

2 Peter 1:3 According as his divine power hath given unto us all things that pertain unto life and godliness, through the knowledge of him that hath called us to glory and virtue:

2 Peter 3:14 Wherefore, beloved, seeing that ye look for such things, be diligent that ye may be found of him in peace, without spot, and blameless.

1 John 1:5 This then is the message which we have heard of him, and declare unto you, that God is light, and in him is no darkness at all.

1 John 2:27 But the anointing which ye have received of him abideth in you, and ye need not that any man teach you: but as the same anointing teacheth you of all things, and is truth, and is no lie, and even as it hath taught you, ye shall abide in him.

1 John 2:29 If ye know that he is righteous, ye know that every one that doeth righteousness is born of him.

1 John 3:22 And whatsoever we ask, we receive of him, because we keep his commandments, and do those things that are pleasing in his sight.

1 John 5:1 Whosoever believeth that Jesus is the Christ is born of God: and every one that loveth him that begat loveth him also that is begotten of him.

1 John 5:15 And if we know that he hear us, whatsoever we ask, we know that we have the petitions that we desired of him.

THROUGH CHRIST

Romans 5:1 Therefore being justified by faith, we have peace with God through our Lord Jesus Christ:

Romans 5:11 And not only so, but we also joy in God through our Lord Jesus Christ, by whom we have now received the atonement.

Romans 6:11 Likewise reckon ye also yourselves to be dead indeed unto sin, but alive unto God through Jesus Christ our Lord.

Romans 6:23 For the wages of sin is death; but the gift of God is eternal life through Jesus Christ our Lord.

Romans 1:8 First, I thank my God through Jesus Christ for you all, that your faith is spoken of throughout the whole world.

Romans 6:11 Likewise reckon ye also yourselves to be dead indeed unto sin, but alive unto God through Jesus Christ our Lord.

Romans 7:25 I thank God through Jesus Christ our Lord. So then with the mind I myself serve the law of God; but with the flesh the law of sin.

Romans 15:17 I have therefore whereof I may glory through Jesus Christ in those things which pertain to God.

Romans 16:27 To God only wise, be glory through Jesus Christ for ever. Amen.

---

1 Corinthians 15:57 But thanks be to God, which gives us the victory through our Lord Jesus Christ.

---

2 Corinthians 3:4And such trust have we through Christ to God-ward:

Galatians 3:13-14 Christ hath redeemed us from the curse of the law, being made a curse for us: for it is written, Cursed is every one that hangs on a tree: That the blessing of Abraham might come on the Gentiles through Jesus Christ; that we might receive the promise of the Spirit through faith.

Galatians 4:7 Wherefore thou art no more a servant, but a son; and if a son, then an heir of God through Christ.

Ephesians 2:7 That in the ages to come he might show the exceeding riches of his grace in his kindness toward us through Christ Jesus.

Philippians 4:6-7 Be careful for nothing; but in every thing by prayer and supplication with thanksgiving let your requests be made known unto God. And the peace of God, which passes all understanding, shall keep your hearts and minds through Christ Jesus.

Philippians 4:13 I can do all things through Christ which strengthens me.

Titus 3:6 Which he shed on us abundantly through Jesus Christ our Saviour;

Hebrews 10:10 By which will we are sanctified through the offering of the body of Jesus Christ once for all.

Hebrews 13:10-21 Now the God of peace, that brought again from the dead our Lord Jesus, that great shepherd of the sheep, through the blood of the everlasting covenant make you perfect in every good work to do his will, working in you that which is well pleasing in his sight, through Jesus Christ; to whom be glory for ever and ever. Amen.

---

1 Peter 4:11 If any man speak, let him speak as the oracles of God; if any man minister, let him do it as of the ability which God giveth: that God in all things may be glorified through Jesus Christ, to whom be praise and dominion for ever and ever. Amen.

THROUGH HIM

John 1:7 The same came for a witness, to bear witness of the Light, that all men through him might believe.

John 3:17 For God sent not his Son into the world to condemn the world; but that the world through him might be saved.

Romans 5:9 Much more then, being now justified by his blood, we shall be saved from wrath through him.

Romans 8:37 Nay, in all these things we are more than conquerors through him that loved us.

Romans 11:36 For of him, and through him, and to him, are all things: to whom be glory for ever. Amen.

Ephesians 2:18 For through him we both have access by one Spirit unto the Father.

1 John 4:9 In this was manifested the love of God toward us, because that God sent his only begotten Son into the world, that we might live through him.

WITH CHRIST

Romans 6:8 Now if we be dead with Christ, we believe that we shall also live with him:

Romans 8:17 And if children, then heirs; heirs of God, and joint-heirs with Christ; if so be that we suffer with him, that we may be also glorified together.

Galatians 2:20 I am crucified with Christ: nevertheless I live; yet not I, but Christ liveth in me: and the life which I now live in the flesh I live by the faith of the Son of God, who loved me, and gave himself for me.

Ephesians 2:5 Even when we were dead in sins, hath quickened us together with Christ, (by grace ye are saved;)

Ephesians 2:12 That at that time ye were without Christ, being aliens from the commonwealth of Israel, and strangers from the covenants of promise, having no hope, and without God in the world:

Philippians 1:23 For I am in a strait betwixt two, having a desire to depart, and to be with Christ; which is far better:

Colossians 2:20 Wherefore if ye be dead with Christ from the rudiments of the world, why, as though living in the world, are ye subject to ordinances,

---

Colossians 3:1 If ye then be risen with Christ, seek those things which are above, where Christ sitteth on the right hand of God.

Colossians 3:3For ye are dead, and your life is hid with Christ in God.

Revelation 20:4And I saw thrones, and they sat upon them, and judgment was given unto them: and I saw the souls of them that were beheaded for the witness of Jesus, and for the word of God, and which had not worshipped the beast, neither his image, neither had received his mark upon their foreheads, or in their hands; and they lived and reigned with Christ a thousand years.

WITH HIM

Romans 6:4 Therefore we are buried with him by baptism into death: that like as Christ was raised up from the dead by the glory of the Father, even so we also should walk in newness of life.

Romans 6:6 Knowing this, that our old man is crucified with him, that the body of sin might be destroyed, that henceforth we should not serve sin.

Romans 6:8 Now if we be dead with Christ, we believe that we shall also live with him:

Romans 8:32 He that spared not his own Son, but delivered him up for us all, how shall he not with him also freely give us all things?

---

2 Corinthians 13:4 For though he was crucified through weakness, yet he lives by the power of God. For we also are weak in him, but we shall live with him by the power of God toward you.

Colossians 2:12 -15 Buried with him in baptism, wherein also ye are risen with him through the faith of the operation of God, who hath raised him from the dead. And you, being dead in your sins and the uncircumcision of your flesh, hath he quickened together with him, having forgiven you all trespasses; Blotting out the handwriting of ordinances that was against us, which was contrary to us, and took it out of the way, nailing it to his cross; And having spoiled principalities and powers, he made a show of them openly, triumphing over them in it.

Colossians 3:4 When Christ, who is our life, shall appear, then shall ye also appear with him in glory.

---

2 Timothy 2:11-12 It is a faithful saying: For if we be dead with him, we shall also live with him: If we suffer, we shall also reign with him: if we deny him, he also will deny us:

BY HIM

John 6:57 As the living Father hath sent me, and I live by the Father: so he that feeds on me, even he shall live by me.

John 14:6 Jesus said to him, "I am the way, the truth, and the life. No one comes to the Father except through Me.

Acts 2:22 Ye men of Israel, hear these words; Jesus of Nazareth, a man approved of God among you by miracles and wonders and signs, which God did by him in the midst of you, as ye yourselves also know:

Acts 3:16 And his name through faith in his name hath made this man strong, whom ye see and know: yea, the faith which is by him hath given him this perfect soundness in the presence of you all.

Acts 4:10 Be it known unto you all, and to all the people of Israel, that by the name of Jesus Christ of Nazareth,

whom ye crucified, whom God raised from the dead, even by him doth this man stand here before you whole.

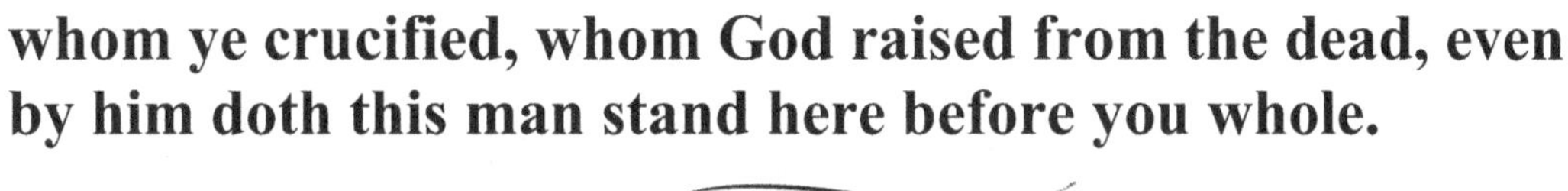

Acts 13:39 And by him all that believe are justified from all things, from which ye could not be justified by the law of Moses.

1 Corinthians 1:5 That in every thing ye are enriched by him, in all utterance, and in all knowledge;

1 Corinthians 8:6 But to us there is but one God, the Father, of whom are all things, and we in him; and one Lord Jesus Christ, by whom are all things, and we by him.

1 Corinthians 16:2 Upon the first day of the week let every one of you lay by him in store, as God hath prospered him, that there be no gatherings when I come.

Ephesians 4:21 If so be that ye have heard him, and have been taught by him, as the truth is in Jesus:

Colossians 1:16 For by him were all things created, that are in heaven, and that are in earth, visible and invisible, whether they be thrones, or dominions, or principalities, or powers: all things were created by him, and for him:

Colossians 1:17 And he is before all things, and by him all things consist.

Colossians 1:20 And, having made peace through the blood of his cross, by him to reconcile all things unto himself; by him, I say, whether they be things in earth, or things in heaven.

Colossians 3:17 And whatsoever ye do in word or deed, do all in the name of the Lord Jesus, giving thanks to God and the Father by him.

Hebrews 1:3 Who being the brightness of his glory, and the express image of his person, and upholding all things by the word of his power, when he had by himself purged our sins, sat down on the right hand of the Majesty on high:

Hebrews 7:21 (For those priests were made without an oath; but this with an oath by him that said unto him, The Lord sware and will not repent, Thou art a priest for ever after the order of Melchisedec:)

Hebrews 7:25 Wherefore he is able also to save them to the uttermost that come unto God by him, seeing he ever liveth to make intercession for them.

Hebrews 13:15 By him therefore let us offer the sacrifice of praise to God continually, that is, the fruit of our lips giving thanks to his name.

1 Peter 1:21 Who by him do believe in God, that raised him up from the dead, and gave him glory; that your faith and hope might be in God.

---

1 Peter 2:14 Or unto governors, as unto them that are sent by him for the punishment of evildoers, and for the praise of them that do well.

Revelation 10:6 And sware by him that liveth for ever and ever, who created heaven, and the things that therein are, and the earth, and the things that therein are, and the sea, and the things which are therein, that there should be time no longer:

IN ME

John 6:56 He that eateth my flesh, and drinketh my blood, dwelleth in me, and I in him.

John 10:38 But if I do, though ye believe not me, believe the works: that ye may know, and believe, that the Father is in me, and I in him.

John 11:25 Jesus said unto her, I am the resurrection, and the life: he that believeth in me, though he were dead, yet shall he live:

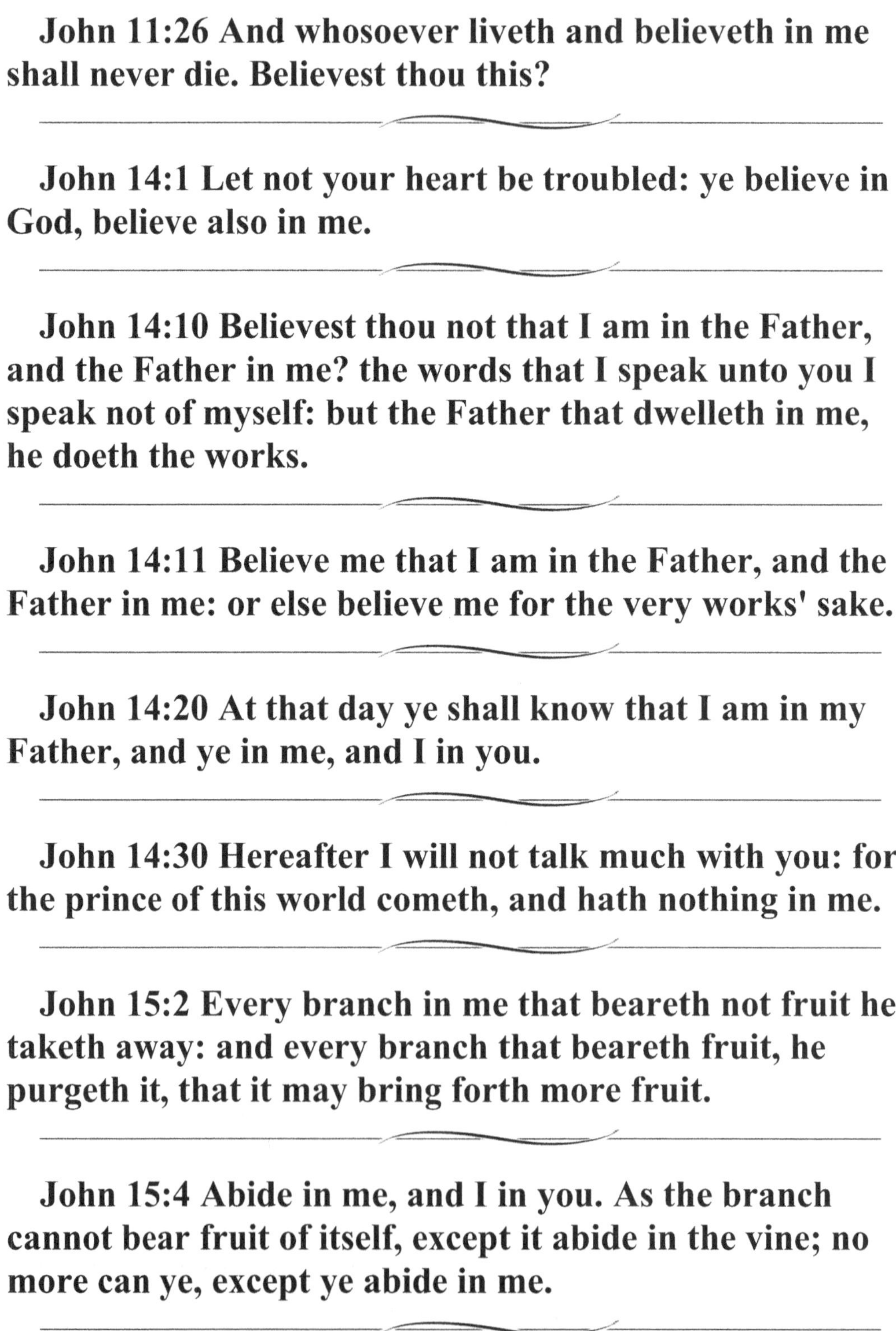

John 11:26 And whosoever liveth and believeth in me shall never die. Believest thou this?

John 14:1 Let not your heart be troubled: ye believe in God, believe also in me.

John 14:10 Believest thou not that I am in the Father, and the Father in me? the words that I speak unto you I speak not of myself: but the Father that dwelleth in me, he doeth the works.

John 14:11 Believe me that I am in the Father, and the Father in me: or else believe me for the very works' sake.

John 14:20 At that day ye shall know that I am in my Father, and ye in me, and I in you.

John 14:30 Hereafter I will not talk much with you: for the prince of this world cometh, and hath nothing in me.

John 15:2 Every branch in me that beareth not fruit he taketh away: and every branch that beareth fruit, he purgeth it, that it may bring forth more fruit.

John 15:4 Abide in me, and I in you. As the branch cannot bear fruit of itself, except it abide in the vine; no more can ye, except ye abide in me.

John 15:5 I am the vine, ye are the branches: He that abideth in me, and I in him, the same bringeth forth much fruit: for without me ye can do nothing.

John 15:6 If a man abide not in me, he is cast forth as a branch, and is withered; and men gather them, and cast them into the fire, and they are burned.

John 15:7 If ye abide in me, and my words abide in you, ye shall ask what ye will, and it shall be done unto you.

John 16:33 These things I have spoken unto you, that in me ye might have peace. In the world ye shall have tribulation: but be of good cheer; I have overcome the world.

John 17:21 That they all may be one; as thou, Father, art in me, and I in thee, that they also may be one in us: that the world may believe that thou hast sent me.

John 17:23I in them, and thou in me, that they may be made perfect in one; and that the world may know that thou hast sent me, and hast loved them, as thou hast loved me.

Galatians 1:16 To reveal his Son in me, that I might preach him among the heathen; immediately I conferred not with flesh and blood:

Galatians 1:24 And they glorified God in me.

Galatians 2:8 (For he that wrought effectually in Peter to the apostleship of the circumcision, the same was mighty in me toward the Gentiles:)

Galatians 2:20 I am crucified with Christ: nevertheless I live; yet not I, but Christ liveth in me: and the life which I now live in the flesh I live by the faith of the Son of God, who loved me, and gave himself for me.

CHAPTER THREE

IN MY LOVE

John 15:9 As the Father hath loved me, so have I loved you: continue ye in my love.

John 15:10 If ye keep my commandments, ye shall abide in my love; even as I have kept my Father's commandments, and abide in his love.

John 17:23 I in them, and thou in me, that they may be made perfect in one; and that the world may know that thou hast sent me, and hast loved them, as thou hast loved me.24 Father, I will that they also, whom thou hast given me, be with me where I am; that they may behold my

glory, which thou hast given me: for thou lovedst me before the foundation of the world.

John 17:26 And I have declared unto them thy name, and will declare it: that the love wherewith thou hast loved me may be in them, and I in them.

1 John 2:28 And now, little children, abide in him; that, when he shall appear, we may have confidence, and not be ashamed before him at his coming.

John 15:11 These things have I spoken unto you, that my joy might remain in you, and that your joy might be full.

Revelation 1:5 And from Jesus Christ, who is the faithful witness, and the first begotten of the dead, and the prince of the kings of the earth. Unto him that loved us, and washed us from our sins in his own blood,

IN HIS NAME

Matthew 18:20 For where two or three are gathered together in My name, I am there in the midst of them."

Mark 16:17-18 And these signs will follow those who believe: In My name they will cast out demons; they will speak with new tongues; 18 they will take up serpents; and if they drink anything deadly, it will by no means hurt them; they will lay hands on the sick, and they will recover."

John 14:13-14 And whatever you ask in My name, that I will do, that the Father may be glorified in the Son. If you ask anything in My name, I will do it.

John 16:23-24 "And in that day you will ask Me nothing. Most assuredly, I say to you, whatever you ask the Father in My name He will give you. Until now you have asked nothing in My name. Ask, and you will receive, that your joy may be full.

---

1 Corinthians 6:11 And such were some of you. But you were washed, but you were sanctified, but you were justified in the name of the Lord Jesus and by the Spirit of our God.

Matthew 12:21 And in his name shall the Gentiles trust.

Luke 24:47 And that repentance and remission of sins should be preached in his name among all nations, beginning at Jerusalem.

John 2:23 Now when he was in Jerusalem at the passover, in the feast day, many believed in his name, when they saw the miracles which he did.

Acts 3:16 And his name through faith in his name hath made this man strong, whom ye see and know: yea, the faith which is by him hath given him this perfect soundness in the presence of you all.

IN MY NAME

Matthew 18:5 And whoso shall receive one such little child in my name receiveth me.

Matthew 18:20 For where two or three are gathered together in my name, there am I in the midst of them.

Matthew 24:5 For many shall come in my name, saying, I am Christ; and shall deceive many.

Mark 9:37 Whosoever shall receive one of such children in my name, receiveth me: and whosoever shall receive me, receiveth not me, but him that sent me.

Mark 9:39 But Jesus said, Forbid him not: for there is no man which shall do a miracle in my name, that can lightly speak evil of me.

Mark 9:41 For whosoever shall give you a cup of water to drink in my name, because ye belong to Christ, verily I say unto you, he shall not lose his reward.

Mark 13:6 For many shall come in my name, saying, I am Christ; and shall deceive many.

Mark 16:17 And these signs shall follow them that believe; In my name shall they cast out devils; they shall speak with new tongues;

Luke 9:48 And said unto them, Whosoever shall receive this child in my name receiveth me: and whosoever shall receive me receiveth him that sent me: for he that is least among you all, the same shall be great.

Luke 21:8 And he said, Take heed that ye be not deceived: for many shall come in my name, saying, I am Christ; and the time draweth near: go ye not therefore after them.

John 14:13 And whatsoever ye shall ask in my name, that will I do, that the Father may be glorified in the Son.

John 14:14 If ye shall ask any thing in my name, I will do it.

John 14:26 But the Comforter, which is the Holy Ghost, whom the Father will send in my name, he shall teach you all things, and bring all things to your remembrance, whatsoever I have said unto you.

John 15:16 Ye have not chosen me, but I have chosen you, and ordained you, that ye should go and bring forth fruit, and that your fruit should remain: that whatsoever ye shall ask of the Father in my name, he may give it you.

John 16:23 And in that day ye shall ask me nothing. Verily, verily, I say unto you, Whatsoever ye shall ask the Father in my name, he will give it you.

John 16:24 Hitherto have ye asked nothing in my name: ask, and ye shall receive, that your joy may be full.

John 16:26 At that day ye shall ask in my name: and I say not unto you, that I will pray the Father for you:

THE FOLLOWING SCRIPTURES DO NOT CONTAIN THE PHRASES IN HIM, IN CHRIST,

ETC. BUT ARE THINGS THAT WE HAVE BECAUSE OF JESUS

Matthew 8:17 at it might be fulfilled which was spoken by Isaiah the prophet, saying:" He Himself took our infirmities and bore our sicknesses."

Matthew 11:28-30 Come to Me, all you who labor and are heavy laden, and I will give you rest. 29 Take My yoke upon you and learn from Me, for I am gentle and lowly in heart, and you will find rest for your souls. 30 For My yoke is easy and My burden is light."

Matthew 18:11 For the Son of Man has come to save that which was lost

Matthew 18:18-20 "Assuredly, I say to you, whatever you bind on earth will be bound in heaven, and whatever you loose on earth will be loosed in heaven." Again I say[to you that if two of you agree on earth concerning anything that they ask, it will be done for them by My Father in heaven. For where two or three are gathered together in My name, I am there in the midst of them."

Matthew 28:18-20 And Jesus came and spoke to them, saying, "All authority has been given to Me in heaven and on earth. Go therefore and make disciples of all the nations, baptizing them in the name of the Father and of the Son and of the Holy Spirit, teaching them to observe all things that I have commanded you; and lo, I am with you always, even to the end of the age." Amen.

Mark 1:8 I indeed baptized you with water, but He will baptize you with the Holy Spirit."

Mark 9:23 Jesus said to him, "If you can believe, all things are possible to him who believes."

Mark 11:23-24 For assuredly, I say to you, whoever says to this mountain, 'Be removed and be cast into the sea,' and does not doubt in his heart, but believes that those things he says will be done, he will have whatever he says. Therefore I say to you, whatever things you ask when you pray, believe that you receive them, and you will have them.

Luke 10:19 Behold, I give you the authority to trample on serpents and scorpions, and over all the power of the enemy, and nothing shall by any means hurt you.

John 4:14 but whoever drinks of the water that I shall give him will never thirst. But the water that I shall give him will become in him a fountain of water springing up into everlasting life."

John 6:40 And this is the will of Him who sent Me, that everyone who sees the Son and believes in Him may have everlasting life; and I will raise him up at the last day."

John 10:10 The thief does not come except to steal, and to kill, and to destroy. I have come that they may have life, and that they may have it more abundantly.

John 14:12 Most assuredly, I say to you, he who believes in Me, the works that I do he will do also; and greater works than these he will do, because I go to My Father.

John 14:23 Jesus answered and said to him, "If anyone loves Me, he will keep My word; and My Father will love him, and We will come to him and make Our home with him.

John 17:23 I in them, and You in Me; that they may be made perfect in one, and that the world may know that You have sent Me, and have loved them as You have loved Me.

Galatians 3:29 And if you are Christ's, then you are Abraham's seed, and heirs according to the promise.

Galatians 5:1 Stand fast therefore in the liberty by which Christ has made us free and do not be entangled again with a yoke of bondage.

Philippians 2:5 Let this mind be in you which was also in Christ Jesus,

---

Colossians 1:13 Who hath delivered us from the power of darkness, and hath translated us into the kingdom of his dear Son:

Colossians 1:26-27 the mystery which has been hidden from ages and from generations, but now has been revealed to His saints. To them God willed to make known what are the riches of the glory of this mystery among the Gentiles: which is Christ in you, the hope of glory.

Titus 2:14 who gave Himself for us, that He might redeem us from every lawless deed and purify for Himself His own special people, zealous for good works.

Titus 3:7 that having been justified by His grace we should become heirs according to the hope of eternal life.

Hebrews 2:9-11 But we see Jesus, who was made a little lower than the angels, for the suffering of death crowned with glory and honor, that He, by the grace of God, might taste death for everyone for it was fitting for Him, for whom are all things and by whom are all things, in bringing many sons to glory, to make the captain of their salvation perfect through sufferings. For both He who sanctifies and those who are being sanctified are all of one, for which reason He is not ashamed to call them brethren,

Hebrews 2:14-15 Inasmuch then as the children have partaken of flesh and blood, He Himself likewise shared in the same, that through death He might destroy him who had the power of death, that is, the devil, and release

those who through fear of death were all their lifetime subject to bondage.

Hebrews 2:18 For in that He Himself has suffered, being tempted, He is able to aid those who are tempted.

Hebrews 4:14-16 Seeing then that we have a great High Priest who has passed through the heavens, Jesus the Son of God, let us hold fast our confession. For we do not have a High Priest who cannot sympathize with our weaknesses, but was in all points tempted as we are, yet without sin. Let us therefore come boldly to the throne of grace that we may obtain mercy and find grace to help in time of need.

Hebrews 7:19-22 for the law made nothing perfect; on the other hand, there is the bringing in of a better hope, through which we draw near to God. And inasmuch as He was not made priest without an oath (for they have become priests without an oath, but He with an oath by Him who said to Him: "The Lord has sworn And will not relent, You are a priest forever According to the order of Melchizedek'"), by so much more Jesus has become a surety of a better covenant.

Hebrews 8:6 But now He has obtained a more excellent ministry, inasmuch as He is also Mediator of a better covenant, which was established on better promises.

Hebrews 9:26 For Christ has not entered the holy places made with hands, which are copies of the true, but

into heaven itself, now to appear in the presence of God for us;

Hebrews 9:28 so Christ was offered once to bear the sins of many. To those who eagerly wait for Him He will appear a second time, apart from sin, for salvation.

Hebrews 10:14 For by one offering He has perfected forever those who are being sanctified.

Hebrews 13:5-6 Let your conduct be without covetousness; be content with such things as you have. For He Himself has said, "I will never leave you nor forsake you."[So we may boldly say: "The Lord is my helper; I will not fear. What can man do to me?"

Hebrews 13:8 Jesus Christ is the same yesterday, today, and forever.

James 4:7 Therefore submit to God. Resist the devil and he will flee from you.

1 Peter 2:9 But you are a chosen generation, a royal priesthood, a holy nation, His own special people, that you may proclaim the praises of Him who called you out of darkness into His marvelous light;

1 Peter 2:21 For to this you were called, because Christ also suffered for us, leaving us[an example, that you should follow His steps:

1 Peter 3:18 For Christ also suffered once for sins, the just for the unjust, that He might bring us to God, being put to death in the flesh but made alive by the Spirit,

1 Peter 5:7 casting all your care upon Him, for He cares for you.

1 John 1:9 If we confess our sins, He is faithful and just to forgive us our sins and to cleanse us from all unrighteousness.

1 John 2:1 My little children, these things I write to you, so that you may not sin. And if anyone sins, we have an Advocate with the Father, Jesus Christ the righteous.

1 John 3:2 Beloved, now we are children of God; and it has not yet been revealed what we shall be, but we know that when He is revealed, we shall be like Him, for we shall see Him as He is.

1 John 3:14 We know that we have passed from death to life, because we love the brethren. He who does not love his brother abides in death.

1 John 4:4 You are of God, little children, and have overcome them, because He who is in you is greater than he who is in the world.

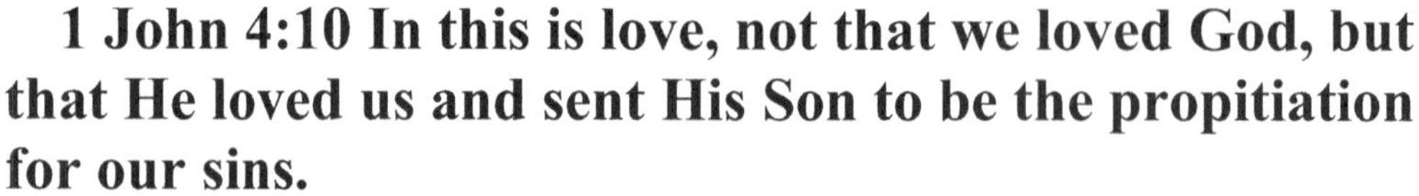

1 John 4:10 In this is love, not that we loved God, but that He loved us and sent His Son to be the propitiation for our sins.

1 John 4:15 Whoever confesses that Jesus is the Son of God, God abides in him, and he in God.

1 John 5:1 Whoever believes that Jesus is the Christ is born of God, and everyone who loves Him who begot also loves him who is begotten of Him.

1 John 5:4-5 For whatever is born of God overcomes the world. And this is the victory that has overcome the world—our faith. Who is he who overcomes the world, but he who believes that Jesus is the Son of God?

1 John 5:11-12 And this is the testimony: that God has given us eternal life, and this life is in His Son. 12 He who has the Son has life; he who does not have the Son of God does not have life.

Revelation 1:5-6 and from Jesus Christ, the faithful witness, the firstborn from the dead, and the ruler over the kings of the earth. To Him who loved us and washed us from our sins in His own blood, and has made us kings and priests to His God and Father, to Him be glory and dominion forever and ever. Amen.

BORN AGAIN BY FAITH IN CHRIST

JOHN 3:3 - JESUS ANSWERED AND SAID UNTO HIM, VERILY, VERILY, I SAY UNTO THEE, EXCEPT A MAN BE BORN AGAIN, HE CANNOT SEE THE KINGDOM OF GOD.

1 PETER 1:23 - BEING BORN AGAIN, NOT OF CORRUPTIBLE SEED, BUT OF INCORRUPTIBLE, BY THE WORD OF GOD, WHICH LIVETH AND ABIDETH FOR EVER.

I AM REDEEMED

EPHESIANS 1:7 - IN WHOM WE HAVE REDEMPTION THROUGH HIS BLOOD, THE FORGIVENESS OF SINS, ACCORDING TO THE RICHES OF HIS GRACE;

COLOSSIANS 1:14 - IN WHOM WE HAVE REDEMPTION THROUGH HIS BLOOD, [EVEN] THE FORGIVENESS OF SINS:

TITUS 2:14 - WHO GAVE HIMSELF FOR US, THAT HE MIGHT REDEEM US FROM ALL INIQUITY, AND PURIFY UNTO HIMSELF A PECULIAR PEOPLE, ZEALOUS OF GOOD WORKS.

1 PETER 1:18-19 - FORASMUCH AS YE KNOW THAT YE WERE NOT REDEEMED WITH CORRUPTIBLE THINGS, [AS] SILVER AND GOLD, FROM YOUR VAIN CONVERSATION [RECEIVED] BY TRADITION FROM

YOUR FATHERS;

JOHN 3:16 - FOR GOD SO LOVED THE WORLD, THAT HE GAVE HIS ONLY BEGOTTEN SON, THAT WHOSOEVER BELIEVETH IN HIM SHOULD NOT PERISH, BUT HAVE EVERLASTING LIFE.

I AM SEATED IN HEAVENLY PLACES

Ephesians 2:6 And hath raised us up together, and made us sit together in heavenly places in Christ Jesus:

I AM BOUGHT WITH A PRICE

1 Corinthians 7:23 Ye are bought with a price; be not ye the servants of men.

1 Corinthians 6:20 For ye are bought with a price: therefore glorify God in your body, and in your spirit, which are God's.

I AM A BRANCH TO BE CONNECTED TO THE VINE

John 15:2 Every branch in me that beareth not fruit he taketh away: and every branch that beareth fruit, he purgeth it, that it may bring forth more fruit.

John 15:4 Abide in me, and I in you. As the branch cannot bear fruit of itself, except it abide in the vine; no more can ye, except ye abide in me.

John 15:5 I am the vine, ye are the branches: He that abideth in me, and I in him, the same bringeth forth much fruit: for without me ye can do nothing.

John 15:6 If a man abide not in me, he is cast forth as a branch, and is withered; and men gather them, and cast them into the fire, and they are burned.

I AM TRANSLATED INTO GODS KINGDOM

Colossians 1:13 Who hath delivered us from the power of darkness, and hath translated us into the kingdom of his dear Son:

Hebrews 11:5 By faith Enoch was translated that he should not see death; and was not found, because God had translated him: for before his translation he had this testimony, that he pleased God.

I AM FEARFULLY AND WONDERFULLY MADE

Psalms 139:14 I will praise thee; for I am fearfully and wonderfully made: marvellous are thy works; and that my soul knoweth right well.

I AM GOD'S HANDIWORK

Ephesians 2:10 For we are his workmanship, created in Christ Jesus unto good works, which God hath before ordained that we should walk in them.

I AM THE APPLE OF HIS EYE

Deuteronomy 32:10 He found him in a desert land, and in the waste howling wilderness; he led him about, he instructed him, he kept him as the apple of his eye.

Zechariah 2:8 For thus saith the LORD of hosts; After the glory hath he sent me unto the nations which spoiled you: for he that toucheth you toucheth the apple of his eye.

I AM HIS CHILD

JOHN 1:12 - BUT AS MANY AS RECEIVED HIM, TO THEM GAVE HE POWER TO BECOME THE SONS OF GOD, [EVEN] TO THEM THAT BELIEVE ON HIS NAME:

GALATIANS 3:26 - FOR YE ARE ALL THE CHILDREN OF GOD BY FAITH IN CHRIST JESUS.

ROMANS 8:17-19 - AND IF CHILDREN, THEN HEIRS; HEIRS OF GOD, AND JOINT-HEIRS WITH CHRIST; IF SO BE THAT WE SUFFER WITH [HIM], THAT WE MAY

BE ALSO GLORIFIED TOGETHER.

ROMANS 8:17 - AND IF CHILDREN, THEN HEIRS; HEIRS OF GOD, AND JOINT-HEIRS WITH CHRIST; IF SO BE THAT WE SUFFER WITH [HIM], THAT WE MAY BE ALSO GLORIFIED TOGETHER.

ROMANS 8:16 - THE SPIRIT ITSELF BEARETH WITNESS WITH OUR SPIRIT, THAT WE ARE THE CHILDREN OF GOD:

I AM AN OVERCOMER BY BLOOD OF THE LAMB

Revelation 3:21 To him that overcometh will I grant to sit with me in my throne, even as I also overcame, and am set down with my Father in his throne.

Revelation 12:11 And they overcame him by the blood of the Lamb, and by the word of their testimony; and they loved not their lives unto the death.

I AM BLESSED WITH ALL SPIRITUAL BLESSINGS

Ephesians 1:3 Blessed be the God and Father of our Lord Jesus Christ, who hath blessed us with all spiritual blessings in heavenly places in Christ:

I AM COMPLETE IN CHRIST

Colossians 2:10 And ye are complete in him, which is the head of all principality and power:

I AM WASHED BY HIS BLOOD

1 JOHN 1:7 - BUT IF WE WALK IN THE LIGHT, AS HE IS IN THE LIGHT, WE HAVE FELLOWSHIP ONE WITH ANOTHER, AND THE BLOOD OF JESUS CHRIST HIS SON CLEANSETH US FROM ALL SIN.

REVELATION 1:5 - AND FROM JESUS CHRIST, [WHO IS] THE FAITHFUL WITNESS, [AND] THE FIRST BEGOTTEN OF THE DEAD, AND THE PRINCE OF THE KINGS OF THE EARTH. UNTO HIM THAT LOVED US, AND WASHED US FROM OUR SINS IN HIS OWN BLOOD,

I AM FORGIVEN

MARK 11:25 - AND WHEN YE STAND PRAYING, FORGIVE, IF YE HAVE OUGHT AGAINST ANY: THAT YOUR FATHER ALSO WHICH IS IN HEAVEN MAY FORGIVE YOU YOUR TRESPASSES.

EPHESIANS 4:32 - AND BE YE KIND ONE TO ANOTHER, TENDERHEARTED, FORGIVING ONE ANOTHER, EVEN AS GOD FOR CHRIST'S SAKE HATH FORGIVEN YOU.

MATTHEW 6:15 - BUT IF YE FORGIVE NOT MEN THEIR TRESPASSES, NEITHER WILL YOUR FATHER FORGIVE YOUR TRESPASSES.

1 JOHN 1:9 - IF WE CONFESS OUR SINS, HE IS FAITHFUL AND JUST TO FORGIVE US [OUR] SINS, AND TO CLEANSE US FROM ALL UNRIGHTEOUSNESS.

I AM HEALED

JEREMIAH 17:14 - HEAL ME, O LORD, AND I SHALL BE HEALED; SAVE ME, AND I SHALL BE SAVED: FOR THOU [ART] MY PRAISE.

JEREMIAH 33:6 - BEHOLD, I WILL BRING IT HEALTH AND CURE, AND I WILL CURE THEM, AND WILL REVEAL UNTO THEM THE ABUNDANCE OF PEACE AND TRUTH.

1 PETER 2:24 - WHO HIS OWN SELF BARE OUR SINS IN HIS OWN BODY ON THE TREE, THAT WE, BEING DEAD TO SINS, SHOULD LIVE UNTO RIGHTEOUSNESS: BY WHOSE STRIPES YE WERE HEALED.

ISAIAH 53:5 - BUT HE [WAS] WOUNDED FOR OUR TRANSGRESSIONS, [HE WAS] BRUISED FOR OUR INIQUITIES: THE CHASTISEMENT OF OUR PEACE [WAS] UPON HIM; AND WITH HIS STRIPES WE ARE HEALED.

JAMES 5:15 - AND THE PRAYER OF FAITH SHALL SAVE THE SICK, AND THE LORD SHALL RAISE HIM UP; AND IF HE HAVE COMMITTED SINS, THEY SHALL BE FORGIVEN HIM.

I AM DELIVERED

JAMES 5:16 - CONFESS [YOUR] FAULTS ONE TO ANOTHER, AND PRAY ONE FOR ANOTHER, THAT YE MAY BE HEALED. THE EFFECTUAL FERVENT PRAYER OF A RIGHTEOUS MAN AVAILETH MUCH.

GALATIANS 5:1 - STAND FAST THEREFORE IN THE LIBERTY WHEREWITH CHRIST HATH MADE US FREE, AND BE NOT ENTANGLED AGAIN WITH THE YOKE OF BONDAGE.

JOEL 2:25-27 - AND I WILL RESTORE TO YOU THE YEARS THAT THE LOCUST HATH EATEN, THE CANKERWORM, AND THE CATERPILLER, AND THE PALMERWORM, MY GREAT ARMY WHICH I SENT AMONG YOU.

PSALMS 40:13 - BE PLEASED, O LORD, TO DELIVER ME: O LORD, MAKE HASTE TO HELP ME.

PSALMS 40:17 - BUT I [AM] POOR AND NEEDY; [YET] THE LORD THINKETH UPON ME: THOU [ART] MY HELP AND MY DELIVERER; MAKE NO TARRYING, O MY GOD.

I AM HEARD BY GOD

JEREMIAH 33:3 - CALL UNTO ME, AND I WILL ANSWER THEE, AND SHEW THEE GREAT AND MIGHTY THINGS, WHICH THOU KNOWEST NOT.

1 JOHN 5:14-15 - AND THIS IS THE CONFIDENCE

THAT WE HAVE IN HIM, THAT, IF WE ASK ANY THING ACCORDING TO HIS WILL, HE HEARETH US:

JAMES 4:3 - YE ASK, AND RECEIVE NOT, BECAUSE YE ASK AMISS, THAT YE MAY CONSUME [IT] UPON YOUR LUSTS.

JOHN 15:7 - IF YE ABIDE IN ME, AND MY WORDS ABIDE IN YOU, YE SHALL ASK WHAT YE WILL, AND IT SHALL BE DONE UNTO YOU.

ISAIAH 65:24 - AND IT SHALL COME TO PASS, THAT BEFORE THEY CALL, I WILL ANSWER; AND WHILE THEY ARE YET SPEAKING, I WILL HEAR.

I AM IN HIS BRIDE

EPHESIANS 5:25-27 - HUSBANDS, LOVE YOUR WIVES, EVEN AS CHRIST ALSO LOVED THE CHURCH, AND GAVE HIMSELF FOR IT;

REVELATION 19:7-9 - LET US BE GLAD AND REJOICE, AND GIVE HONOUR TO HIM: FOR THE MARRIAGE OF THE LAMB IS COME, AND HIS WIFE HATH MADE HERSELF READY.

REVELATION 21:2 - AND I JOHN SAW THE HOLY CITY, NEW JERUSALEM, COMING DOWN FROM GOD OUT OF HEAVEN, PREPARED AS A BRIDE ADORNED FOR HER HUSBAND.

ISAIAH 54:5 - FOR THY MAKER [IS] THINE HUSBAND; THE LORD OF HOSTS [IS] HIS NAME; AND THY REDEEMER THE HOLY ONE OF ISRAEL; THE GOD OF

THE WHOLE EARTH SHALL HE BE CALLED.

REVELATION 21:9 - AND THERE CAME UNTO ME ONE OF THE SEVEN ANGELS WHICH HAD THE SEVEN VIALS FULL OF THE SEVEN LAST PLAGUES, AND TALKED WITH ME, SAYING, COME HITHER, I WILL SHEW THEE THE BRIDE, THE LAMB'S WIFE.

2 CORINTHIANS 11:2 - FOR I AM JEALOUS OVER YOU WITH GODLY JEALOUSY: FOR I HAVE ESPOUSED YOU TO ONE HUSBAND, THAT I MAY PRESENT [YOU AS] A CHASTE VIRGIN TO CHRIST.

I AM GOD'S POSSESSION

MALACHI 3:17 - AND THEY SHALL BE MINE, SAITH THE LORD OF HOSTS, IN THAT DAY WHEN I MAKE UP MY JEWELS; AND I WILL SPARE THEM, AS A MAN SPARETH HIS OWN SON THAT SERVETH HIM.

1 Corinthians 6:20 For ye are bought with a price: therefore glorify God in your body, and in your spirit, which are God's.

1 Corinthians 7:23 Ye are bought with a price; be not ye the servants of men.

I AM NOT MY OWN

1 Corinthians 6:19 What? know ye not that your body is the temple of the Holy Ghost which is in you, which ye have of God, and ye are not your own?

2 Corinthians 13:5 Examine yourselves, whether ye be in the faith; prove your own selves. Know ye not your own selves, how that Jesus Christ is in you, except ye be reprobates?

I AM THE TEMPLE OF THE HOLY SPIRIT

1 CORINTHIANS 3:16-17 - KNOW YE NOT THAT YE ARE THE TEMPLE OF GOD, AND [THAT] THE SPIRIT OF GOD DWELLETH IN YOU?

1 CORINTHIANS 3:16 - KNOW YE NOT THAT YE ARE THE TEMPLE OF GOD, AND [THAT] THE SPIRIT OF GOD DWELLETH IN YOU?

2 CORINTHIANS 6:16 - AND WHAT AGREEMENT HATH THE TEMPLE OF GOD WITH IDOLS? FOR YE ARE THE TEMPLE OF THE LIVING GOD; AS GOD HATH SAID, I WILL DWELL IN THEM, AND WALK IN [THEM]; AND I WILL BE THEIR GOD, AND THEY SHALL BE MY PEOPLE.

I AM RECONCILED TO GOD

EPHESIANS 4:32 - AND BE YE KIND ONE TO ANOTHER, TENDERHEARTED, FORGIVING ONE ANOTHER, EVEN AS GOD FOR CHRIST'S SAKE HATH FORGIVEN YOU.

2 CORINTHIANS 5:18 - AND ALL THINGS [ARE] OF GOD, WHO HATH RECONCILED US TO HIMSELF BY JESUS CHRIST, AND HATH GIVEN TO US THE MINISTRY OF RECONCILIATION;

2 CORINTHIANS 5:18-21 - AND ALL THINGS [ARE] OF GOD, WHO HATH RECONCILED US TO HIMSELF BY JESUS CHRIST, AND HATH GIVEN TO US THE MINISTRY OF RECONCILIATION;

ROMANS 5:10 - FOR IF, WHEN WE WERE ENEMIES, WE WERE RECONCILED TO GOD BY THE DEATH OF HIS SON, MUCH MORE, BEING RECONCILED, WE SHALL BE SAVED BY HIS LIFE.

COLOSSIANS 1:20 - AND, HAVING MADE PEACE THROUGH THE BLOOD OF HIS CROSS, BY HIM TO RECONCILE ALL THINGS UNTO HIMSELF; BY HIM, [I SAY], WHETHER [THEY BE] THINGS IN EARTH, OR THINGS IN HEAVEN.

COLOSSIANS 1:20-22 - AND, HAVING MADE PEACE THROUGH THE BLOOD OF HIS CROSS, BY HIM TO RECONCILE ALL THINGS UNTO HIMSELF; BY HIM, [I SAY], WHETHER [THEY BE] THINGS IN EARTH, OR THINGS IN HEAVEN.

CHAPTER FOUR

I AM EMPOWERED BY CHRIST

DEUTERONOMY 31:6 - BE STRONG AND OF A GOOD COURAGE, FEAR NOT, NOR BE AFRAID OF THEM: FOR THE LORD THY GOD, HE [IT IS] THAT DOTH GO WITH THEE; HE WILL NOT FAIL THEE, NOR FORSAKE THEE.

ACTS 1:8 - BUT YE SHALL RECEIVE POWER, AFTER THAT THE HOLY GHOST IS COME UPON YOU: AND YE SHALL BE WITNESSES UNTO ME BOTH IN JERUSALEM, AND IN ALL JUDAEA, AND IN SAMARIA, AND UNTO THE UTTERMOST PART OF THE EARTH.

1 JOHN 4:4 - YE ARE OF GOD, LITTLE CHILDREN, AND HAVE OVERCOME THEM: BECAUSE GREATER IS HE THAT IS IN YOU, THAN HE THAT IS IN THE WORLD.

LUKE 10:19-20 - BEHOLD, I GIVE UNTO YOU POWER TO TREAD ON SERPENTS AND SCORPIONS, AND OVER

ALL THE POWER OF THE ENEMY: AND NOTHING SHALL BY ANY MEANS HURT YOU.

2 PETER 1:3-4 - ACCORDING AS HIS DIVINE POWER HATH GIVEN UNTO US ALL THINGS THAT [PERTAIN] UNTO LIFE AND GODLINESS, THROUGH THE KNOWLEDGE OF HIM THAT HATH CALLED US TO GLORY AND VIRTUE:

2 TIMOTHY 3:16 - ALL SCRIPTURE [IS] GIVEN BY INSPIRATION OF GOD, AND [IS] PROFITABLE FOR DOCTRINE, FOR REPROOF, FOR CORRECTION, FOR INSTRUCTION IN RIGHTEOUSNESS:

ISAIAH 41:10-13 - FEAR THOU NOT; FOR I [AM] WITH THEE: BE NOT DISMAYED; FOR I [AM] THY GOD: I WILL STRENGTHEN THEE; YEA, I WILL HELP THEE; YEA, I WILL UPHOLD THEE WITH THE RIGHT HAND OF MY RIGHTEOUSNESS.

I AM AN HEIR AND JOINT HEIRS WITH CHRIST

Romans 8:17 And if children, then heirs; heirs of God, and joint-heirs with Christ; if so be that we suffer with him, that we may be also glorified together.

Galatians 3:29 And if ye be Christ's, then are ye Abraham's seed, and heirs according to the promise.

Titus 3:7 That being justified by his grace, we should be made heirs according to the hope of eternal life.

Hebrews 1:14 Are they not all ministering spirits, sent forth to minister for them who shall be heirs of salvation?

Hebrews 6:17 Wherein God, willing more abundantly to shew unto the heirs of promise the immutability of his counsel, confirmed it by an oath:

I AM CHOSEN BY GOD

1 PETER 2:9 - BUT YE [ARE] A CHOSEN GENERATION, A ROYAL PRIESTHOOD, AN HOLY NATION, A PECULIAR PEOPLE; THAT YE SHOULD SHEW FORTH THE PRAISES OF HIM WHO HATH CALLED YOU OUT OF DARKNESS INTO HIS MARVELLOUS LIGHT:

JOHN 15:16 - YE HAVE NOT CHOSEN ME, BUT I HAVE CHOSEN YOU, AND ORDAINED YOU, THAT YE SHOULD GO AND BRING FORTH FRUIT, AND [THAT] YOUR FRUIT SHOULD REMAIN: THAT WHATSOEVER YE SHALL ASK OF THE FATHER IN MY NAME, HE MAY GIVE IT YOU.

JEREMIAH 1:5 - BEFORE I FORMED THEE IN THE BELLY I KNEW THEE; AND BEFORE THOU CAMEST FORTH OUT OF THE WOMB I SANCTIFIED THEE, [AND] I ORDAINED THEE A PROPHET UNTO THE NATIONS.

EPHESIANS 1:3-4 - BLESSED [BE] THE GOD AND FATHER OF OUR LORD JESUS CHRIST, WHO HATH BLESSED US WITH ALL SPIRITUAL BLESSINGS IN HEAVENLY [PLACES] IN CHRIST:

DEUTERONOMY 14:2 - FOR THOU [ART] AN HOLY PEOPLE UNTO THE LORD THY GOD, AND THE LORD HATH CHOSEN THEE TO BE A PECULIAR PEOPLE UNTO HIMSELF, ABOVE ALL THE NATIONS THAT [ARE] UPON THE EARTH.

ISAIAH 43:10 - YE [ARE] MY WITNESSES, SAITH THE LORD, AND MY SERVANT WHOM I HAVE CHOSEN: THAT YE MAY KNOW AND BELIEVE ME, AND UNDERSTAND THAT I [AM] HE: BEFORE ME THERE WAS NO GOD FORMED, NEITHER SHALL THERE BE AFTER ME.

2 THESSALONIANS 2:14 - WHEREUNTO HE CALLED YOU BY OUR GOSPEL, TO THE OBTAINING OF THE GLORY OF OUR LORD JESUS CHRIST.

JOHN 3:16 - FOR GOD SO LOVED THE WORLD, THAT HE GAVE HIS ONLY BEGOTTEN SON, THAT WHOSOEVER BELIEVETH IN HIM SHOULD NOT PERISH, BUT HAVE EVERLASTING LIFE.

I AM MORE THAN A CONQUEROR

ROMANS 8:37 - NAY, IN ALL THESE THINGS WE ARE MORE THAN CONQUERORS THROUGH HIM THAT LOVED US.

ROMANS 8:35-37 - WHO SHALL SEPARATE US FROM THE LOVE OF CHRIST? [SHALL] TRIBULATION, OR DISTRESS, OR PERSECUTION, OR FAMINE, OR NAKEDNESS, OR PERIL, OR SWORD?

EPHESIANS 6:10-12 - FINALLY, MY BRETHREN, BE STRONG IN THE LORD, AND IN THE POWER OF HIS MIGHT.

ROMANS 12:1 - I BESEECH YOU THEREFORE, BRETHREN, BY THE MERCIES OF GOD, THAT YE PRESENT YOUR BODIES A LIVING SACRIFICE, HOLY, ACCEPTABLE UNTO GOD, [WHICH IS] YOUR REASONABLE SERVICE.

JEREMIAH 29:11 - FOR I KNOW THE THOUGHTS THAT I THINK TOWARD YOU, SAITH THE LORD, THOUGHTS OF PEACE, AND NOT OF EVIL, TO GIVE YOU AN EXPECTED END.

1 JOHN 5:4 - FOR WHATSOEVER IS BORN OF GOD OVERCOMETH THE WORLD: AND THIS IS THE VICTORY THAT OVERCOMETH THE WORLD, [EVEN] OUR FAITH.

ROMANS 8:11 - BUT IF THE SPIRIT OF HIM THAT RAISED UP JESUS FROM THE DEAD DWELL IN YOU, HE THAT RAISED UP CHRIST FROM THE DEAD SHALL ALSO QUICKEN YOUR MORTAL BODIES BY HIS SPIRIT THAT DWELLETH IN YOU.

1 CORINTHIANS 15:57 - BUT THANKS [BE] TO GOD, WHICH GIVETH US THE VICTORY THROUGH OUR LORD JESUS CHRIST.

ROMANS 8:35-39 - WHO SHALL SEPARATE US FROM THE LOVE OF CHRIST? [SHALL] TRIBULATION, OR DISTRESS, OR PERSECUTION, OR FAMINE, OR NAKEDNESS, OR PERIL, OR SWORD?

I AM HIDDEN WITH CHRIST IN GOD

Isaiah 45:3 And I will give thee the treasures of darkness, and hidden riches of secret places, that thou mayest know that I, the LORD, which call thee by thy name, am the God of Israel.

Isaiah 48:6 Thou hast heard, see all this; and will not ye declare it? I have shewed thee new things from this time, even hidden things, and thou didst not know them.

1 Corinthians 2:7 But we speak the wisdom of God in a mystery, even the hidden wisdom, which God ordained before the world unto our glory:

1 Peter 3:4 But let it be the hidden man of the heart, in that which is not corruptible, even the ornament of a meek and quiet spirit, which is in the sight of God of great price.

Colossians 3:3 For ye are dead, and your life is hid with Christ in God.

I AM IN THE BOOK OF LIFE

REVELATION 13:8 - AND ALL THAT DWELL UPON THE EARTH SHALL WORSHIP HIM, WHOSE NAMES ARE NOT WRITTEN IN THE BOOK OF LIFE OF THE LAMB SLAIN FROM THE FOUNDATION OF THE WORLD.

REVELATION 20:12 - AND I SAW THE DEAD, SMALL AND GREAT, STAND BEFORE GOD; AND THE BOOKS

WERE OPENED: AND ANOTHER BOOK WAS OPENED, WHICH IS [THE BOOK] OF LIFE: AND THE DEAD WERE JUDGED OUT OF THOSE THINGS WHICH WERE WRITTEN IN THE BOOKS, ACCORDING TO THEIR WORKS.

REVELATION 3:5 - HE THAT OVERCOMETH, THE SAME SHALL BE CLOTHED IN WHITE RAIMENT; AND I WILL NOT BLOT OUT HIS NAME OUT OF THE BOOK OF LIFE, BUT I WILL CONFESS HIS NAME BEFORE MY FATHER, AND BEFORE HIS ANGELS.

REVELATION 21:27 - AND THERE SHALL IN NO WISE ENTER INTO IT ANY THING THAT DEFILETH, NEITHER [WHATSOEVER] WORKETH ABOMINATION, OR [MAKETH] A LIE: BUT THEY WHICH ARE WRITTEN IN THE LAMB'S BOOK OF LIFE.

REVELATION 20:15 - AND WHOSOEVER WAS NOT FOUND WRITTEN IN THE BOOK OF LIFE WAS CAST INTO THE LAKE OF FIRE.

LUKE 10:20 - NOTWITHSTANDING IN THIS REJOICE NOT, THAT THE SPIRITS ARE SUBJECT UNTO YOU; BUT RATHER REJOICE, BECAUSE YOUR NAMES ARE WRITTEN IN HEAVEN.

EXODUS 32:33 - AND THE LORD SAID UNTO MOSES, WHOSOEVER HATH SINNED AGAINST ME, HIM WILL I BLOT OUT OF MY BOOK.

PSALMS 69:28 - LET THEM BE BLOTTED OUT OF THE BOOK OF THE LIVING, AND NOT BE WRITTEN WITH THE RIGHTEOUS.

MALACHI 3:16 - THEN THEY THAT FEARED THE LORD SPAKE OFTEN ONE TO ANOTHER: AND THE LORD HEARKENED, AND HEARD [IT], AND A BOOK OF REMEMBRANCE WAS WRITTEN BEFORE HIM FOR THEM THAT FEARED THE LORD, AND THAT THOUGHT UPON HIS NAME.

REVELATION 17:8 - THE BEAST THAT THOU SAWEST WAS, AND IS NOT; AND SHALL ASCEND OUT OF THE BOTTOMLESS PIT, AND GO INTO PERDITION: AND THEY THAT DWELL ON THE EARTH SHALL WONDER, WHOSE NAMES WERE NOT WRITTEN IN THE BOOK OF LIFE FROM THE FOUNDATION OF THE WORLD, WHEN THEY BEHOLD THE BEAST THAT WAS, AND IS NOT, AND YET IS.

PHILIPPIANS 4:3 - AND I INTREAT THEE ALSO, TRUE YOKEFELLOW, HELP THOSE WOMEN WHICH LABOURED WITH ME IN THE GOSPEL, WITH CLEMENT ALSO, AND [WITH] OTHER MY FELLOWLABOURERS, WHOSE NAMES [ARE] IN THE BOOK OF LIFE.

DANIEL 12:1 - AND AT THAT TIME SHALL MICHAEL STAND UP, THE GREAT PRINCE WHICH STANDETH FOR THE CHILDREN OF THY PEOPLE: AND THERE SHALL BE A TIME OF TROUBLE, SUCH AS NEVER WAS SINCE THERE WAS A NATION [EVEN] TO THAT SAME TIME: AND AT THAT TIME THY PEOPLE SHALL BE DELIVERED, EVERY ONE THAT SHALL BE FOUND WRITTEN IN THE BOOK.

I AM BLESSED AND HIGHLY FAVORED

PSALMS 5:12 - FOR THOU, LORD, WILT BLESS THE RIGHTEOUS; WITH FAVOUR WILT THOU COMPASS HIM AS [WITH] A SHIELD.

PSALMS 90:17 - AND LET THE BEAUTY OF THE LORD OUR GOD BE UPON US: AND ESTABLISH THOU THE WORK OF OUR HANDS UPON US; YEA, THE WORK OF OUR HANDS ESTABLISH THOU IT.

PSALMS 84:11 - FOR THE LORD GOD [IS] A SUN AND SHIELD: THE LORD WILL GIVE GRACE AND GLORY: NO GOOD [THING] WILL HE WITHHOLD FROM THEM THAT WALK UPRIGHTLY.

EPHESIANS 1:11 - IN WHOM ALSO WE HAVE OBTAINED AN INHERITANCE, BEING PREDESTINATED ACCORDING TO THE PURPOSE OF HIM WHO WORKETH ALL THINGS AFTER THE COUNSEL OF HIS OWN WILL:

PSALMS 30:5 - FOR HIS ANGER [ENDURETH BUT] A MOMENT; IN HIS FAVOUR [IS] LIFE: WEEPING MAY ENDURE FOR A NIGHT, BUT JOY [COMETH] IN THE MORNING.

GENESIS 6:8 - BUT NOAH FOUND GRACE IN THE EYES OF THE LORD.

ISAIAH 58:11 - AND THE LORD SHALL GUIDE THEE CONTINUALLY, AND SATISFY THY SOUL IN DROUGHT, AND MAKE FAT THY BONES: AND THOU SHALT BE LIKE A WATERED GARDEN, AND LIKE A SPRING OF WATER, WHOSE WATERS FAIL NOT.

ESTHER 2:15-18 - NOW WHEN THE TURN OF ESTHER, THE DAUGHTER OF ABIHAIL THE UNCLE OF

MORDECAI, WHO HAD TAKEN HER FOR HIS DAUGHTER, WAS COME TO GO IN UNTO THE KING, SHE REQUIRED NOTHING BUT WHAT HEGAI THE KING'S CHAMBERLAIN, THE KEEPER OF THE WOMEN, APPOINTED. AND ESTHER OBTAINED FAVOUR IN THE SIGHT OF ALL THEM THAT LOOKED UPON HER. *(READ MORE...)*

PSALMS 102:13 - THOU SHALT ARISE, [AND] HAVE MERCY UPON ZION: FOR THE TIME TO FAVOUR HER, YEA, THE SET TIME, IS COME.

LUKE 2:52 - AND JESUS INCREASED IN WISDOM AND STATURE, AND IN FAVOUR WITH GOD AND MAN.

GENESIS 39:4 - AND JOSEPH FOUND GRACE IN HIS SIGHT, AND HE SERVED HIM: AND HE MADE HIM OVERSEER OVER HIS HOUSE, AND ALL [THAT] HE HAD HE PUT INTO HIS HAND.

I AM ADOPTED AS GOD'S SON

EPHESIANS 1:5 - HAVING PREDESTINATED US UNTO THE ADOPTION OF CHILDREN BY JESUS CHRIST TO HIMSELF, ACCORDING TO THE GOOD PLEASURE OF HIS WILL,

GALATIANS 4:5-7 - TO REDEEM THEM THAT WERE UNDER THE LAW, THAT WE MIGHT RECEIVE THE ADOPTION OF SONS. *(READ MORE...)*

ROMANS 9:8 - THAT IS, THEY WHICH ARE THE CHILDREN OF THE FLESH, THESE [ARE] NOT THE

CHILDREN OF GOD: BUT THE CHILDREN OF THE PROMISE ARE COUNTED FOR THE SEED.

JOHN 1:12 - BUT AS MANY AS RECEIVED HIM, TO THEM GAVE HE POWER TO BECOME THE SONS OF GOD, [EVEN] TO THEM THAT BELIEVE ON HIS NAME:

1 JOHN 3:1 - BEHOLD, WHAT MANNER OF LOVE THE FATHER HATH BESTOWED UPON US, THAT WE SHOULD BE CALLED THE SONS OF GOD: THEREFORE THE WORLD KNOWETH US NOT, BECAUSE IT KNEW HIM NOT.

ROMANS 8:14-19 - FOR AS MANY AS ARE LED BY THE SPIRIT OF GOD, THEY ARE THE SONS OF GOD. *(READ MORE...)*

GALATIANS 3:26 - FOR YE ARE ALL THE CHILDREN OF GOD BY FAITH IN CHRIST JESUS.

JOHN 1:13 - WHICH WERE BORN, NOT OF BLOOD, NOR OF THE WILL OF THE FLESH, NOR OF THE WILL OF MAN, BUT OF GOD.

1 JOHN 3:2 - BELOVED, NOW ARE WE THE SONS OF GOD, AND IT DOTH NOT YET APPEAR WHAT WE SHALL BE: BUT WE KNOW THAT, WHEN HE SHALL APPEAR, WE SHALL BE LIKE HIM; FOR WE SHALL SEE HIM AS HE IS.

ROMANS 8:15 - FOR YE HAVE NOT RECEIVED THE SPIRIT OF BONDAGE AGAIN TO FEAR; BUT YE HAVE RECEIVED THE SPIRIT OF ADOPTION, WHEREBY WE CRY, ABBA, FATHER.

I AM THE HEAD AND NOT THE TAIL

Deuteronomy 28:13 And the LORD shall make thee the head, and not the tail; and thou shalt be above only, and thou shalt not be beneath; if that thou hearken unto the commandments of the LORD thy God, which I command thee this day, to observe and to do them:

Deuteronomy 28:44 He shall lend to thee, and thou shalt not lend to him: he shall be the head, and thou shalt be the tail.

I AM ACCEPTED IN THE BELOVED

ROMANS 15:7 - WHEREFORE RECEIVE YE ONE ANOTHER, AS CHRIST ALSO RECEIVED US TO THE GLORY OF GOD.

JOHN 6:37 - ALL THAT THE FATHER GIVETH ME SHALL COME TO ME; AND HIM THAT COMETH TO ME I WILL IN NO WISE CAST OUT.

GALATIANS 5:1 - STAND FAST THEREFORE IN THE LIBERTY WHEREWITH CHRIST HATH MADE US FREE, AND BE NOT ENTANGLED AGAIN WITH THE YOKE OF BONDAGE.

Ephesians 1:6 To the praise of the glory of his grace, wherein he hath made us accepted in the beloved.

I AM A ROYAL PRIESTHOOD

1 PETER 2:9 - BUT YE [ARE] A CHOSEN GENERATION, A ROYAL PRIESTHOOD, AN HOLY NATION, A PECULIAR PEOPLE; THAT YE SHOULD SHEW FORTH THE PRAISES OF HIM WHO HATH CALLED YOU OUT OF DARKNESS INTO HIS MARVELLOUS LIGHT:

1 PETER 2:4-10 - TO WHOM COMING, [AS UNTO] A LIVING STONE, DISALLOWED INDEED OF MEN, BUT CHOSEN OF GOD, [AND] PRECIOUS, *(READ MORE...)*

REVELATION 1:6 - AND HATH MADE US KINGS AND PRIESTS UNTO GOD AND HIS FATHER; TO HIM [BE] GLORY AND DOMINION FOR EVER AND EVER. AMEN.

1 PETER 2:5 - YE ALSO, AS LIVELY STONES, ARE BUILT UP A SPIRITUAL HOUSE, AN HOLY PRIESTHOOD, TO OFFER UP SPIRITUAL SACRIFICES, ACCEPTABLE TO GOD BY JESUS CHRIST.

1 PETER 2:9-10 - BUT YE [ARE] A CHOSEN GENERATION, A ROYAL PRIESTHOOD, AN HOLY NATION, A PECULIAR PEOPLE; THAT YE SHOULD SHEW FORTH THE PRAISES OF HIM WHO HATH CALLED YOU OUT OF DARKNESS INTO HIS MARVELLOUS LIGHT: *(READ MORE...)*

EXODUS 19:6 - AND YE SHALL BE UNTO ME A KINGDOM OF PRIESTS, AND AN HOLY NATION. THESE [ARE] THE WORDS WHICH THOU SHALT SPEAK UNTO THE CHILDREN OF ISRAEL.

REVELATION 5:10 - AND HAST MADE US UNTO OUR

GOD KINGS AND PRIESTS: AND WE SHALL REIGN ON THE EARTH.

JOHN 15:16 - YE HAVE NOT CHOSEN ME, BUT I HAVE CHOSEN YOU, AND ORDAINED YOU, THAT YE SHOULD GO AND BRING FORTH FRUIT, AND [THAT] YOUR FRUIT SHOULD REMAIN: THAT WHATSOEVER YE SHALL ASK OF THE FATHER IN MY NAME, HE MAY GIVE IT YOU.

1 PETER 2:1-25 - WHEREFORE LAYING ASIDE ALL MALICE, AND ALL GUILE, AND HYPOCRISIES, AND ENVIES, AND ALL EVIL SPEAKINGS, *(READ MORE...)*

2 TIMOTHY 1:9 - WHO HATH SAVED US, AND CALLED [US] WITH AN HOLY CALLING, NOT ACCORDING TO OUR WORKS, BUT ACCORDING TO HIS OWN PURPOSE AND GRACE, WHICH WAS GIVEN US IN CHRIST JESUS BEFORE THE WORLD BEGAN,

JEREMIAH 1:5 - BEFORE I FORMED THEE IN THE BELLY I KNEW THEE; AND BEFORE THOU CAMEST FORTH OUT OF THE WOMB I SANCTIFIED THEE, [AND] I ORDAINED THEE A PROPHET UNTO THE NATIONS.

DEUTERONOMY 7:6-9 - FOR THOU [ART] AN HOLY PEOPLE UNTO THE LORD THY GOD: THE LORD THY GOD HATH CHOSEN THEE TO BE A SPECIAL PEOPLE UNTO HIMSELF, ABOVE ALL PEOPLE THAT [ARE] UPON THE FACE OF THE EARTH. *(READ MORE...)*

1 THESSALONIANS 1:4 - KNOWING, BRETHREN BELOVED, YOUR ELECTION OF GOD.

I AM LOVED

JOHN 3:16 - FOR GOD SO LOVED THE WORLD, THAT HE GAVE HIS ONLY BEGOTTEN SON, THAT WHOSOEVER BELIEVETH IN HIM SHOULD NOT PERISH, BUT HAVE EVERLASTING LIFE.

ROMANS 5:8 - BUT GOD COMMENDETH HIS LOVE TOWARD US, IN THAT, WHILE WE WERE YET SINNERS, CHRIST DIED FOR US.

1 JOHN 4:19 - WE LOVE HIM, BECAUSE HE FIRST LOVED US.

ISAIAH 41:13 - FOR I THE LORD THY GOD WILL HOLD THY RIGHT HAND, SAYING UNTO THEE, FEAR NOT; I WILL HELP THEE.

1 JOHN 4:10 - HEREIN IS LOVE, NOT THAT WE LOVED GOD, BUT THAT HE LOVED US, AND SENT HIS SON [TO BE] THE PROPITIATION FOR OUR SINS.

ROMANS 8:35-39 - WHO SHALL SEPARATE US FROM THE LOVE OF CHRIST? [SHALL] TRIBULATION, OR DISTRESS, OR PERSECUTION, OR FAMINE, OR NAKEDNESS, OR PERIL, OR SWORD? *(READ MORE...)*

JEREMIAH 31:3 - THE LORD HATH APPEARED OF OLD UNTO ME, [SAYING], YEA, I HAVE LOVED THEE WITH AN EVERLASTING LOVE: THEREFORE WITH LOVINGKINDNESS HAVE I DRAWN THEE.

GALATIANS 2:20 - I AM CRUCIFIED WITH CHRIST: NEVERTHELESS I LIVE; YET NOT I, BUT CHRIST LIVETH IN ME: AND THE LIFE WHICH I NOW LIVE IN

THE FLESH I LIVE BY THE FAITH OF THE SON OF GOD, WHO LOVED ME, AND GAVE HIMSELF FOR ME.

1 JOHN 3:1 - BEHOLD, WHAT MANNER OF LOVE THE FATHER HATH BESTOWED UPON US, THAT WE SHOULD BE CALLED THE SONS OF GOD: THEREFORE THE WORLD KNOWETH US NOT, BECAUSE IT KNEW HIM NOT.

ZEPHANIAH 3:17 - THE LORD THY GOD IN THE MIDST OF THEE [IS] MIGHTY; HE WILL SAVE, HE WILL REJOICE OVER THEE WITH JOY; HE WILL REST IN HIS LOVE, HE WILL JOY OVER THEE WITH SINGING.

JOHN 15:13 - GREATER LOVE HATH NO MAN THAN THIS, THAT A MAN LAY DOWN HIS LIFE FOR HIS FRIENDS.

EPHESIANS 3:19 - AND TO KNOW THE LOVE OF CHRIST, WHICH PASSETH KNOWLEDGE, THAT YE MIGHT BE FILLED WITH ALL THE FULNESS OF GOD.

I AM A PARTAKER OF THE SAINTS IN LIGHT

Colossians 1:12 Giving thanks unto the Father, which hath made us meet to be partakers of the inheritance of the saints in light:

John 12:36 While ye have light, believe in the light, that ye may be the children of light. These things spake Jesus, and departed, and did hide himself from them.

Romans 1:7 - To all that be in Rome, beloved of God,

called [to be] saints: Grace to you and peace from God our Father, and the Lord Jesus Christ.

1 Timothy 2:5 - For [there is] one God, and one mediator between God and men, the man Christ Jesus;

Revelation 5:8 - And when he had taken the book, the four beasts and four [and] twenty elders fell down before the Lamb, having every one of them harps, and golden vials full of odours, which are the prayers of saints.

1 Corinthians 14:33 - For God is not [the author] of confusion, but of peace, as in all churches of the saints.

Revelation 14:12 - Here is the patience of the saints: here [are] they that keep the commandments of God, and the faith of Jesus.

Hebrews 12:1 - Wherefore seeing we also are compassed about with so great a cloud of witnesses, let us lay aside every weight, and the sin which doth so easily beset [us], and let us run with patience the race that is set before us,

Romans 12:2 - And be not conformed to this world: but be ye transformed by the renewing of your mind, that ye may prove what [is] that good, and acceptable, and perfect, will of God.

Psalms 30:4 - Sing unto the LORD, O ye saints of his, and give thanks at the remembrance of his holiness.

2 Corinthians 5:17 - Therefore if any man [be] in Christ, [he is] a new creature: old things are passed away; behold, all things are become new.

Revelation 8:3 - And another angel came and stood at the altar, having a golden censer; and there was given unto him much incense, that he should offer [it] with the prayers of all saints upon the golden altar which was before the throne.

John 17:20-23 - Neither pray I for these alone, but for them also which shall believe on me through their word; *(Read More...)*

Matthew 7:21-23 - Not every one that saith unto me, Lord, Lord, shall enter into the kingdom of heaven; but he that doeth the will of my Father which is in heaven. *(Read More...)*

I AM FREE FROM THE LAW OF SIN AND DEATH

Romans 8:2 For the law of the Spirit of life in Christ Jesus hath made me free from the law of sin and death.

I AM A CHILD OF THE KING

JOHN 1:12 - BUT AS MANY AS RECEIVED HIM, TO THEM GAVE HE POWER TO BECOME THE SONS OF GOD, [EVEN] TO THEM THAT BELIEVE ON HIS NAME:

GALATIANS 3:26 - FOR YE ARE ALL THE CHILDREN OF GOD BY FAITH IN CHRIST JESUS.

1 JOHN 2:28 - 3:10 - AND NOW, LITTLE CHILDREN,

ABIDE IN HIM; THAT, WHEN HE SHALL APPEAR, WE MAY HAVE CONFIDENCE, AND NOT BE ASHAMED BEFORE HIM AT HIS COMING. *(READ MORE...)*

ROMANS 8:17-19 - AND IF CHILDREN, THEN HEIRS; HEIRS OF GOD, AND JOINT-HEIRS WITH CHRIST; IF SO BE THAT WE SUFFER WITH [HIM], THAT WE MAY BE ALSO GLORIFIED TOGETHER. *(READ MORE...)*

1 PETER 2:10 - WHICH IN TIME PAST [WERE] NOT A PEOPLE, BUT [ARE] NOW THE PEOPLE OF GOD: WHICH HAD NOT OBTAINED MERCY, BUT NOW HAVE OBTAINED MERCY.

ROMANS 8:14-19 - FOR AS MANY AS ARE LED BY THE SPIRIT OF GOD, THEY ARE THE SONS OF GOD. *(READ MORE...)*

ROMANS 8:28 - AND WE KNOW THAT ALL THINGS WORK TOGETHER FOR GOOD TO THEM THAT LOVE GOD, TO THEM WHO ARE THE CALLED ACCORDING TO [HIS] PURPOSE.

ROMANS 8:17 - AND IF CHILDREN, THEN HEIRS; HEIRS OF GOD, AND JOINT-HEIRS WITH CHRIST; IF SO BE THAT WE SUFFER WITH [HIM], THAT WE MAY BE ALSO GLORIFIED TOGETHER.

MATTHEW 5:9 - BLESSED [ARE] THE PEACEMAKERS: FOR THEY SHALL BE CALLED THE CHILDREN OF GOD.

ROMANS 5:1-21 - THEREFORE BEING JUSTIFIED BY FAITH, WE HAVE PEACE WITH GOD THROUGH OUR LORD JESUS CHRIST: *(READ MORE...)*

ROMANS 8:16 - THE SPIRIT ITSELF BEARETH WITNESS WITH OUR SPIRIT, THAT WE ARE THE CHILDREN OF GOD:

ROMANS 5:8 - BUT GOD COMMENDETH HIS LOVE TOWARD US, IN THAT, WHILE WE WERE YET SINNERS, CHRIST DIED FOR US.

ROMANS 12:2 - AND BE NOT CONFORMED TO THIS WORLD: BUT BE YE TRANSFORMED BY THE RENEWING OF YOUR MIND, THAT YE MAY PROVE WHAT [IS] THAT GOOD, AND ACCEPTABLE, AND PERFECT, WILL OF GOD.

GALATIANS 3:28 - THERE IS NEITHER JEW NOR GREEK, THERE IS NEITHER BOND NOR FREE, THERE IS NEITHER MALE NOR FEMALE: FOR YE ARE ALL ONE IN CHRIST JESUS.

I AM LIKE THE WIND

John 3:8 **The wind bloweth where it listeth, and thou hearest the sound thereof, but canst not tell whence it cometh, and whither it goeth: so is every one that is born of the Spirit.**

I AM BORN NOT OF FLESH

John 1:13 Which were born, not of blood, nor of the will of the flesh, nor of the will of man, but of God.

I AM SAVED BY THE POWER OF GOD

Psalms 106:8 Nevertheless he saved them for his name's sake, that he might make his mighty power to be known.

1 Corinthians 1:18 For the preaching of the cross is to them that perish foolishness; but unto us which are saved it is the power of God.

2 Corinthians 13:4 For though he was crucified through weakness, yet he liveth by the power of God. For we also are weak in him, but we shall live with him by the power of God toward you.

Ephesians 1:19 And what is the exceeding greatness of his power to us-ward who believe, according to the working of his mighty power,

---

I AM MADE ALIVE IN ONENESS WITH CHRIST

1 CORINTHIANS 12:13 - FOR BY ONE SPIRIT ARE WE ALL BAPTIZED INTO ONE BODY, WHETHER [WE BE] JEWS OR GENTILES, WHETHER [WE BE] BOND OR FREE; AND HAVE BEEN ALL MADE TO DRINK INTO ONE SPIRIT.

EPHESIANS 4:5 - ONE LORD, ONE FAITH, ONE BAPTISM,

JOHN 10:30 - I AND [MY] FATHER ARE ONE.

1 JOHN 5:20 - AND WE KNOW THAT THE SON OF GOD IS COME, AND HATH GIVEN US AN UNDERSTANDING, THAT WE MAY KNOW HIM THAT IS TRUE, AND WE ARE IN HIM THAT IS TRUE, [EVEN] IN HIS SON JESUS CHRIST. THIS IS THE TRUE GOD, AND ETERNAL LIFE.

GENESIS 1:26 - AND GOD SAID, LET US MAKE MAN IN OUR IMAGE, AFTER OUR LIKENESS: AND LET THEM HAVE DOMINION OVER THE FISH OF THE SEA, AND OVER THE FOWL OF THE AIR, AND OVER THE CATTLE, AND OVER ALL THE EARTH, AND OVER EVERY CREEPING THING THAT CREEPETH UPON THE EARTH.

I HAVE THE VERY LIFE OF CHRIST HIMSELF

JOHN 14:6 - JESUS SAITH UNTO HIM, I AM THE WAY, THE TRUTH, AND THE LIFE: NO MAN COMETH UNTO THE FATHER, BUT BY ME.

JOHN 3:16 - FOR GOD SO LOVED THE WORLD, THAT HE GAVE HIS ONLY BEGOTTEN SON, THAT WHOSOEVER BELIEVETH IN HIM SHOULD NOT PERISH, BUT HAVE EVERLASTING LIFE.

ROMANS 6:23 - FOR THE WAGES OF SIN [IS] DEATH; BUT THE GIFT OF GOD [IS] ETERNAL LIFE THROUGH JESUS CHRIST OUR LORD.

GALATIANS 2:20 - I AM CRUCIFIED WITH CHRIST: NEVERTHELESS I LIVE; YET NOT I, BUT CHRIST LIVETH IN ME: AND THE LIFE WHICH I NOW LIVE IN THE FLESH I LIVE BY THE FAITH OF THE SON OF GOD, WHO LOVED ME, AND GAVE HIMSELF FOR ME.

I HAVE THE SAME SPIRIT THAT CHRIST

Romans 8:11 But if the Spirit of him that raised up Jesus from the dead dwell in you, he that raised up Christ from the dead shall also quicken your mortal bodies by his Spirit that dwelleth in you.

1 John 5:6 This is he that came by water and blood, even Jesus Christ; not by water only, but by water and blood. And it is the Spirit that beareth witness, because the Spirit is truth.

I AM CALLED

2 Timothy 1:9 - Who hath saved us, and called [us] with an holy calling, not according to our works, but according to his own purpose and grace, which was given us in Christ Jesus before the world began,

Matthew 22:14 - For many are called, but few [are] chosen.

John 6:44 - No man can come to me, except the Father which hath sent me draw him: and I will raise him up at the last day.

Romans 8:28-30 - And we know that all things work together for good to them that love God, to them who are the called according to [his] purpose. *(Read More...)*

1 Corinthians 1:26 - For ye see your calling, brethren, how that not many wise men after the flesh, not many mighty, not many noble, [are called]:

Philippians 1:6 - Being confident of this very thing, that he which hath begun a good work in you will perform [it] until the day of Jesus Christ:

Luke 12:32 - Fear not, little flock; for it is your Father's good pleasure to give you the kingdom.

1 Timothy 1:12 - And I thank Christ Jesus our Lord, who hath enabled me, for that he counted me faithful, putting me into the ministry;

1 Corinthians 7:17-24 - But as God hath distributed to every man, as the Lord hath called every one, so let him walk. And so ordain I in all churches. *(Read More...)*

Matthew 28:19-20 - Go ye therefore, and teach all nations, baptizing them in the name of the Father, and of the Son, and of the Holy Ghost: *(Read More...)*

CHAPTER FIVE

I AM EMPOWERED OVER ALL POWER OF ENEMY

2 CORINTHIANS 12:9 - AND HE SAID UNTO ME, MY GRACE IS SUFFICIENT FOR THEE: FOR MY STRENGTH IS MADE PERFECT IN WEAKNESS. MOST GLADLY THEREFORE WILL I RATHER GLORY IN MY INFIRMITIES, THAT THE POWER OF CHRIST MAY REST UPON ME.

DEUTERONOMY 31:6 - BE STRONG AND OF A GOOD COURAGE, FEAR NOT, NOR BE AFRAID OF THEM: FOR THE LORD THY GOD, HE [IT IS] THAT DOTH GO WITH THEE; HE WILL NOT FAIL THEE, NOR FORSAKE THEE.

ACTS 1:8 - BUT YE SHALL RECEIVE POWER, AFTER THAT THE HOLY GHOST IS COME UPON YOU: AND YE SHALL BE WITNESSES UNTO ME BOTH IN JERUSALEM, AND IN ALL JUDAEA, AND IN SAMARIA, AND UNTO THE

UTTERMOST PART OF THE EARTH.

1 JOHN 4:4 - YE ARE OF GOD, LITTLE CHILDREN, AND HAVE OVERCOME THEM: BECAUSE GREATER IS HE THAT IS IN YOU, THAN HE THAT IS IN THE WORLD.

LUKE 10:19-20 - BEHOLD, I GIVE UNTO YOU POWER TO TREAD ON SERPENTS AND SCORPIONS, AND OVER ALL THE POWER OF THE ENEMY: AND NOTHING SHALL BY ANY MEANS HURT YOU. *(READ MORE...)*

2 PETER 1:3-4 - ACCORDING AS HIS DIVINE POWER HATH GIVEN UNTO US ALL THINGS THAT [PERTAIN] UNTO LIFE AND GODLINESS, THROUGH THE KNOWLEDGE OF HIM THAT HATH CALLED US TO GLORY AND VIRTUE: *(READ MORE...)*

MATTHEW 28:18-20 - AND JESUS CAME AND SPAKE UNTO THEM, SAYING, ALL POWER IS GIVEN UNTO ME IN HEAVEN AND IN EARTH. *(READ MORE...)*

ISAIAH 41:10-13 - FEAR THOU NOT; FOR I [AM] WITH THEE: BE NOT DISMAYED; FOR I [AM] THY GOD: I WILL STRENGTHEN THEE; YEA, I WILL HELP THEE; YEA, I WILL UPHOLD THEE WITH THE RIGHT HAND OF MY RIGHTEOUSNESS.

I AM NO LONGER A SLAVE

GALATIANS 5:1 - STAND FAST THEREFORE IN THE LIBERTY WHEREWITH CHRIST HATH MADE US FREE, AND BE NOT ENTANGLED AGAIN WITH THE YOKE OF BONDAGE.

GALATIANS 3:28 - THERE IS NEITHER JEW NOR GREEK, THERE IS NEITHER BOND NOR FREE, THERE IS NEITHER MALE NOR FEMALE: FOR YE ARE ALL ONE IN CHRIST JESUS.

LUKE 4:18 - THE SPIRIT OF THE LORD [IS] UPON ME, BECAUSE HE HATH ANOINTED ME TO PREACH THE GOSPEL TO THE POOR; HE HATH SENT ME TO HEAL THE BROKENHEARTED, TO PREACH DELIVERANCE TO THE CAPTIVES, AND RECOVERING OF SIGHT TO THE BLIND, TO SET AT LIBERTY THEM THAT ARE BRUISED,

PHILEMON 1:16 - NOT NOW AS A SERVANT, BUT ABOVE A SERVANT, A BROTHER BELOVED, SPECIALLY TO ME, BUT HOW MUCH MORE UNTO THEE, BOTH IN THE FLESH, AND IN THE LORD?

I AM CREATED IN HIS IMAGE

GENESIS 1:27 - SO GOD CREATED MAN IN HIS [OWN] IMAGE, IN THE IMAGE OF GOD CREATED HE HIM; MALE AND FEMALE CREATED HE THEM.

COLOSSIANS 3:10 - AND HAVE PUT ON THE NEW [MAN], WHICH IS RENEWED IN KNOWLEDGE AFTER THE IMAGE OF HIM THAT CREATED HIM:

GENESIS 1:26-27 - AND GOD SAID, LET US MAKE MAN IN OUR IMAGE, AFTER OUR LIKENESS: AND LET THEM HAVE DOMINION OVER THE FISH OF THE SEA, AND OVER THE FOWL OF THE AIR, AND OVER THE CATTLE, AND OVER ALL THE EARTH, AND OVER EVERY CREEPING THING THAT CREEPETH UPON THE

EARTH. *(READ MORE...)*

GENESIS 9:6 - WHOSO SHEDDETH MAN'S BLOOD, BY MAN SHALL HIS BLOOD BE SHED: FOR IN THE IMAGE OF GOD MADE HE MAN.

GENESIS 1:26 - AND GOD SAID, LET US MAKE MAN IN OUR IMAGE, AFTER OUR LIKENESS: AND LET THEM HAVE DOMINION OVER THE FISH OF THE SEA, AND OVER THE FOWL OF THE AIR, AND OVER THE CATTLE, AND OVER ALL THE EARTH, AND OVER EVERY CREEPING THING THAT CREEPETH UPON THE EARTH.

2 CORINTHIANS 4:4 - IN WHOM THE GOD OF THIS WORLD HATH BLINDED THE MINDS OF THEM WHICH BELIEVE NOT, LEST THE LIGHT OF THE GLORIOUS GOSPEL OF CHRIST, WHO IS THE IMAGE OF GOD, SHOULD SHINE UNTO THEM.

JAMES 3:8-10 - BUT THE TONGUE CAN NO MAN TAME; [IT IS] AN UNRULY EVIL, FULL OF DEADLY POISON. *(READ MORE...)*

2 CORINTHIANS 4:3-4 - BUT IF OUR GOSPEL BE HID, IT IS HID TO THEM THAT ARE LOST: *(READ MORE...)*

2 CORINTHIANS 3:15-18 - BUT EVEN UNTO THIS DAY, WHEN MOSES IS READ, THE VAIL IS UPON THEIR HEART. *(READ MORE...)*

1 CORINTHIANS 11:7 - FOR A MAN INDEED OUGHT NOT TO COVER [HIS] HEAD, FORASMUCH AS HE IS THE IMAGE AND GLORY OF GOD: BUT THE WOMAN IS THE GLORY OF THE MAN.

I AM LIVING ETERNALLY

JOHN 3:16 - FOR GOD SO LOVED THE WORLD, THAT HE GAVE HIS ONLY BEGOTTEN SON, THAT WHOSOEVER BELIEVETH IN HIM SHOULD NOT PERISH, BUT HAVE EVERLASTING LIFE.

ROMANS 6:23 - FOR THE WAGES OF SIN [IS] DEATH; BUT THE GIFT OF GOD [IS] ETERNAL LIFE THROUGH JESUS CHRIST OUR LORD.

JOHN 17:3 - AND THIS IS LIFE ETERNAL, THAT THEY MIGHT KNOW THEE THE ONLY TRUE GOD, AND JESUS CHRIST, WHOM THOU HAST SENT.

MATTHEW 25:46 - AND THESE SHALL GO AWAY INTO EVERLASTING PUNISHMENT: BUT THE RIGHTEOUS INTO LIFE ETERNAL.

ROMANS 10:13 - FOR WHOSOEVER SHALL CALL UPON THE NAME OF THE LORD SHALL BE SAVED.

JOHN 6:50-71 - THIS IS THE BREAD WHICH COMETH DOWN FROM HEAVEN, THAT A MAN MAY EAT THEREOF, AND NOT DIE. *(READ MORE...)*

1 JOHN 1:9 - IF WE CONFESS OUR SINS, HE IS FAITHFUL AND JUST TO FORGIVE US [OUR] SINS, AND TO CLEANSE US FROM ALL UNRIGHTEOUSNESS.

MATTHEW 7:21-23 - NOT EVERY ONE THAT SAITH UNTO ME, LORD, LORD, SHALL ENTER INTO THE KINGDOM OF HEAVEN; BUT HE THAT DOETH THE WILL

OF MY FATHER WHICH IS IN HEAVEN. *(READ MORE...)*

JOHN 5:24 - VERILY, VERILY, I SAY UNTO YOU, HE THAT HEARETH MY WORD, AND BELIEVETH ON HIM THAT SENT ME, HATH EVERLASTING LIFE, AND SHALL NOT COME INTO CONDEMNATION; BUT IS PASSED FROM DEATH UNTO LIFE.

REVELATION 21:8 - BUT THE FEARFUL, AND UNBELIEVING, AND THE ABOMINABLE, AND MURDERERS, AND WHOREMONGERS, AND SORCERERS, AND IDOLATERS, AND ALL LIARS, SHALL HAVE THEIR PART IN THE LAKE WHICH BURNETH WITH FIRE AND BRIMSTONE: WHICH IS THE SECOND DEATH.

I AM TO BE

ALL OF THIS CAN ONLY BE DONE BY FAITH

I AM TO BE LIKE JESUS

1 JOHN 2:6 - HE THAT SAITH HE ABIDETH IN HIM OUGHT HIMSELF ALSO SO TO WALK, EVEN AS HE WALKED.

1 CORINTHIANS 11:1 - BE YE FOLLOWERS OF ME, EVEN AS I ALSO [AM] OF CHRIST.

1 PETER 2:21 - FOR EVEN HEREUNTO WERE YE CALLED: BECAUSE CHRIST ALSO SUFFERED FOR US, LEAVING US AN EXAMPLE, THAT YE SHOULD FOLLOW HIS STEPS:

EPHESIANS 5:1-2 - BE YE THEREFORE FOLLOWERS OF GOD, AS DEAR CHILDREN; *(READ MORE...)*

JOHN 13:13-17 - YE CALL ME MASTER AND LORD: AND YE SAY WELL; FOR [SO] I AM. *(READ MORE...)*

JOHN 14:15 - IF YE LOVE ME, KEEP MY COMMANDMENTS.

EPHESIANS 4:22-24 - THAT YE PUT OFF CONCERNING THE FORMER CONVERSATION THE OLD MAN, WHICH IS CORRUPT ACCORDING TO THE DECEITFUL LUSTS; *(READ MORE...)*

GALATIANS 3:27 - FOR AS MANY OF YOU AS HAVE BEEN BAPTIZED INTO CHRIST HAVE PUT ON CHRIST.

TITUS 3:1-8 - PUT THEM IN MIND TO BE SUBJECT TO PRINCIPALITIES AND POWERS, TO OBEY MAGISTRATES, TO BE READY TO EVERY GOOD WORK, *(READ MORE...)*

ROMANS 8:29 - FOR WHOM HE DID FOREKNOW, HE ALSO DID PREDESTINATE [TO BE] CONFORMED TO THE IMAGE OF HIS SON, THAT HE MIGHT BE THE FIRSTBORN AMONG MANY BRETHREN.

PROVERBS 3:5-6 - TRUST IN THE LORD WITH ALL THINE HEART; AND LEAN NOT UNTO THINE OWN

UNDERSTANDING. *(READ MORE...)*

ROMANS 8:2-8 - FOR THE LAW OF THE SPIRIT OF LIFE IN CHRIST JESUS HATH MADE ME FREE FROM THE LAW OF SIN AND DEATH. *(READ MORE...)*

PHILIPPIANS 2:5 - LET THIS MIND BE IN YOU, WHICH WAS ALSO IN CHRIST JESUS:

MATTHEW 11:29 - TAKE MY YOKE UPON YOU, AND LEARN OF ME; FOR I AM MEEK AND LOWLY IN HEART: AND YE SHALL FIND REST UNTO YOUR SOULS.

I AM TO BE HAVING THE MIND OF CHRIST

1 CORINTHIANS 2:16 - FOR WHO HATH KNOWN THE MIND OF THE LORD, THAT HE MAY INSTRUCT HIM? BUT WE HAVE THE MIND OF CHRIST.

ROMANS 12:2 - AND BE NOT CONFORMED TO THIS WORLD: BUT BE YE TRANSFORMED BY THE RENEWING OF YOUR MIND, THAT YE MAY PROVE WHAT [IS] THAT GOOD, AND ACCEPTABLE, AND PERFECT, WILL OF GOD.

1 CORINTHIANS 2:14-16 - BUT THE NATURAL MAN RECEIVETH NOT THE THINGS OF THE SPIRIT OF GOD: FOR THEY ARE FOOLISHNESS UNTO HIM: NEITHER CAN HE KNOW [THEM], BECAUSE THEY ARE SPIRITUALLY DISCERNED. *(READ MORE...)*

PHILIPPIANS 2:5 - LET THIS MIND BE IN YOU, WHICH WAS ALSO IN CHRIST JESUS:

1 CORINTHIANS 2:13-16 - WHICH THINGS ALSO WE SPEAK, NOT IN THE WORDS WHICH MAN'S WISDOM TEACHETH, BUT WHICH THE HOLY GHOST TEACHETH; COMPARING SPIRITUAL THINGS WITH SPIRITUAL. *(READ MORE...)*

2 TIMOTHY 1:7 - FOR GOD HATH NOT GIVEN US THE SPIRIT OF FEAR; BUT OF POWER, AND OF LOVE, AND OF A SOUND MIND.

1 PETER 1:13 - WHEREFORE GIRD UP THE LOINS OF YOUR MIND, BE SOBER, AND HOPE TO THE END FOR THE GRACE THAT IS TO BE BROUGHT UNTO YOU AT THE REVELATION OF JESUS CHRIST;

PHILIPPIANS 2:5-11 - LET THIS MIND BE IN YOU, WHICH WAS ALSO IN CHRIST JESUS: *(READ MORE...)*

1 PETER 4:17 - FOR THE TIME [IS COME] THAT JUDGMENT MUST BEGIN AT THE HOUSE OF GOD: AND IF [IT] FIRST [BEGIN] AT US, WHAT SHALL THE END [BE] OF THEM THAT OBEY NOT THE GOSPEL OF GOD?

1 PETER 1:3 - BLESSED [BE] THE GOD AND FATHER OF OUR LORD JESUS CHRIST, WHICH ACCORDING TO HIS ABUNDANT MERCY HATH BEGOTTEN US AGAIN UNTO A LIVELY HOPE BY THE RESURRECTION OF JESUS CHRIST FROM THE DEAD,

JOHN 5:30 - I CAN OF MINE OWN SELF DO NOTHING: AS I HEAR, I JUDGE: AND MY JUDGMENT IS JUST; BECAUSE I SEEK NOT MINE OWN WILL, BUT THE WILL OF THE FATHER WHICH HATH SENT ME.

EPHESIANS 5:1 - BE YE THEREFORE FOLLOWERS OF

GOD, AS DEAR CHILDREN;

1 JOHN 2:6 - HE THAT SAITH HE ABIDETH IN HIM OUGHT HIMSELF ALSO SO TO WALK, EVEN AS HE WALKED.

ROMANS 8:1-39 - [THERE IS] THEREFORE NOW NO CONDEMNATION TO THEM WHICH ARE IN CHRIST JESUS, WHO WALK NOT AFTER THE FLESH, BUT AFTER THE SPIRIT. *(READ MORE...)*

PHILIPPIANS 4:8 - FINALLY, BRETHREN, WHATSOEVER THINGS ARE TRUE, WHATSOEVER THINGS [ARE] HONEST, WHATSOEVER THINGS [ARE] JUST, WHATSOEVER THINGS [ARE] PURE, WHATSOEVER THINGS [ARE] LOVELY, WHATSOEVER THINGS [ARE] OF GOOD REPORT; IF [THERE BE] ANY VIRTUE, AND IF [THERE BE] ANY PRAISE, THINK ON THESE THINGS.

JAMES 1:27 - PURE RELIGION AND UNDEFILED BEFORE GOD AND THE FATHER IS THIS, TO VISIT THE FATHERLESS AND WIDOWS IN THEIR AFFLICTION, [AND] TO KEEP HIMSELF UNSPOTTED FROM THE WORLD.

MATTHEW 28:18 - AND JESUS CAME AND SPAKE UNTO THEM, SAYING, ALL POWER IS GIVEN UNTO ME IN HEAVEN AND IN EARTH.

GALATIANS 5:19-21 - NOW THE WORKS OF THE FLESH ARE MANIFEST, WHICH ARE [THESE]; ADULTERY, FORNICATION, UNCLEANNESS, LASCIVIOUSNESS, *(READ MORE...)*

I AM TO BE LOVING

1 CORINTHIANS 13:4-8 - CHARITY SUFFERETH LONG, [AND] IS KIND; CHARITY ENVIETH NOT; CHARITY VAUNTETH NOT ITSELF, IS NOT PUFFED UP, *(READ MORE...)*

1 CORINTHIANS 16:14 - LET ALL YOUR THINGS BE DONE WITH CHARITY.

1 JOHN 4:8 - HE THAT LOVETH NOT KNOWETH NOT GOD; FOR GOD IS LOVE.

MARK 12:29-31 - AND JESUS ANSWERED HIM, THE FIRST OF ALL THE COMMANDMENTS [IS], HEAR, O ISRAEL; THE LORD OUR GOD IS ONE LORD: *(READ MORE...)*

MATTHEW 22:36-40 - MASTER, WHICH [IS] THE GREAT COMMANDMENT IN THE LAW? *(READ MORE...)*

JOHN 13:34-35 - A NEW COMMANDMENT I GIVE UNTO YOU, THAT YE LOVE ONE ANOTHER; AS I HAVE LOVED YOU, THAT YE ALSO LOVE ONE ANOTHER. *(READ MORE...)*

COLOSSIANS 3:14 - AND ABOVE ALL THESE THINGS [PUT ON] CHARITY, WHICH IS THE BOND OF PERFECTNESS.

JOHN 15:13 - GREATER LOVE HATH NO MAN THAN THIS, THAT A MAN LAY DOWN HIS LIFE FOR HIS FRIENDS.

JOHN 3:16 - FOR GOD SO LOVED THE WORLD, THAT HE GAVE HIS ONLY BEGOTTEN SON, THAT WHOSOEVER BELIEVETH IN HIM SHOULD NOT PERISH, BUT HAVE EVERLASTING LIFE.

1 JOHN 4:19 - WE LOVE HIM, BECAUSE HE FIRST LOVED US.

1 JOHN 4:7 - BELOVED, LET US LOVE ONE ANOTHER: FOR LOVE IS OF GOD; AND EVERY ONE THAT LOVETH IS BORN OF GOD, AND KNOWETH GOD.

1 PETER 4:8 - AND ABOVE ALL THINGS HAVE FERVENT CHARITY AMONG YOURSELVES: FOR CHARITY SHALL COVER THE MULTITUDE OF SINS.

JOHN 14:15 - IF YE LOVE ME, KEEP MY COMMANDMENTS.

1 JOHN 4:18 - THERE IS NO FEAR IN LOVE; BUT PERFECT LOVE CASTETH OUT FEAR: BECAUSE FEAR HATH TORMENT. HE THAT FEARETH IS NOT MADE PERFECT IN LOVE.

1 CORINTHIANS 13:1-13 - THOUGH I SPEAK WITH THE TONGUES OF MEN AND OF ANGELS, AND HAVE NOT CHARITY, I AM BECOME [AS] SOUNDING BRASS, OR A TINKLING CYMBAL. *(READ MORE...)*

1 CORINTHIANS 13:13 - AND NOW ABIDETH FAITH, HOPE, CHARITY, THESE THREE; BUT THE GREATEST OF THESE [IS] CHARITY.

I AM TO BE JOYFUL

PROVERBS 17:22 - A MERRY HEART DOETH GOOD [LIKE] A MEDICINE: BUT A BROKEN SPIRIT DRIETH THE BONES.

ROMANS 15:13 - NOW THE GOD OF HOPE FILL YOU WITH ALL JOY AND PEACE IN BELIEVING, THAT YE MAY ABOUND IN HOPE, THROUGH THE POWER OF THE HOLY GHOST.

ROMANS 12:12 - REJOICING IN HOPE; PATIENT IN TRIBULATION; CONTINUING INSTANT IN PRAYER;

PSALMS 28:7 - THE LORD [IS] MY STRENGTH AND MY SHIELD; MY HEART TRUSTED IN HIM, AND I AM HELPED: THEREFORE MY HEART GREATLY REJOICETH; AND WITH MY SONG WILL I PRAISE HIM.

PSALMS 100:2 - SERVE THE LORD WITH GLADNESS: COME BEFORE HIS PRESENCE WITH SINGING.

PSALMS 21:6 - FOR THOU HAST MADE HIM MOST BLESSED FOR EVER: THOU HAST MADE HIM EXCEEDING GLAD WITH THY COUNTENANCE.

PHILIPPIANS 4:4 - REJOICE IN THE LORD ALWAY: [AND] AGAIN I SAY, REJOICE.

PSALMS 64:10 - THE RIGHTEOUS SHALL BE GLAD IN THE LORD, AND SHALL TRUST IN HIM; AND ALL THE UPRIGHT IN HEART SHALL GLORY.

JAMES 5:13 - IS ANY AMONG YOU AFFLICTED? LET HIM PRAY. IS ANY MERRY? LET HIM SING PSALMS.

JOHN 14:27 - PEACE I LEAVE WITH YOU, MY PEACE I GIVE UNTO YOU: NOT AS THE WORLD GIVETH, GIVE I UNTO YOU. LET NOT YOUR HEART BE TROUBLED, NEITHER LET IT BE AFRAID.

DEUTERONOMY 28:1-68 - AND IT SHALL COME TO PASS, IF THOU SHALT HEARKEN DILIGENTLY UNTO THE VOICE OF THE LORD THY GOD, TO OBSERVE [AND] TO DO ALL HIS COMMANDMENTS WHICH I COMMAND THEE THIS DAY, THAT THE LORD THY GOD WILL SET THEE ON HIGH ABOVE ALL NATIONS OF THE EARTH: *(READ MORE...)*

PSALMS 5:11 - BUT LET ALL THOSE THAT PUT THEIR TRUST IN THEE REJOICE: LET THEM EVER SHOUT FOR JOY, BECAUSE THOU DEFENDEST THEM: LET THEM ALSO THAT LOVE THY NAME BE JOYFUL IN THEE.

1 THESSALONIANS 5:16 - REJOICE EVERMORE.

JOHN 16:22 - AND YE NOW THEREFORE HAVE SORROW: BUT I WILL SEE YOU AGAIN, AND YOUR HEART SHALL REJOICE, AND YOUR JOY NO MAN TAKETH FROM YOU.

PSALMS 30:5 - FOR HIS ANGER [ENDURETH BUT] A MOMENT; IN HIS FAVOUR [IS] LIFE: WEEPING MAY ENDURE FOR A NIGHT, BUT JOY [COMETH] IN THE MORNING.

EPHESIANS 5:19 - SPEAKING TO YOURSELVES IN PSALMS AND HYMNS AND SPIRITUAL SONGS, SINGING AND MAKING MELODY IN YOUR HEART TO THE LORD;

HEBREWS 1:1-14 - GOD, WHO AT SUNDRY TIMES

AND IN DIVERS MANNERS SPAKE IN TIME PAST UNTO THE FATHERS BY THE PROPHETS, *(READ MORE...)*

ISAIAH 12:6 - CRY OUT AND SHOUT, THOU INHABITANT OF ZION: FOR GREAT [IS] THE HOLY ONE OF ISRAEL IN THE MIDST OF THEE.

1 JOHN 4:18 - THERE IS NO FEAR IN LOVE; BUT PERFECT LOVE CASTETH OUT FEAR: BECAUSE FEAR HATH TORMENT. HE THAT FEARETH IS NOT MADE PERFECT IN LOVE.

ISAIAH 61:10 - I WILL GREATLY REJOICE IN THE LORD, MY SOUL SHALL BE JOYFUL IN MY GOD; FOR HE HATH CLOTHED ME WITH THE GARMENTS OF SALVATION, HE HATH COVERED ME WITH THE ROBE OF RIGHTEOUSNESS, AS A BRIDEGROOM DECKETH [HIMSELF] WITH ORNAMENTS, AND AS A BRIDE ADORNETH [HERSELF] WITH HER JEWELS.

ZEPHANIAH 3:17 - THE LORD THY GOD IN THE MIDST OF THEE [IS] MIGHTY; HE WILL SAVE, HE WILL REJOICE OVER THEE WITH JOY; HE WILL REST IN HIS LOVE, HE WILL JOY OVER THEE WITH SINGING.

PSALMS 104:34 - MY MEDITATION OF HIM SHALL BE SWEET: I WILL BE GLAD IN THE LORD.

NEHEMIAH 8:10 - THEN HE SAID UNTO THEM, GO YOUR WAY, EAT THE FAT, AND DRINK THE SWEET, AND SEND PORTIONS UNTO THEM FOR WHOM NOTHING IS PREPARED: FOR [THIS] DAY [IS] HOLY UNTO OUR LORD: NEITHER BE YE SORRY; FOR THE JOY OF THE LORD IS YOUR STRENGTH.

I AM TO BE FULL OF GODS PEACE

2 THESSALONIANS 3:16 - NOW THE LORD OF PEACE HIMSELF GIVE YOU PEACE ALWAYS BY ALL MEANS. THE LORD [BE] WITH YOU ALL.

JOHN 16:33 - THESE THINGS I HAVE SPOKEN UNTO YOU, THAT IN ME YE MIGHT HAVE PEACE. IN THE WORLD YE SHALL HAVE TRIBULATION: BUT BE OF GOOD CHEER; I HAVE OVERCOME THE WORLD.

PHILIPPIANS 4:6 - BE CAREFUL FOR NOTHING; BUT IN EVERY THING BY PRAYER AND SUPPLICATION WITH THANKSGIVING LET YOUR REQUESTS BE MADE KNOWN UNTO GOD.

ISAIAH 26:3 - THOU WILT KEEP [HIM] IN PERFECT PEACE, [WHOSE] MIND [IS] STAYED [ON THEE]: BECAUSE HE TRUSTETH IN THEE.

1 PETER 5:7 - CASTING ALL YOUR CARE UPON HIM; FOR HE CARETH FOR YOU.

MATTHEW 5:9 - BLESSED [ARE] THE PEACEMAKERS: FOR THEY SHALL BE CALLED THE CHILDREN OF GOD.

ROMANS 12:18 - IF IT BE POSSIBLE, AS MUCH AS LIETH IN YOU, LIVE PEACEABLY WITH ALL MEN.

MATTHEW 10:34-36 - THINK NOT THAT I AM COME TO SEND PEACE ON EARTH: I CAME NOT TO SEND PEACE, BUT A SWORD. *(READ MORE...)*

1 PETER 3:11 - LET HIM ESCHEW EVIL, AND DO GOOD; LET HIM SEEK PEACE, AND ENSUE IT.

ROMANS 15:13 - NOW THE GOD OF HOPE FILL YOU WITH ALL JOY AND PEACE IN BELIEVING, THAT YE MAY ABOUND IN HOPE, THROUGH THE POWER OF THE HOLY GHOST.

HEBREWS 12:14 - FOLLOW PEACE WITH ALL [MEN], AND HOLINESS, WITHOUT WHICH NO MAN SHALL SEE THE LORD:

1 PETER 5:6-7 - HUMBLE YOURSELVES THEREFORE UNDER THE MIGHTY HAND OF GOD, THAT HE MAY EXALT YOU IN DUE TIME: *(READ MORE...)*

PSALMS 4:8 - I WILL BOTH LAY ME DOWN IN PEACE, AND SLEEP: FOR THOU, LORD, ONLY MAKEST ME DWELL IN SAFETY.

PROVERBS 12:20 - DECEIT [IS] IN THE HEART OF THEM THAT IMAGINE EVIL: BUT TO THE COUNSELLORS OF PEACE [IS] JOY.

ISAIAH 12:2 - BEHOLD, GOD [IS] MY SALVATION; I WILL TRUST, AND NOT BE AFRAID: FOR THE LORD JEHOVAH [IS] MY STRENGTH AND [MY] SONG; HE ALSO IS BECOME MY SALVATION.

1 CORINTHIANS 14:33 - FOR GOD IS NOT [THE AUTHOR] OF CONFUSION, BUT OF PEACE, AS IN ALL CHURCHES OF THE SAINTS.

I AM TO BE LONGSUFFERING

2 PETER 3:9 - THE LORD IS NOT SLACK CONCERNING HIS PROMISE, AS SOME MEN COUNT SLACKNESS; BUT IS LONGSUFFERING TO US-WARD, NOT WILLING THAT ANY SHOULD PERISH, BUT THAT ALL SHOULD COME TO REPENTANCE.

EPHESIANS 4:2 - WITH ALL LOWLINESS AND MEEKNESS, WITH LONGSUFFERING, FORBEARING ONE ANOTHER IN LOVE;

GALATIANS 5:22 - BUT THE FRUIT OF THE SPIRIT IS LOVE, JOY, PEACE, LONGSUFFERING, GENTLENESS, GOODNESS, FAITH,

ROMANS 8:28 - AND WE KNOW THAT ALL THINGS WORK TOGETHER FOR GOOD TO THEM THAT LOVE GOD, TO THEM WHO ARE THE CALLED ACCORDING TO [HIS] PURPOSE.

ROMANS 5:3-4 - AND NOT ONLY [SO], BUT WE GLORY IN TRIBULATIONS ALSO: KNOWING THAT TRIBULATION WORKETH PATIENCE; *(READ MORE...)*

HEBREWS 2:10 - FOR IT BECAME HIM, FOR WHOM [ARE] ALL THINGS, AND BY WHOM [ARE] ALL THINGS, IN BRINGING MANY SONS UNTO GLORY, TO MAKE THE CAPTAIN OF THEIR SALVATION PERFECT THROUGH SUFFERINGS.

ROMANS 2:4 - OR DESPISEST THOU THE RICHES OF HIS GOODNESS AND FORBEARANCE AND LONGSUFFERING; NOT KNOWING THAT THE GOODNESS OF GOD LEADETH THEE TO REPENTANCE?

2 PETER 3:1-18 - THIS SECOND EPISTLE, BELOVED, I

NOW WRITE UNTO YOU; IN [BOTH] WHICH I STIR UP YOUR PURE MINDS BY WAY OF REMEMBRANCE: *(READ MORE...)*

ROMANS 9:22 - [WHAT] IF GOD, WILLING TO SHEW [HIS] WRATH, AND TO MAKE HIS POWER KNOWN, ENDURED WITH MUCH LONGSUFFERING THE VESSELS OF WRATH FITTED TO DESTRUCTION:

JOB 1:1-22 - THERE WAS A MAN IN THE LAND OF UZ, WHOSE NAME [WAS] JOB; AND THAT MAN WAS PERFECT AND UPRIGHT, AND ONE THAT FEARED GOD, AND ESCHEWED EVIL. *(READ MORE...)*

COLOSSIANS 3:12 - PUT ON THEREFORE, AS THE ELECT OF GOD, HOLY AND BELOVED, BOWELS OF MERCIES, KINDNESS, HUMBLENESS OF MIND, MEEKNESS, LONGSUFFERING;

1 CORINTHIANS 2:9 - BUT AS IT IS WRITTEN, EYE HATH NOT SEEN, NOR EAR HEARD, NEITHER HAVE ENTERED INTO THE HEART OF MAN, THE THINGS WHICH GOD HATH PREPARED FOR THEM THAT LOVE HIM.

HEBREWS 4:15 - FOR WE HAVE NOT AN HIGH PRIEST WHICH CANNOT BE TOUCHED WITH THE FEELING OF OUR INFIRMITIES; BUT WAS IN ALL POINTS TEMPTED LIKE AS [WE ARE, YET] WITHOUT SIN.

I AM TO BE GENTLE

TITUS 3:2 - TO SPEAK EVIL OF NO MAN, TO BE NO BRAWLERS, [BUT] GENTLE, SHEWING ALL MEEKNESS UNTO ALL MEN.

1 PETER 3:15 - BUT SANCTIFY THE LORD GOD IN YOUR HEARTS: AND [BE] READY ALWAYS TO [GIVE] AN ANSWER TO EVERY MAN THAT ASKETH YOU A REASON OF THE HOPE THAT IS IN YOU WITH MEEKNESS AND FEAR:

PSALMS 18:35 - THOU HAST ALSO GIVEN ME THE SHIELD OF THY SALVATION: AND THY RIGHT HAND HATH HOLDEN ME UP, AND THY GENTLENESS HATH MADE ME GREAT.

2 TIMOTHY 2:24-26 - AND THE SERVANT OF THE LORD MUST NOT STRIVE; BUT BE GENTLE UNTO ALL [MEN], APT TO TEACH, PATIENT, *(READ MORE...)*

JAMES 3:17 - BUT THE WISDOM THAT IS FROM ABOVE IS FIRST PURE, THEN PEACEABLE, GENTLE, [AND] EASY TO BE INTREATED, FULL OF MERCY AND GOOD FRUITS, WITHOUT PARTIALITY, AND WITHOUT HYPOCRISY.

PROVERBS 15:1 - A SOFT ANSWER TURNETH AWAY WRATH: BUT GRIEVOUS WORDS STIR UP ANGER.

GALATIANS 5:22-23 - BUT THE FRUIT OF THE SPIRIT IS LOVE, JOY, PEACE, LONGSUFFERING, GENTLENESS, GOODNESS, FAITH, *(READ MORE...)*

GALATIANS 6:1 - BRETHREN, IF A MAN BE OVERTAKEN IN A FAULT, YE WHICH ARE SPIRITUAL, RESTORE SUCH AN ONE IN THE SPIRIT OF MEEKNESS;

CONSIDERING THYSELF, LEST THOU ALSO BE TEMPTED.

MATTHEW 11:29 - TAKE MY YOKE UPON YOU, AND LEARN OF ME; FOR I AM MEEK AND LOWLY IN HEART: AND YE SHALL FIND REST UNTO YOUR SOULS.

EPHESIANS 4:2 - WITH ALL LOWLINESS AND MEEKNESS, WITH LONGSUFFERING, FORBEARING ONE ANOTHER IN LOVE;

JAMES 1:19-20 - WHEREFORE, MY BELOVED BRETHREN, LET EVERY MAN BE SWIFT TO HEAR, SLOW TO SPEAK, SLOW TO WRATH: *(READ MORE...)*

2 SAMUEL 22:36 - THOU HAST ALSO GIVEN ME THE SHIELD OF THY SALVATION: AND THY GENTLENESS HATH MADE ME GREAT.

1 CORINTHIANS 13:4-5 - CHARITY SUFFERETH LONG, [AND] IS KIND; CHARITY ENVIETH NOT; CHARITY VAUNTETH NOT ITSELF, IS NOT PUFFED UP, *(READ MORE...)*

ISAIAH 40:11 - HE SHALL FEED HIS FLOCK LIKE A SHEPHERD: HE SHALL GATHER THE LAMBS WITH HIS ARM, AND CARRY [THEM] IN HIS BOSOM, [AND] SHALL GENTLY LEAD THOSE THAT ARE WITH YOUNG.

GALATIANS 5:22 - BUT THE FRUIT OF THE SPIRIT IS LOVE, JOY, PEACE, LONGSUFFERING, GENTLENESS, GOODNESS, FAITH,

---

I AM TO BE GOOD

GALATIANS 6:9 - AND LET US NOT BE WEARY IN WELL DOING: FOR IN DUE SEASON WE SHALL REAP, IF WE FAINT NOT.

PSALMS 37:3 - TRUST IN THE LORD, AND DO GOOD; [SO] SHALT THOU DWELL IN THE LAND, AND VERILY THOU SHALT BE FED.

EPHESIANS 2:10 - FOR WE ARE HIS WORKMANSHIP, CREATED IN CHRIST JESUS UNTO GOOD WORKS, WHICH GOD HATH BEFORE ORDAINED THAT WE SHOULD WALK IN THEM.

MATTHEW 5:16 - LET YOUR LIGHT SO SHINE BEFORE MEN, THAT THEY MAY SEE YOUR GOOD WORKS, AND GLORIFY YOUR FATHER WHICH IS IN HEAVEN.

LUKE 12:33-34 - SELL THAT YE HAVE, AND GIVE ALMS; PROVIDE YOURSELVES BAGS WHICH WAX NOT OLD, A TREASURE IN THE HEAVENS THAT FAILETH NOT, WHERE NO THIEF APPROACHETH, NEITHER MOTH CORRUPTETH. *(READ MORE...)*

JAMES 2:14-17 - WHAT [DOTH IT] PROFIT, MY BRETHREN, THOUGH A MAN SAY HE HATH FAITH, AND HAVE NOT WORKS? CAN FAITH SAVE HIM? *(READ MORE...)*

1 TIMOTHY 6:17-19 - CHARGE THEM THAT ARE RICH IN THIS WORLD, THAT THEY BE NOT HIGHMINDED, NOR TRUST IN UNCERTAIN RICHES, BUT IN THE LIVING GOD, WHO GIVETH US RICHLY ALL THINGS TO ENJOY; *(READ MORE...)*

JOHN 3:16 - FOR GOD SO LOVED THE WORLD, THAT HE GAVE HIS ONLY BEGOTTEN SON, THAT WHOSOEVER BELIEVETH IN HIM SHOULD NOT PERISH, BUT HAVE EVERLASTING LIFE.

2 THESSALONIANS 3:13 - BUT YE, BRETHREN, BE NOT WEARY IN WELL DOING.

LUKE 15:7 - I SAY UNTO YOU, THAT LIKEWISE JOY SHALL BE IN HEAVEN OVER ONE SINNER THAT REPENTETH, MORE THAN OVER NINETY AND NINE JUST PERSONS, WHICH NEED NO REPENTANCE.

GALATIANS 5:19-26 - NOW THE WORKS OF THE FLESH ARE MANIFEST, WHICH ARE [THESE]; ADULTERY, FORNICATION, UNCLEANNESS, LASCIVIOUSNESS, *(READ MORE...)*

ROMANS 2:6-10 - WHO WILL RENDER TO EVERY MAN ACCORDING TO HIS DEEDS: *(READ MORE...)*

GALATIANS 2:16 - KNOWING THAT A MAN IS NOT JUSTIFIED BY THE WORKS OF THE LAW, BUT BY THE FAITH OF JESUS CHRIST, EVEN WE HAVE BELIEVED IN JESUS CHRIST, THAT WE MIGHT BE JUSTIFIED BY THE FAITH OF CHRIST, AND NOT BY THE WORKS OF THE LAW: FOR BY THE WORKS OF THE LAW SHALL NO FLESH BE JUSTIFIED.

I AM TO BE FAITHFUL

PROVERBS 28:20 - A FAITHFUL MAN SHALL ABOUND WITH BLESSINGS: BUT HE THAT MAKETH HASTE TO BE RICH SHALL NOT BE INNOCENT.

LUKE 16:10-12 - HE THAT IS FAITHFUL IN THAT WHICH IS LEAST IS FAITHFUL ALSO IN MUCH: AND HE THAT IS UNJUST IN THE LEAST IS UNJUST ALSO IN MUCH. *(READ MORE...)*

DEUTERONOMY 28:1-68 - AND IT SHALL COME TO PASS, IF THOU SHALT HEARKEN DILIGENTLY UNTO THE VOICE OF THE LORD THY GOD, TO OBSERVE [AND] TO DO ALL HIS COMMANDMENTS WHICH I COMMAND THEE THIS DAY, THAT THE LORD THY GOD WILL SET THEE ON HIGH ABOVE ALL NATIONS OF THE EARTH: *(READ MORE...)*

2 CORINTHIANS 5:7 - (FOR WE WALK BY FAITH, NOT BY SIGHT:)

HEBREWS 13:8 - JESUS CHRIST THE SAME YESTERDAY, AND TO DAY, AND FOR EVER.

GALATIANS 5:22-23 - BUT THE FRUIT OF THE SPIRIT IS LOVE, JOY, PEACE, LONGSUFFERING, GENTLENESS, GOODNESS, FAITH, *(READ MORE...)*

LUKE 12:42-44 - AND THE LORD SAID, WHO THEN IS THAT FAITHFUL AND WISE STEWARD, WHOM [HIS] LORD SHALL MAKE RULER OVER HIS HOUSEHOLD, TO GIVE [THEM THEIR] PORTION OF MEAT IN DUE SEASON? *(READ MORE...)*

1 JOHN 1:9 - IF WE CONFESS OUR SINS, HE IS FAITHFUL AND JUST TO FORGIVE US [OUR] SINS, AND TO CLEANSE US FROM ALL UNRIGHTEOUSNESS.

1 CORINTHIANS 10:13 - THERE HATH NO TEMPTATION TAKEN YOU BUT SUCH AS IS COMMON

TO MAN: BUT GOD [IS] FAITHFUL, WHO WILL NOT SUFFER YOU TO BE TEMPTED ABOVE THAT YE ARE ABLE; BUT WILL WITH THE TEMPTATION ALSO MAKE A WAY TO ESCAPE, THAT YE MAY BE ABLE TO BEAR [IT].

JOHN 14:15 - IF YE LOVE ME, KEEP MY COMMANDMENTS.

1 CORINTHIANS 4:2 - MOREOVER IT IS REQUIRED IN STEWARDS, THAT A MAN BE FOUND FAITHFUL.

PROVERBS 3:3-4 - LET NOT MERCY AND TRUTH FORSAKE THEE: BIND THEM ABOUT THY NECK; WRITE THEM UPON THE TABLE OF THINE HEART: *(READ MORE...)*

PSALMS 89:33 - NEVERTHELESS MY LOVINGKINDNESS WILL I NOT UTTERLY TAKE FROM HIM, NOR SUFFER MY FAITHFULNESS TO FAIL.

2 TIMOTHY 2:13 - IF WE BELIEVE NOT, [YET] HE ABIDETH FAITHFUL: HE CANNOT DENY HIMSELF.

I AM TO BE MEEK

MATTHEW 5:5 - BLESSED [ARE] THE MEEK: FOR THEY SHALL INHERIT THE EARTH.

TITUS 3:2 - TO SPEAK EVIL OF NO MAN, TO BE NO BRAWLERS, [BUT] GENTLE, SHEWING ALL MEEKNESS UNTO ALL MEN.

MATTHEW 11:29 - TAKE MY YOKE UPON YOU, AND

LEARN OF ME; FOR I AM MEEK AND LOWLY IN HEART: AND YE SHALL FIND REST UNTO YOUR SOULS.

PSALMS 37:11 - BUT THE MEEK SHALL INHERIT THE EARTH; AND SHALL DELIGHT THEMSELVES IN THE ABUNDANCE OF PEACE.

PSALMS 25:9 - THE MEEK WILL HE GUIDE IN JUDGMENT: AND THE MEEK WILL HE TEACH HIS WAY.

JAMES 3:13 - WHO [IS] A WISE MAN AND ENDUED WITH KNOWLEDGE AMONG YOU? LET HIM SHEW OUT OF A GOOD CONVERSATION HIS WORKS WITH MEEKNESS OF WISDOM.

1 PETER 3:4 - BUT [LET IT BE] THE HIDDEN MAN OF THE HEART, IN THAT WHICH IS NOT CORRUPTIBLE, [EVEN THE ORNAMENT] OF A MEEK AND QUIET SPIRIT, WHICH IS IN THE SIGHT OF GOD OF GREAT PRICE.

ROMANS 12:14 - BLESS THEM WHICH PERSECUTE YOU: BLESS, AND CURSE NOT.

1 PETER 3:15 - BUT SANCTIFY THE LORD GOD IN YOUR HEARTS: AND [BE] READY ALWAYS TO [GIVE] AN ANSWER TO EVERY MAN THAT ASKETH YOU A REASON OF THE HOPE THAT IS IN YOU WITH MEEKNESS AND FEAR:

GALATIANS 5:22 - BUT THE FRUIT OF THE SPIRIT IS LOVE, JOY, PEACE, LONGSUFFERING, GENTLENESS, GOODNESS, FAITH,

CHAPTER SIX

I AM TO BE THINKING LIKE GOD

PHILIPPIANS 4:8 - FINALLY, BRETHREN, WHATSOEVER THINGS ARE TRUE, WHATSOEVER THINGS [ARE] HONEST, WHATSOEVER THINGS [ARE] JUST, WHATSOEVER THINGS [ARE] PURE, WHATSOEVER THINGS [ARE] LOVELY, WHATSOEVER THINGS [ARE] OF GOOD REPORT; IF [THERE BE] ANY VIRTUE, AND IF [THERE BE] ANY PRAISE, THINK ON THESE THINGS.

ROMANS 8:5-6 - FOR THEY THAT ARE AFTER THE FLESH DO MIND THE THINGS OF THE FLESH; BUT THEY THAT ARE AFTER THE SPIRIT THE THINGS OF THE SPIRIT. *(READ MORE...)*

ROMANS 12:2 - AND BE NOT CONFORMED TO THIS

WORLD: BUT BE YE TRANSFORMED BY THE RENEWING OF YOUR MIND, THAT YE MAY PROVE WHAT [IS] THAT GOOD, AND ACCEPTABLE, AND PERFECT, WILL OF GOD.

COLOSSIANS 3:2 - SET YOUR AFFECTION ON THINGS ABOVE, NOT ON THINGS ON THE EARTH.

1 CORINTHIANS 3:18 - LET NO MAN DECEIVE HIMSELF. IF ANY MAN AMONG YOU SEEMETH TO BE WISE IN THIS WORLD, LET HIM BECOME A FOOL, THAT HE MAY BE WISE.

PROVERBS 15:28 - THE HEART OF THE RIGHTEOUS STUDIETH TO ANSWER: BUT THE MOUTH OF THE WICKED POURETH OUT EVIL THINGS.

2 TIMOTHY 2:7 - CONSIDER WHAT I SAY; AND THE LORD GIVE THEE UNDERSTANDING IN ALL THINGS.

JEREMIAH 29:11 - FOR I KNOW THE THOUGHTS THAT I THINK TOWARD YOU, SAITH THE LORD, THOUGHTS OF PEACE, AND NOT OF EVIL, TO GIVE YOU AN EXPECTED END.

2 CORINTHIANS 10:5 - CASTING DOWN IMAGINATIONS, AND EVERY HIGH THING THAT EXALTETH ITSELF AGAINST THE KNOWLEDGE OF GOD, AND BRINGING INTO CAPTIVITY EVERY THOUGHT TO THE OBEDIENCE OF CHRIST;

PSALMS 104:34 - MY MEDITATION OF HIM SHALL BE SWEET: I WILL BE GLAD IN THE LORD.

I AM TO BE SPEAKING LIKE GOD

HEBREWS 4:12 - FOR THE WORD OF GOD [IS] QUICK, AND POWERFUL, AND SHARPER THAN ANY TWOEDGED SWORD, PIERCING EVEN TO THE DIVIDING ASUNDER OF SOUL AND SPIRIT, AND OF THE JOINTS AND MARROW, AND [IS] A DISCERNER OF THE THOUGHTS AND INTENTS OF THE HEART.

2 TIMOTHY 3:16-17 - ALL SCRIPTURE [IS] GIVEN BY INSPIRATION OF GOD, AND [IS] PROFITABLE FOR DOCTRINE, FOR REPROOF, FOR CORRECTION, FOR INSTRUCTION IN RIGHTEOUSNESS: *(READ MORE...)*

2 PETER 1:20-21 - KNOWING THIS FIRST, THAT NO PROPHECY OF THE SCRIPTURE IS OF ANY PRIVATE INTERPRETATION. *(READ MORE...)*

1 JOHN 1:9 - IF WE CONFESS OUR SINS, HE IS FAITHFUL AND JUST TO FORGIVE US [OUR] SINS, AND TO CLEANSE US FROM ALL UNRIGHTEOUSNESS.

1 THESSALONIANS 2:13 - FOR THIS CAUSE ALSO THANK WE GOD WITHOUT CEASING, BECAUSE, WHEN YE RECEIVED THE WORD OF GOD WHICH YE HEARD OF US, YE RECEIVED [IT] NOT [AS] THE WORD OF MEN, BUT AS IT IS IN TRUTH, THE WORD OF GOD, WHICH EFFECTUALLY WORKETH ALSO IN YOU THAT BELIEVE.

1 CORINTHIANS 14:1-40 - FOLLOW AFTER CHARITY, AND DESIRE SPIRITUAL [GIFTS], BUT RATHER THAT YE MAY PROPHESY. *(READ MORE...)*

MARK 13:9 - BUT TAKE HEED TO YOURSELVES: FOR THEY SHALL DELIVER YOU UP TO COUNCILS; AND IN

THE SYNAGOGUES YE SHALL BE BEATEN: AND YE SHALL BE BROUGHT BEFORE RULERS AND KINGS FOR MY SAKE, FOR A TESTIMONY AGAINST THEM.

LUKE 12:40 - BE YE THEREFORE READY ALSO: FOR THE SON OF MAN COMETH AT AN HOUR WHEN YE THINK NOT.

1 JOHN 1:8 - IF WE SAY THAT WE HAVE NO SIN, WE DECEIVE OURSELVES, AND THE TRUTH IS NOT IN US.

I AM TO BE LIVING RIGHTEOUSLY

JAMES 1:19-20 - WHEREFORE, MY BELOVED BRETHREN, LET EVERY MAN BE SWIFT TO HEAR, SLOW TO SPEAK, SLOW TO WRATH: *(READ MORE...)*

JAMES 1:22-27 - BUT BE YE DOERS OF THE WORD, AND NOT HEARERS ONLY, DECEIVING YOUR OWN SELVES. *(READ MORE...)*

COLOSSIANS 3:5 - MORTIFY THEREFORE YOUR MEMBERS WHICH ARE UPON THE EARTH; FORNICATION, UNCLEANNESS, INORDINATE AFFECTION, EVIL CONCUPISCENCE, AND COVETOUSNESS, WHICH IS IDOLATRY:

MATTHEW 25:31-46 - WHEN THE SON OF MAN SHALL COME IN HIS GLORY, AND ALL THE HOLY ANGELS WITH HIM, THEN SHALL HE SIT UPON THE THRONE OF HIS GLORY: *(READ MORE...)*

PHILIPPIANS 4:8-9 - FINALLY, BRETHREN,

WHATSOEVER THINGS ARE TRUE, WHATSOEVER THINGS [ARE] HONEST, WHATSOEVER THINGS [ARE] JUST, WHATSOEVER THINGS [ARE] PURE, WHATSOEVER THINGS [ARE] LOVELY, WHATSOEVER THINGS [ARE] OF GOOD REPORT; IF [THERE BE] ANY VIRTUE, AND IF [THERE BE] ANY PRAISE, THINK ON THESE THINGS. *(READ MORE...)*

REVELATION 22:11-12 - HE THAT IS UNJUST, LET HIM BE UNJUST STILL: AND HE WHICH IS FILTHY, LET HIM BE FILTHY STILL: AND HE THAT IS RIGHTEOUS, LET HIM BE RIGHTEOUS STILL: AND HE THAT IS HOLY, LET HIM BE HOLY STILL. *(READ MORE...)*

GALATIANS 5:16-26 - [THIS] I SAY THEN, WALK IN THE SPIRIT, AND YE SHALL NOT FULFIL THE LUST OF THE FLESH. *(READ MORE...)*

EPHESIANS 4:31-32 - LET ALL BITTERNESS, AND WRATH, AND ANGER, AND CLAMOUR, AND EVIL SPEAKING, BE PUT AWAY FROM YOU, WITH ALL MALICE: *(READ MORE...)*

PROVERBS 16:28 - A FROWARD MAN SOWETH STRIFE: AND A WHISPERER SEPARATETH CHIEF FRIENDS.

HEBREWS 13:18 - PRAY FOR US: FOR WE TRUST WE HAVE A GOOD CONSCIENCE, IN ALL THINGS WILLING TO LIVE HONESTLY.

PSALMS 5:12 - FOR THOU, LORD, WILT BLESS THE RIGHTEOUS; WITH FAVOUR WILT THOU COMPASS HIM AS [WITH] A SHIELD.

COLOSSIANS 3:7-8 - IN THE WHICH YE ALSO WALKED SOME TIME, WHEN YE LIVED IN THEM. *(READ MORE...)*

GALATIANS 6:7-8 - BE NOT DECEIVED; GOD IS NOT MOCKED: FOR WHATSOEVER A MAN SOWETH, THAT SHALL HE ALSO REAP. *(READ MORE...)*

EPHESIANS 5:8 - FOR YE WERE SOMETIMES DARKNESS, BUT NOW [ARE YE] LIGHT IN THE LORD: WALK AS CHILDREN OF LIGHT:

ROMANS 13:11-14 - AND THAT, KNOWING THE TIME, THAT NOW [IT IS] HIGH TIME TO AWAKE OUT OF SLEEP: FOR NOW [IS] OUR SALVATION NEARER THAN WHEN WE BELIEVED. *(READ MORE...)*

I AM TO BE SELF-CONTROLED

PROVERBS 25:28 - HE THAT [HATH] NO RULE OVER HIS OWN SPIRIT [IS LIKE] A CITY [THAT IS] BROKEN DOWN, [AND] WITHOUT WALLS.

GALATIANS 5:19-25 - NOW THE WORKS OF THE FLESH ARE MANIFEST, WHICH ARE [THESE]; ADULTERY, FORNICATION, UNCLEANNESS, LASCIVIOUSNESS, *(READ MORE...)*

TITUS 1:8 - BUT A LOVER OF HOSPITALITY, A LOVER OF GOOD MEN, SOBER, JUST, HOLY, TEMPERATE;

2 PETER 1:5-6 - AND BESIDE THIS, GIVING ALL DILIGENCE, ADD TO YOUR FAITH VIRTUE; AND TO VIRTUE KNOWLEDGE; *(READ MORE...)*

1 PETER 4:7 - BUT THE END OF ALL THINGS IS AT HAND: BE YE THEREFORE SOBER, AND WATCH UNTO PRAYER.

TITUS 2:6 - YOUNG MEN LIKEWISE EXHORT TO BE SOBER MINDED.

ROMANS 12:19 - DEARLY BELOVED, AVENGE NOT YOURSELVES, BUT [RATHER] GIVE PLACE UNTO WRATH: FOR IT IS WRITTEN, VENGEANCE [IS] MINE; I WILL REPAY, SAITH THE LORD.

1 PETER 5:8 - BE SOBER, BE VIGILANT; BECAUSE YOUR ADVERSARY THE DEVIL, AS A ROARING LION, WALKETH ABOUT, SEEKING WHOM HE MAY DEVOUR:

JAMES 1:20 - FOR THE WRATH OF MAN WORKETH NOT THE RIGHTEOUSNESS OF GOD.

2 TIMOTHY 1:7 - FOR GOD HATH NOT GIVEN US THE SPIRIT OF FEAR; BUT OF POWER, AND OF LOVE, AND OF A SOUND MIND.

GALATIANS 5:22-23 - BUT THE FRUIT OF THE SPIRIT IS LOVE, JOY, PEACE, LONGSUFFERING, GENTLENESS, GOODNESS, FAITH, *(READ MORE...)*

ROMANS 12:1-2 - I BESEECH YOU THEREFORE, BRETHREN, BY THE MERCIES OF GOD, THAT YE PRESENT YOUR BODIES A LIVING SACRIFICE, HOLY, ACCEPTABLE UNTO GOD, [WHICH IS] YOUR REASONABLE SERVICE. *(READ MORE...)*

GALATIANS 5:23 - MEEKNESS, TEMPERANCE: AGAINST SUCH THERE IS NO LAW.

TOOTH: *(READ MORE...)*

PROVERBS 25:26 - A RIGHTEOUS MAN FALLING DOWN BEFORE THE WICKED [IS AS] A TROUBLED FOUNTAIN, AND A CORRUPT SPRING.

I AM TO BE HOLY AS HE IS HOLY

1 PETER 1:16 - BECAUSE IT IS WRITTEN, BE YE HOLY; FOR I AM HOLY.

1 PETER 1:15 - BUT AS HE WHICH HATH CALLED YOU IS HOLY, SO BE YE HOLY IN ALL MANNER OF CONVERSATION;

LEVITICUS 11:44 - FOR I [AM] THE LORD YOUR GOD: YE SHALL THEREFORE SANCTIFY YOURSELVES, AND YE SHALL BE HOLY; FOR I [AM] HOLY: NEITHER SHALL YE DEFILE YOURSELVES WITH ANY MANNER OF CREEPING THING THAT CREEPETH UPON THE EARTH.

LEVITICUS 1:2 - SPEAK UNTO THE CHILDREN OF ISRAEL, AND SAY UNTO THEM, IF ANY MAN OF YOU BRING AN OFFERING UNTO THE LORD, YE SHALL BRING YOUR OFFERING OF THE CATTLE, [EVEN] OF THE HERD, AND OF THE FLOCK.

LEVITICUS 19:2 - SPEAK UNTO ALL THE CONGREGATION OF THE CHILDREN OF ISRAEL, AND SAY UNTO THEM, YE SHALL BE HOLY: FOR I THE LORD YOUR GOD [AM] HOLY.

LEVITICUS 11:45 - FOR I [AM] THE LORD THAT

BRINGETH YOU UP OUT OF THE LAND OF EGYPT, TO BE YOUR GOD: YE SHALL THEREFORE BE HOLY, FOR I [AM] HOLY.

ISAIAH 6:3 - AND ONE CRIED UNTO ANOTHER, AND SAID, HOLY, HOLY, HOLY, [IS] THE LORD OF HOSTS: THE WHOLE EARTH [IS] FULL OF HIS GLORY.

PHILIPPIANS 4:4-9 - REJOICE IN THE LORD ALWAY: [AND] AGAIN I SAY, REJOICE. *(READ MORE...)*

ACTS 22:16 - AND NOW WHY TARRIEST THOU? ARISE, AND BE BAPTIZED, AND WASH AWAY THY SINS, CALLING ON THE NAME OF THE LORD.

HEBREWS 11:7 - BY FAITH NOAH, BEING WARNED OF GOD OF THINGS NOT SEEN AS YET, MOVED WITH FEAR, PREPARED AN ARK TO THE SAVING OF HIS HOUSE; BY THE WHICH HE CONDEMNED THE WORLD, AND BECAME HEIR OF THE RIGHTEOUSNESS WHICH IS BY FAITH.

1 PETER 1:1-25 - PETER, AN APOSTLE OF JESUS CHRIST, TO THE STRANGERS SCATTERED THROUGHOUT PONTUS, GALATIA, CAPPADOCIA, ASIA, AND BITHYNIA, *(READ MORE...)*

EPHESIANS 2:8-9 - FOR BY GRACE ARE YE SAVED THROUGH FAITH; AND THAT NOT OF YOURSELVES: [IT IS] THE GIFT OF GOD: *(READ MORE...)*

HEBREWS 12:14 - FOLLOW PEACE WITH ALL [MEN], AND HOLINESS, WITHOUT WHICH NO MAN SHALL SEE THE LORD:

JUDGES 13:2-14 - AND THERE WAS A CERTAIN MAN OF ZORAH, OF THE FAMILY OF THE DANITES, WHOSE NAME [WAS] MANOAH; AND HIS WIFE [WAS] BARREN, AND BARE NOT. *(READ MORE...)*

ACTS 2:38 - THEN PETER SAID UNTO THEM, REPENT, AND BE BAPTIZED EVERY ONE OF YOU IN THE NAME OF JESUS CHRIST FOR THE REMISSION OF SINS, AND YE SHALL RECEIVE THE GIFT OF THE HOLY GHOST.

PSALMS 96:9 - O WORSHIP THE LORD IN THE BEAUTY OF HOLINESS: FEAR BEFORE HIM, ALL THE EARTH.

JAMES 2:24 - YE SEE THEN HOW THAT BY WORKS A MAN IS JUSTIFIED, AND NOT BY FAITH ONLY.

ISAIAH 6:2-3 - ABOVE IT STOOD THE SERAPHIMS: EACH ONE HAD SIX WINGS; WITH TWAIN HE COVERED HIS FACE, AND WITH TWAIN HE COVERED HIS FEET, AND WITH TWAIN HE DID FLY. *(READ MORE...)*

JAMES 2:18 - YEA, A MAN MAY SAY, THOU HAST FAITH, AND I HAVE WORKS: SHEW ME THY FAITH WITHOUT THY WORKS, AND I WILL SHEW THEE MY FAITH BY MY WORKS.

PSALMS 30:4 - SING UNTO THE LORD, O YE SAINTS OF HIS, AND GIVE THANKS AT THE REMEMBRANCE OF HIS HOLINESS.

REVELATION 22:11 - HE THAT IS UNJUST, LET HIM BE UNJUST STILL: AND HE WHICH IS FILTHY, LET HIM BE FILTHY STILL: AND HE THAT IS RIGHTEOUS, LET

HIM BE RIGHTEOUS STILL: AND HE THAT IS HOLY, LET HIM BE HOLY STILL.

I AM TO BE WALKING BY FAITH

2 CORINTHIANS 5:7 - (FOR WE WALK BY FAITH, NOT BY SIGHT:)

PROVERBS 3:5-6 - TRUST IN THE LORD WITH ALL THINE HEART; AND LEAN NOT UNTO THINE OWN UNDERSTANDING. *(READ MORE...)*

HEBREWS 11:6 - BUT WITHOUT FAITH [IT IS] IMPOSSIBLE TO PLEASE [HIM]: FOR HE THAT COMETH TO GOD MUST BELIEVE THAT HE IS, AND [THAT] HE IS A REWARDER OF THEM THAT DILIGENTLY SEEK HIM.

2 CORINTHIANS 4:16-18 - FOR WHICH CAUSE WE FAINT NOT; BUT THOUGH OUR OUTWARD MAN PERISH, YET THE INWARD [MAN] IS RENEWED DAY BY DAY. *(READ MORE...)*

ROMANS 10:17 - SO THEN FAITH [COMETH] BY HEARING, AND HEARING BY THE WORD OF GOD.

HEBREWS 11:1 - NOW FAITH IS THE SUBSTANCE OF THINGS HOPED FOR, THE EVIDENCE OF THINGS NOT SEEN.

HEBREWS 11:1-40 - NOW FAITH IS THE SUBSTANCE OF THINGS HOPED FOR, THE EVIDENCE OF THINGS NOT SEEN. *(READ MORE...)*

ROMANS 1:17 - FOR THEREIN IS THE RIGHTEOUSNESS OF GOD REVEALED FROM FAITH TO FAITH: AS IT IS WRITTEN, THE JUST SHALL LIVE BY FAITH.

1 PETER 3:15 - BUT SANCTIFY THE LORD GOD IN YOUR HEARTS: AND [BE] READY ALWAYS TO [GIVE] AN ANSWER TO EVERY MAN THAT ASKETH YOU A REASON OF THE HOPE THAT IS IN YOU WITH MEEKNESS AND FEAR:

EPHESIANS 2:8-9 - FOR BY GRACE ARE YE SAVED THROUGH FAITH; AND THAT NOT OF YOURSELVES: [IT IS] THE GIFT OF GOD: *(READ MORE...)*

ROMANS 4:1-25 - WHAT SHALL WE SAY THEN THAT ABRAHAM OUR FATHER, AS PERTAINING TO THE FLESH, HATH FOUND? *(READ MORE...)*

PSALMS 91:1-16 - HE THAT DWELLETH IN THE SECRET PLACE OF THE MOST HIGH SHALL ABIDE UNDER THE SHADOW OF THE ALMIGHTY. *(READ MORE...)*

HEBREWS 11:3 - THROUGH FAITH WE UNDERSTAND THAT THE WORLDS WERE FRAMED BY THE WORD OF GOD, SO THAT THINGS WHICH ARE SEEN WERE NOT MADE OF THINGS WHICH DO APPEAR.

I AM TO BE SHEWING FORTH PRAISES OF CHRIST

PSALMS 150:1 - 127:6 - PRAISE YE THE LORD. PRAISE GOD IN HIS SANCTUARY: PRAISE HIM IN THE

FIRMAMENT OF HIS POWER. *(READ MORE...)*

PSALMS 95:1-11 - O COME, LET US SING UNTO THE LORD: LET US MAKE A JOYFUL NOISE TO THE ROCK OF OUR SALVATION. *(READ MORE...)*

JAMES 5:13 - IS ANY AMONG YOU AFFLICTED? LET HIM PRAY. IS ANY MERRY? LET HIM SING PSALMS.

PSALMS 115:1 - NOT UNTO US, O LORD, NOT UNTO US, BUT UNTO THY NAME GIVE GLORY, FOR THY MERCY, [AND] FOR THY TRUTH'S SAKE.

PSALMS 24:8-10 - WHO [IS] THIS KING OF GLORY? THE LORD STRONG AND MIGHTY, THE LORD MIGHTY IN BATTLE. *(READ MORE...)*

2 SAMUEL 22:50 - THEREFORE I WILL GIVE THANKS UNTO THEE, O LORD, AMONG THE HEATHEN, AND I WILL SING PRAISES UNTO THY NAME.

PSALMS 103:2 - BLESS THE LORD, O MY SOUL, AND FORGET NOT ALL HIS BENEFITS:

MARK 10:27 - AND JESUS LOOKING UPON THEM SAITH, WITH MEN [IT IS] IMPOSSIBLE, BUT NOT WITH GOD: FOR WITH GOD ALL THINGS ARE POSSIBLE.

PSALMS 1:1-6 - BLESSED [IS] THE MAN THAT WALKETH NOT IN THE COUNSEL OF THE UNGODLY, NOR STANDETH IN THE WAY OF SINNERS, NOR SITTETH IN THE SEAT OF THE SCORNFUL. *(READ MORE...)*

HEBREWS 13:8 - JESUS CHRIST THE SAME

YESTERDAY, AND TO DAY, AND FOR EVER.

PSALMS 91:1-16 - HE THAT DWELLETH IN THE SECRET PLACE OF THE MOST HIGH SHALL ABIDE UNDER THE SHADOW OF THE ALMIGHTY. *(READ MORE...)*

2 TIMOTHY 1:7 - FOR GOD HATH NOT GIVEN US THE SPIRIT OF FEAR; BUT OF POWER, AND OF LOVE, AND OF A SOUND MIND.

PSALMS 103:1-2 - ([A PSALM] OF DAVID.) BLESS THE LORD, O MY SOUL: AND ALL THAT IS WITHIN ME, [BLESS] HIS HOLY NAME. *(READ MORE...)*

PSALMS 144:1 - ([A PSALM] OF DAVID.) BLESSED [BE] THE LORD MY STRENGTH, WHICH TEACHETH MY HANDS TO WAR, [AND] MY FINGERS TO FIGHT:

PSALMS 22:3 - BUT THOU [ART] HOLY, [O THOU] THAT INHABITEST THE PRAISES OF ISRAEL.

I AM TO BE DOING GOOD WORKS.

MATTHEW 5:16 - LET YOUR LIGHT SO SHINE BEFORE MEN, THAT THEY MAY SEE YOUR GOOD WORKS, AND GLORIFY YOUR FATHER WHICH IS IN HEAVEN.

JAMES 2:14-17 - WHAT [DOTH IT] PROFIT, MY BRETHREN, THOUGH A MAN SAY HE HATH FAITH, AND HAVE NOT WORKS? CAN FAITH SAVE HIM? *(READ MORE...)*

EPHESIANS 2:10 - FOR WE ARE HIS WORKMANSHIP, CREATED IN CHRIST JESUS UNTO GOOD WORKS, WHICH GOD HATH BEFORE ORDAINED THAT WE SHOULD WALK IN THEM.

EPHESIANS 2:8-9 - FOR BY GRACE ARE YE SAVED THROUGH FAITH; AND THAT NOT OF YOURSELVES: [IT IS] THE GIFT OF GOD: *(READ MORE...)*

JAMES 2:26 - FOR AS THE BODY WITHOUT THE SPIRIT IS DEAD, SO FAITH WITHOUT WORKS IS DEAD ALSO.

HEBREWS 13:16 - BUT TO DO GOOD AND TO COMMUNICATE FORGET NOT: FOR WITH SUCH SACRIFICES GOD IS WELL PLEASED.

COLOSSIANS 3:23-24 - AND WHATSOEVER YE DO, DO [IT] HEARTILY, AS TO THE LORD, AND NOT UNTO MEN; *(READ MORE...)*

JAMES 2:18 - YEA, A MAN MAY SAY, THOU HAST FAITH, AND I HAVE WORKS: SHEW ME THY FAITH WITHOUT THY WORKS, AND I WILL SHEW THEE MY FAITH BY MY WORKS.

1 TIMOTHY 6:17-19 - CHARGE THEM THAT ARE RICH IN THIS WORLD, THAT THEY BE NOT HIGHMINDED, NOR TRUST IN UNCERTAIN RICHES, BUT IN THE LIVING GOD, WHO GIVETH US RICHLY ALL THINGS TO ENJOY; *(READ MORE...)*

JOHN 6:28-29 - THEN SAID THEY UNTO HIM, WHAT SHALL WE DO, THAT WE MIGHT WORK THE WORKS OF GOD? *(READ MORE...)*

GALATIANS 6:9 - AND LET US NOT BE WEARY IN WELL DOING: FOR IN DUE SEASON WE SHALL REAP, IF WE FAINT NOT.

PROVERBS 3:27-28 - WITHHOLD NOT GOOD FROM THEM TO WHOM IT IS DUE, WHEN IT IS IN THE POWER OF THINE HAND TO DO [IT]. *(READ MORE...)*

JAMES 4:17 - THEREFORE TO HIM THAT KNOWETH TO DO GOOD, AND DOETH [IT] NOT, TO HIM IT IS SIN.

1 CORINTHIANS 16:14 - LET ALL YOUR THINGS BE DONE WITH CHARITY.

ROMANS 2:6-10 - WHO WILL RENDER TO EVERY MAN ACCORDING TO HIS DEEDS: *(READ MORE...)*

I AM TO BE LAYING DOWN MY LIFE

John 10:15 As the Father knoweth me, even so know I the Father: and I lay down my life for the sheep.

John 10:17 Therefore doth my Father love me, because I lay down my life, that I might take it again.

John 15:13 Greater love hath no man than this, that a man lay down his life for his friends.

1 John 3:16 Hereby perceive we the love of God, because he laid down his life for us: and we ought to lay down our lives for the brethren.

I AM TO BE TRUSTING MY KING

PROVERBS 3:5 - TRUST IN THE LORD WITH ALL THINE HEART; AND LEAN NOT UNTO THINE OWN UNDERSTANDING.

PSALMS 37:4-6 - DELIGHT THYSELF ALSO IN THE LORD; AND HE SHALL GIVE THEE THE DESIRES OF THINE HEART. *(READ MORE...)*

ROMANS 8:28 - AND WE KNOW THAT ALL THINGS WORK TOGETHER FOR GOOD TO THEM THAT LOVE GOD, TO THEM WHO ARE THE CALLED ACCORDING TO [HIS] PURPOSE.

PROVERBS 3:6 - IN ALL THY WAYS ACKNOWLEDGE HIM, AND HE SHALL DIRECT THY PATHS.

PSALMS 46:10 - BE STILL, AND KNOW THAT I [AM] GOD: I WILL BE EXALTED AMONG THE HEATHEN, I WILL BE EXALTED IN THE EARTH.

JEREMIAH 29:11 - FOR I KNOW THE THOUGHTS THAT I THINK TOWARD YOU, SAITH THE LORD, THOUGHTS OF PEACE, AND NOT OF EVIL, TO GIVE YOU AN EXPECTED END.

MATTHEW 6:25 - THEREFORE I SAY UNTO YOU, TAKE NO THOUGHT FOR YOUR LIFE, WHAT YE SHALL EAT, OR WHAT YE SHALL DRINK; NOR YET FOR YOUR BODY, WHAT YE SHALL PUT ON. IS NOT THE LIFE MORE THAN MEAT, AND THE BODY THAN RAIMENT?

PSALMS 28:7 - THE LORD [IS] MY STRENGTH AND MY

SHIELD; MY HEART TRUSTED IN HIM, AND I AM HELPED: THEREFORE MY HEART GREATLY REJOICETH; AND WITH MY SONG WILL I PRAISE HIM.

HEBREWS 13:8 - JESUS CHRIST THE SAME YESTERDAY, AND TO DAY, AND FOR EVER.

ROMANS 15:13 - NOW THE GOD OF HOPE FILL YOU WITH ALL JOY AND PEACE IN BELIEVING, THAT YE MAY ABOUND IN HOPE, THROUGH THE POWER OF THE HOLY GHOST.

PSALMS 112:7 - HE SHALL NOT BE AFRAID OF EVIL TIDINGS: HIS HEART IS FIXED, TRUSTING IN THE LORD.

MARK 5:36 - AS SOON AS JESUS HEARD THE WORD THAT WAS SPOKEN, HE SAITH UNTO THE RULER OF THE SYNAGOGUE, BE NOT AFRAID, ONLY BELIEVE.

PSALMS 9:10 - AND THEY THAT KNOW THY NAME WILL PUT THEIR TRUST IN THEE: FOR THOU, LORD, HAST NOT FORSAKEN THEM THAT SEEK THEE.

ROMANS 12:19 - DEARLY BELOVED, AVENGE NOT YOURSELVES, BUT [RATHER] GIVE PLACE UNTO WRATH: FOR IT IS WRITTEN, VENGEANCE [IS] MINE; I WILL REPAY, SAITH THE LORD.

DEUTERONOMY 28:1-68 - AND IT SHALL COME TO PASS, IF THOU SHALT HEARKEN DILIGENTLY UNTO THE VOICE OF THE LORD THY GOD, TO OBSERVE [AND] TO DO ALL HIS COMMANDMENTS WHICH I COMMAND THEE THIS DAY, THAT THE LORD THY GOD WILL SET THEE ON HIGH ABOVE ALL NATIONS OF THE

EARTH: *(READ MORE...)*

I AM TO BE OBEYING MY KING

JOHN 14:15 - IF YE LOVE ME, KEEP MY COMMANDMENTS.

LUKE 6:46 - AND WHY CALL YE ME, LORD, LORD, AND DO NOT THE THINGS WHICH I SAY?

ROMANS 6:16 - KNOW YE NOT, THAT TO WHOM YE YIELD YOURSELVES SERVANTS TO OBEY, HIS SERVANTS YE ARE TO WHOM YE OBEY; WHETHER OF SIN UNTO DEATH, OR OF OBEDIENCE UNTO RIGHTEOUSNESS?

MATTHEW 7:21 - NOT EVERY ONE THAT SAITH UNTO ME, LORD, LORD, SHALL ENTER INTO THE KINGDOM OF HEAVEN; BUT HE THAT DOETH THE WILL OF MY FATHER WHICH IS IN HEAVEN.

JAMES 1:22 - BUT BE YE DOERS OF THE WORD, AND NOT HEARERS ONLY, DECEIVING YOUR OWN SELVES.

ISAIAH 1:19 - IF YE BE WILLING AND OBEDIENT, YE SHALL EAT THE GOOD OF THE LAND:

1 SAMUEL 15:22 - AND SAMUEL SAID, HATH THE LORD [AS GREAT] DELIGHT IN BURNT OFFERINGS AND SACRIFICES, AS IN OBEYING THE VOICE OF THE LORD? BEHOLD, TO OBEY [IS] BETTER THAN SACRIFICE, [AND] TO HEARKEN THAN THE FAT OF RAMS.

EPHESIANS 6:5-9 - SERVANTS, BE OBEDIENT TO THEM THAT ARE [YOUR] MASTERS ACCORDING TO THE FLESH, WITH FEAR AND TREMBLING, IN SINGLENESS OF YOUR HEART, AS UNTO CHRIST; *(READ MORE...)*

ROMANS 8:28 - AND WE KNOW THAT ALL THINGS WORK TOGETHER FOR GOOD TO THEM THAT LOVE GOD, TO THEM WHO ARE THE CALLED ACCORDING TO [HIS] PURPOSE.

JAMES 2:24 - YE SEE THEN HOW THAT BY WORKS A MAN IS JUSTIFIED, AND NOT BY FAITH ONLY.

JOHN 14:21 - HE THAT HATH MY COMMANDMENTS, AND KEEPETH THEM, HE IT IS THAT LOVETH ME: AND HE THAT LOVETH ME SHALL BE LOVED OF MY FATHER, AND I WILL LOVE HIM, AND WILL MANIFEST MYSELF TO HIM.

MATTHEW 7:14 - BECAUSE STRAIT [IS] THE GATE, AND NARROW [IS] THE WAY, WHICH LEADETH UNTO LIFE, AND FEW THERE BE THAT FIND IT.

2 CORINTHIANS 2:9 - FOR TO THIS END ALSO DID I WRITE, THAT I MIGHT KNOW THE PROOF OF YOU, WHETHER YE BE OBEDIENT IN ALL THINGS.

LUKE 5:1-39 - AND IT CAME TO PASS, THAT, AS THE PEOPLE PRESSED UPON HIM TO HEAR THE WORD OF GOD, HE STOOD BY THE LAKE OF GENNESARET, *(READ MORE...)*

I AM TO BE THE FRIEND OF JESUS

JOHN 15:15 - HENCEFORTH I CALL YOU NOT SERVANTS; FOR THE SERVANT KNOWETH NOT WHAT HIS LORD DOETH: BUT I HAVE CALLED YOU FRIENDS; FOR ALL THINGS THAT I HAVE HEARD OF MY FATHER I HAVE MADE KNOWN UNTO YOU.

JOHN 15:13 - GREATER LOVE HATH NO MAN THAN THIS, THAT A MAN LAY DOWN HIS LIFE FOR HIS FRIENDS.

JOHN 15:14 - YE ARE MY FRIENDS, IF YE DO WHATSOEVER I COMMAND YOU.

JAMES 2:23 - AND THE SCRIPTURE WAS FULFILLED WHICH SAITH, ABRAHAM BELIEVED GOD, AND IT WAS IMPUTED UNTO HIM FOR RIGHTEOUSNESS: AND HE WAS CALLED THE FRIEND OF GOD.

PROVERBS 18:24 - A MAN [THAT HATH] FRIENDS MUST SHEW HIMSELF FRIENDLY: AND THERE IS A FRIEND [THAT] STICKETH CLOSER THAN A BROTHER.

PROVERBS 17:17 - A FRIEND LOVETH AT ALL TIMES, AND A BROTHER IS BORN FOR ADVERSITY.

1 JOHN 3:1 - BEHOLD, WHAT MANNER OF LOVE THE FATHER HATH BESTOWED UPON US, THAT WE SHOULD BE CALLED THE SONS OF GOD: THEREFORE THE WORLD KNOWETH US NOT, BECAUSE IT KNEW HIM NOT.

REVELATION 3:20 - BEHOLD, I STAND AT THE DOOR, AND KNOCK: IF ANY MAN HEAR MY VOICE, AND OPEN THE DOOR, I WILL COME IN TO HIM, AND WILL SUP

WITH HIM, AND HE WITH ME.

PHILIPPIANS 2:1-30 - IF [THERE BE] THEREFORE ANY CONSOLATION IN CHRIST, IF ANY COMFORT OF LOVE, IF ANY FELLOWSHIP OF THE SPIRIT, IF ANY BOWELS AND MERCIES, *(READ MORE...)*

ROMANS 5:8 - BUT GOD COMMENDETH HIS LOVE TOWARD US, IN THAT, WHILE WE WERE YET SINNERS, CHRIST DIED FOR US.

JAMES 4:8 - DRAW NIGH TO GOD, AND HE WILL DRAW NIGH TO YOU. CLEANSE [YOUR] HANDS, [YE] SINNERS; AND PURIFY [YOUR] HEARTS, [YE] DOUBLE MINDED.

I AM TO BE VICTORIOUS!

DEUTERONOMY 20:4 - FOR THE LORD YOUR GOD [IS] HE THAT GOETH WITH YOU, TO FIGHT FOR YOU AGAINST YOUR ENEMIES, TO SAVE YOU.

PHILIPPIANS 4:13 - I CAN DO ALL THINGS THROUGH CHRIST WHICH STRENGTHENETH ME.

JOHN 16:33 - THESE THINGS I HAVE SPOKEN UNTO YOU, THAT IN ME YE MIGHT HAVE PEACE. IN THE WORLD YE SHALL HAVE TRIBULATION: BUT BE OF GOOD CHEER; I HAVE OVERCOME THE WORLD.

JAMES 1:12-14 - BLESSED [IS] THE MAN THAT ENDURETH TEMPTATION: FOR WHEN HE IS TRIED, HE SHALL RECEIVE THE CROWN OF LIFE, WHICH THE LORD HATH PROMISED TO THEM THAT LOVE HIM. *(READ MORE...)*

PSALMS 108:13 - THROUGH GOD WE SHALL DO VALIANTLY: FOR HE [IT IS THAT] SHALL TREAD DOWN OUR ENEMIES.

1 CORINTHIANS 10:13 - THERE HATH NO TEMPTATION TAKEN YOU BUT SUCH AS IS COMMON TO MAN: BUT GOD [IS] FAITHFUL, WHO WILL NOT SUFFER YOU TO BE TEMPTED ABOVE THAT YE ARE ABLE; BUT WILL WITH THE TEMPTATION ALSO MAKE A WAY TO ESCAPE, THAT YE MAY BE ABLE TO BEAR [IT].

DEUTERONOMY 20:1-4 - WHEN THOU GOEST OUT TO BATTLE AGAINST THINE ENEMIES, AND SEEST HORSES, AND CHARIOTS, [AND] A PEOPLE MORE THAN THOU, BE NOT AFRAID OF THEM: FOR THE LORD THY GOD [IS] WITH THEE, WHICH BROUGHT THEE UP OUT OF THE LAND OF EGYPT. *(READ MORE...)*

2 CORINTHIANS 12:9-10 - AND HE SAID UNTO ME, MY GRACE IS SUFFICIENT FOR THEE: FOR MY STRENGTH IS MADE PERFECT IN WEAKNESS. MOST GLADLY THEREFORE WILL I RATHER GLORY IN MY INFIRMITIES, THAT THE POWER OF CHRIST MAY REST UPON ME. *(READ MORE...)*

1 CORINTHIANS 15:57 - BUT THANKS [BE] TO GOD, WHICH GIVETH US THE VICTORY THROUGH OUR LORD JESUS CHRIST.

EPHESIANS 6:13 - WHEREFORE TAKE UNTO YOU THE WHOLE ARMOUR OF GOD, THAT YE MAY BE ABLE TO WITHSTAND IN THE EVIL DAY, AND HAVING DONE ALL, TO STAND.

EPHESIANS 6:10 - FINALLY, MY BRETHREN, BE STRONG IN THE LORD, AND IN THE POWER OF HIS MIGHT.

REVELATION 21:6-7 - AND HE SAID UNTO ME, IT IS DONE. I AM ALPHA AND OMEGA, THE BEGINNING AND THE END. I WILL GIVE UNTO HIM THAT IS ATHIRST OF THE FOUNTAIN OF THE WATER OF LIFE FREELY. *(READ MORE...)*

PROVERBS 24:16 - FOR A JUST [MAN] FALLETH SEVEN TIMES, AND RISETH UP AGAIN: BUT THE WICKED SHALL FALL INTO MISCHIEF.
REVELATION 12:10 - AND I HEARD A LOUD VOICE SAYING IN HEAVEN, NOW IS COME SALVATION, AND STRENGTH, AND THE KINGDOM OF OUR GOD, AND THE POWER OF HIS CHRIST: FOR THE ACCUSER OF OUR BRETHREN IS CAST DOWN, WHICH ACCUSED THEM BEFORE OUR GOD DAY AND NIGHT.

CHAPTER SEVEN

I AM TO BE LIVING LIKE A NEW CREATION,

2 CORINTHIANS 5:17 - THEREFORE IF ANY MAN [BE] IN CHRIST, [HE IS] A NEW CREATURE: OLD THINGS ARE PASSED AWAY; BEHOLD, ALL THINGS ARE BECOME NEW.

EPHESIANS 2:8-9 - FOR BY GRACE ARE YE SAVED THROUGH FAITH; AND THAT NOT OF YOURSELVES: [IT IS] THE GIFT OF GOD: *(READ MORE...)*

1 PETER 1:23 - BEING BORN AGAIN, NOT OF CORRUPTIBLE SEED, BUT OF INCORRUPTIBLE, BY THE WORD OF GOD, WHICH LIVETH AND ABIDETH FOR EVER.

REVELATION 21:1-27 - AND I SAW A NEW HEAVEN

AND A NEW EARTH: FOR THE FIRST HEAVEN AND THE FIRST EARTH WERE PASSED AWAY; AND THERE WAS NO MORE SEA. *(READ MORE...)*

1 JOHN 1:9 - IF WE CONFESS OUR SINS, HE IS FAITHFUL AND JUST TO FORGIVE US [OUR] SINS, AND TO CLEANSE US FROM ALL UNRIGHTEOUSNESS.

ROMANS 8:1 - [THERE IS] THEREFORE NOW NO CONDEMNATION TO THEM WHICH ARE IN CHRIST JESUS, WHO WALK NOT AFTER THE FLESH, BUT AFTER THE SPIRIT.

ACTS 2:38-39 - THEN PETER SAID UNTO THEM, REPENT, AND BE BAPTIZED EVERY ONE OF YOU IN THE NAME OF JESUS CHRIST FOR THE REMISSION OF SINS, AND YE SHALL RECEIVE THE GIFT OF THE HOLY GHOST. *(READ MORE...)*

JOHN 3:16 - FOR GOD SO LOVED THE WORLD, THAT HE GAVE HIS ONLY BEGOTTEN SON, THAT WHOSOEVER BELIEVETH IN HIM SHOULD NOT PERISH, BUT HAVE EVERLASTING LIFE.

EPHESIANS 2:10 - FOR WE ARE HIS WORKMANSHIP, CREATED IN CHRIST JESUS UNTO GOOD WORKS, WHICH GOD HATH BEFORE ORDAINED THAT WE SHOULD WALK IN THEM.

2 CORINTHIANS 5:21 - FOR HE HATH MADE HIM [TO BE] SIN FOR US, WHO KNEW NO SIN; THAT WE MIGHT BE MADE THE RIGHTEOUSNESS OF GOD IN HIM.

1 CORINTHIANS 5:7 - PURGE OUT THEREFORE THE OLD LEAVEN, THAT YE MAY BE A NEW LUMP, AS YE

ARE UNLEAVENED. FOR EVEN CHRIST OUR PASSOVER IS SACRIFICED FOR US:

1 PETER 3:18-22 - FOR CHRIST ALSO HATH ONCE SUFFERED FOR SINS, THE JUST FOR THE UNJUST, THAT HE MIGHT BRING US TO GOD, BEING PUT TO DEATH IN THE FLESH, BUT QUICKENED BY THE SPIRIT: *(READ MORE...)*

JOHN 5:24 - VERILY, VERILY, I SAY UNTO YOU, HE THAT HEARETH MY WORD, AND BELIEVETH ON HIM THAT SENT ME, HATH EVERLASTING LIFE, AND SHALL NOT COME INTO CONDEMNATION; BUT IS PASSED FROM DEATH UNTO LIFE.

ROMANS 8:1-39 - [THERE IS] THEREFORE NOW NO CONDEMNATION TO THEM WHICH ARE IN CHRIST JESUS, WHO WALK NOT AFTER THE FLESH, BUT AFTER THE SPIRIT. *(READ MORE...)*

PHILIPPIANS 4:13 - I CAN DO ALL THINGS THROUGH CHRIST WHICH STRENGTHENETH ME.

1 JOHN 4:4 - YE ARE OF GOD, LITTLE CHILDREN, AND HAVE OVERCOME THEM: BECAUSE GREATER IS HE THAT IS IN YOU, THAN HE THAT IS IN THE WORLD.

I AM TO BE LIKE A TREE

JEREMIAH 17:8 - FOR HE SHALL BE AS A TREE PLANTED BY THE WATERS, AND [THAT] SPREADETH OUT HER ROOTS BY THE RIVER, AND SHALL NOT SEE WHEN HEAT COMETH, BUT HER LEAF SHALL BE GREEN; AND SHALL NOT BE CAREFUL IN THE YEAR OF

DROUGHT, NEITHER SHALL CEASE FROM YIELDING FRUIT.

PSALMS 1:3 - AND HE SHALL BE LIKE A TREE PLANTED BY THE RIVERS OF WATER, THAT BRINGETH FORTH HIS FRUIT IN HIS SEASON; HIS LEAF ALSO SHALL NOT WITHER; AND WHATSOEVER HE DOETH SHALL PROSPER.

JOB 14:7 - FOR THERE IS HOPE OF A TREE, IF IT BE CUT DOWN, THAT IT WILL SPROUT AGAIN, AND THAT THE TENDER BRANCH THEREOF WILL NOT CEASE.

1 CHRONICLES 16:33 - THEN SHALL THE TREES OF THE WOOD SING OUT AT THE PRESENCE OF THE LORD, BECAUSE HE COMETH TO JUDGE THE EARTH.

MATTHEW 7:17 - EVEN SO EVERY GOOD TREE BRINGETH FORTH GOOD FRUIT; BUT A CORRUPT TREE BRINGETH FORTH EVIL FRUIT.

DANIEL 4:10-12 - THUS [WERE] THE VISIONS OF MINE HEAD IN MY BED; I SAW, AND BEHOLD A TREE IN THE MIDST OF THE EARTH, AND THE HEIGHT THEREOF [WAS] GREAT. *(READ MORE...)*

REVELATION 22:14 - BLESSED [ARE] THEY THAT DO HIS COMMANDMENTS, THAT THEY MAY HAVE RIGHT TO THE TREE OF LIFE, AND MAY ENTER IN THROUGH THE GATES INTO THE CITY.

PROVERBS 13:12 - HOPE DEFERRED MAKETH THE HEART SICK: BUT [WHEN] THE DESIRE COMETH, [IT IS] A TREE OF LIFE.

COLOSSIANS 2:7 - ROOTED AND BUILT UP IN HIM, AND STABLISHED IN THE FAITH, AS YE HAVE BEEN TAUGHT, ABOUNDING THEREIN WITH THANKSGIVING.

REVELATION 22:2 - IN THE MIDST OF THE STREET OF IT, AND ON EITHER SIDE OF THE RIVER, [WAS THERE] THE TREE OF LIFE, WHICH BARE TWELVE [MANNER OF] FRUITS, [AND] YIELDED HER FRUIT EVERY MONTH: AND THE LEAVES OF THE TREE [WERE] FOR THE HEALING OF THE NATIONS.

PSALMS 52:8 - BUT I [AM] LIKE A GREEN OLIVE TREE IN THE HOUSE OF GOD: I TRUST IN THE MERCY OF GOD FOR EVER AND EVER.

I AM TO BE FAR FROM OPPRESSION

Isaiah 54:14 In righteousness shalt thou be established: thou shalt be far from oppression; for thou shalt not fear: and from terror; for it shall not come near thee.

PROVERBS 3:25-26 - BE NOT AFRAID OF SUDDEN FEAR, NEITHER OF THE DESOLATION OF THE WICKED, WHEN IT COMETH.FOR THE LORD SHALL BE THY CONFIDENCE, AND SHALL KEEP THY FOOT FROM BEING TAKEN.

ISAIAH 2:4 - AND HE SHALL JUDGE AMONG THE NATIONS, AND SHALL REBUKE MANY PEOPLE: AND THEY SHALL BEAT THEIR SWORDS INTO PLOWSHARES, AND THEIR SPEARS INTO PRUNINGHOOKS: NATION SHALL NOT LIFT UP SWORD AGAINST NATION, NEITHER SHALL THEY LEARN WAR

ANY MORE.

ISAIAH 9:4 - FOR THOU HAST BROKEN THE YOKE OF HIS BURDEN, AND THE STAFF OF HIS SHOULDER, THE ROD OF HIS OPPRESSOR, AS IN THE DAY OF MIDIAN.

ISAIAH 45:24 - SURELY, SHALL *ONE* SAY, IN THE LORD HAVE I RIGHTEOUSNESS AND STRENGTH: *EVEN* TO HIM SHALL *MEN* COME; AND ALL THAT ARE INCENSED AGAINST HIM SHALL BE ASHAMED.

ISAIAH 51:13 - AND FORGETTEST THE LORD THY MAKER, THAT HATH STRETCHED FORTH THE HEAVENS, AND LAID THE FOUNDATIONS OF THE EARTH; AND HAST FEARED CONTINUALLY EVERY DAY BECAUSE OF THE FURY OF THE OPPRESSOR, AS IF HE WERE READY TO DESTROY? AND WHERE *IS* THE FURY OF THE OPPRESSOR?

ISAIAH 52:1 - AWAKE, AWAKE; PUT ON THY STRENGTH, O ZION; PUT ON THY BEAUTIFUL GARMENTS, O JERUSALEM, THE HOLY CITY: FOR HENCEFORTH THERE SHALL NO MORE COME INTO THEE THE UNCIRCUMCISED AND THE UNCLEAN.

ISAIAH 60:21 - THY PEOPLE ALSO *SHALL BE* ALL RIGHTEOUS: THEY SHALL INHERIT THE LAND FOR EVER, THE BRANCH OF MY PLANTING, THE WORK OF MY HANDS, THAT I MAY BE GLORIFIED.

JEREMIAH 23:3-4 - AND I WILL GATHER THE REMNANT OF MY FLOCK OUT OF ALL COUNTRIES WHITHER I HAVE DRIVEN THEM, AND WILL BRING

THEM AGAIN TO THEIR FOLDS; AND THEY SHALL BE FRUITFUL AND INCREASE.AND I WILL SET UP SHEPHERDS OVER THEM WHICH SHALL FEED THEM: AND THEY SHALL FEAR NO MORE, NOR BE DISMAYED, NEITHER SHALL THEY BE LACKING, SAITH THE LORD.

JEREMIAH 30:10 - THEREFORE FEAR THOU NOT, O MY SERVANT JACOB, SAITH THE LORD; NEITHER BE DISMAYED, O ISRAEL: FOR, LO, I WILL SAVE THEE FROM AFAR, AND THY SEED FROM THE LAND OF THEIR CAPTIVITY; AND JACOB SHALL RETURN, AND SHALL BE IN REST, AND BE QUIET, AND NONE SHALL MAKE *HIM* AFRAID.

JEREMIAH 31:23 - THUS SAITH THE LORD OF HOSTS, THE GOD OF ISRAEL; AS YET THEY SHALL USE THIS SPEECH IN THE LAND OF JUDAH AND IN THE CITIES THEREOF, WHEN I SHALL BRING AGAIN THEIR CAPTIVITY; THE LORD BLESS THEE, O HABITATION OF JUSTICE, *AND* MOUNTAIN OF HOLINESS.

EZEKIEL 36:27-28 - AND I WILL PUT MY SPIRIT WITHIN YOU, AND CAUSE YOU TO WALK IN MY STATUTES, AND YE SHALL KEEP MY JUDGMENTS, AND DO *THEM*.AND YE SHALL DWELL IN THE LAND THAT I GAVE TO YOUR FATHERS; AND YE SHALL BE MY PEOPLE, AND I WILL BE YOUR GOD.

JOEL 3:17-21 - SO SHALL YE KNOW THAT I *AM* THE LORD YOUR GOD DWELLING IN ZION, MY HOLY MOUNTAIN: THEN SHALL JERUSALEM BE HOLY, AND THERE SHALL NO STRANGERS PASS THROUGH HER ANY MORE.AND IT SHALL COME TO PASS IN THAT DAY, *THAT* THE MOUNTAINS SHALL DROP DOWN NEW

WINE, AND THE HILLS SHALL FLOW WITH MILK, AND ALL THE RIVERS OF JUDAH SHALL FLOW WITH WATERS, AND A FOUNTAIN SHALL COME FORTH OF THE HOUSE OF THE LORD, AND SHALL WATER THE VALLEY OF SHITTIM.

MICAH 4:3-4 - AND HE SHALL JUDGE AMONG MANY PEOPLE, AND REBUKE STRONG NATIONS AFAR OFF; AND THEY SHALL BEAT THEIR SWORDS INTO PLOWSHARES, AND THEIR SPEARS INTO PRUNINGHOOKS: NATION SHALL NOT LIFT UP A SWORD AGAINST NATION, NEITHER SHALL THEY LEARN WAR ANY MORE.BUT THEY SHALL SIT EVERY MAN UNDER HIS VINE AND UNDER HIS FIG TREE; AND NONE SHALL MAKE *THEM* AFRAID: FOR THE MOUTH OF THE LORD OF HOSTS HATH SPOKEN *IT*.

ZECHARIAH 2:4-5 - AND SAID UNTO HIM, RUN, SPEAK TO THIS YOUNG MAN, SAYING, JERUSALEM SHALL BE INHABITED *AS* TOWNS WITHOUT WALLS FOR THE MULTITUDE OF MEN AND CATTLE THEREIN:FOR I, SAITH THE LORD, WILL BE UNTO HER A WALL OF FIRE ROUND ABOUT, AND WILL BE THE GLORY IN THE MIDST OF HER.

ZECHARIAH 8:3 - THUS SAITH THE LORD; I AM RETURNED UNTO ZION, AND WILL DWELL IN THE MIDST OF JERUSALEM: AND JERUSALEM SHALL BE CALLED A CITY OF TRUTH; AND THE MOUNTAIN OF THE LORD OF HOSTS THE HOLY MOUNTAIN.

ZECHARIAH 9:8 - AND I WILL ENCAMP ABOUT MINE HOUSE BECAUSE OF THE ARMY, BECAUSE OF HIM THAT PASSETH BY, AND BECAUSE OF HIM THAT RETURNETH: AND NO OPPRESSOR SHALL PASS

THROUGH THEM ANY MORE: FOR NOW HAVE I SEEN WITH MINE EYES.

2 PETER 3:13 - NEVERTHELESS WE, ACCORDING TO HIS PROMISE, LOOK FOR NEW HEAVENS AND A NEW EARTH, WHEREIN DWELLETH RIGHTEOUSNESS.

I AM TO BE AS JESUS IS, IN THIS WORLD.

1 JOHN 2:6 - HE THAT SAITH HE ABIDETH IN HIM OUGHT HIMSELF ALSO SO TO WALK, EVEN AS HE WALKED.

1 CORINTHIANS 11:1 - BE YE FOLLOWERS OF ME, EVEN AS I ALSO [AM] OF CHRIST.

1 PETER 2:21 - FOR EVEN HEREUNTO WERE YE CALLED: BECAUSE CHRIST ALSO SUFFERED FOR US, LEAVING US AN EXAMPLE, THAT YE SHOULD FOLLOW HIS STEPS:

EPHESIANS 5:1-2 - BE YE THEREFORE FOLLOWERS OF GOD, AS DEAR CHILDREN; *(READ MORE...)*

JOHN 13:13-17 - YE CALL ME MASTER AND LORD: AND YE SAY WELL; FOR [SO] I AM. *(READ MORE...)*

JOHN 14:15 - IF YE LOVE ME, KEEP MY COMMANDMENTS.

EPHESIANS 4:22-24 - THAT YE PUT OFF CONCERNING THE FORMER CONVERSATION THE OLD MAN, WHICH IS CORRUPT ACCORDING TO THE

DECEITFUL LUSTS; *(READ MORE...)*

GALATIANS 3:27 - FOR AS MANY OF YOU AS HAVE BEEN BAPTIZED INTO CHRIST HAVE PUT ON CHRIST.

ROMANS 8:29 - FOR WHOM HE DID FOREKNOW, HE ALSO DID PREDESTINATE [TO BE] CONFORMED TO THE IMAGE OF HIS SON, THAT HE MIGHT BE THE FIRSTBORN AMONG MANY BRETHREN.

PHILIPPIANS 2:5 - LET THIS MIND BE IN YOU, WHICH WAS ALSO IN CHRIST JESUS:

I AM TO BE DEAD WITH CHRIST

Romans 6:8 Now if we be dead with Christ, we believe that we shall also live with him:

Colossians 3:3 For ye are dead, and your life is hid with Christ in God.

2 Corinthians 5:14 For the love of Christ constraineth us; because we thus judge, that if one died for all, then were all dead:

I AM TO BE SUBMITTED TO GOD,

JAMES 4:7 - SUBMIT YOURSELVES THEREFORE TO GOD. RESIST THE DEVIL, AND HE WILL FLEE FROM YOU.

ROMANS 8:7 - BECAUSE THE CARNAL MIND [IS] ENMITY AGAINST GOD: FOR IT IS NOT SUBJECT TO THE LAW OF GOD, NEITHER INDEED CAN BE.

PROVERBS 3:5-6 - TRUST IN THE LORD WITH ALL THINE HEART; AND LEAN NOT UNTO THINE OWN UNDERSTANDING. *(READ MORE...)*

EPHESIANS 5:21 - SUBMITTING YOURSELVES ONE TO ANOTHER IN THE FEAR OF GOD.

1 PETER 5:6 - HUMBLE YOURSELVES THEREFORE UNDER THE MIGHTY HAND OF GOD, THAT HE MAY EXALT YOU IN DUE TIME:

1 PETER 5:5 - LIKEWISE, YE YOUNGER, SUBMIT YOURSELVES UNTO THE ELDER. YEA, ALL [OF YOU] BE SUBJECT ONE TO ANOTHER, AND BE CLOTHED WITH HUMILITY: FOR GOD RESISTETH THE PROUD, AND GIVETH GRACE TO THE HUMBLE.

I AM TO BE WALKING IN GODS WILL

2 CORINTHIANS 5:7 - (FOR WE WALK BY FAITH, NOT BY SIGHT:)

PROVERBS 3:5-6 - TRUST IN THE LORD WITH ALL THINE HEART; AND LEAN NOT UNTO THINE OWN UNDERSTANDING. *(READ MORE...)*

PSALMS 119:105 - NUN. THY WORD [IS] A LAMP UNTO MY FEET, AND A LIGHT UNTO MY PATH.

DEUTERONOMY 5:33 - YE SHALL WALK IN ALL THE

WAYS WHICH THE LORD YOUR GOD HATH COMMANDED YOU, THAT YE MAY LIVE, AND [THAT IT MAY BE] WELL WITH YOU, AND [THAT] YE MAY PROLONG [YOUR] DAYS IN THE LAND WHICH YE SHALL POSSESS.

PSALMS 119:127 - THEREFORE I LOVE THY COMMANDMENTS ABOVE GOLD; YEA, ABOVE FINE GOLD.

EPHESIANS 2:10 - FOR WE ARE HIS WORKMANSHIP, CREATED IN CHRIST JESUS UNTO GOOD WORKS, WHICH GOD HATH BEFORE ORDAINED THAT WE SHOULD WALK IN THEM.

JAMES 4:7 - SUBMIT YOURSELVES THEREFORE TO GOD. RESIST THE DEVIL, AND HE WILL FLEE FROM YOU.

MICAH 6:8 - HE HATH SHEWED THEE, O MAN, WHAT [IS] GOOD; AND WHAT DOTH THE LORD REQUIRE OF THEE, BUT TO DO JUSTLY, AND TO LOVE MERCY, AND TO WALK HUMBLY WITH THY GOD?

GENESIS 6:9 - THESE [ARE] THE GENERATIONS OF NOAH: NOAH WAS A JUST MAN [AND] PERFECT IN HIS GENERATIONS, [AND] NOAH WALKED WITH GOD.

JAMES 4:8 - DRAW NIGH TO GOD, AND HE WILL DRAW NIGH TO YOU. CLEANSE [YOUR] HANDS, [YE] SINNERS; AND PURIFY [YOUR] HEARTS, [YE] DOUBLE MINDED.

AMOS 3:3 - CAN TWO WALK TOGETHER, EXCEPT THEY BE AGREED?

ZECHARIAH 3:7 - THUS SAITH THE LORD OF HOSTS; IF THOU WILT WALK IN MY WAYS, AND IF THOU WILT KEEP MY CHARGE, THEN THOU SHALT ALSO JUDGE MY HOUSE, AND SHALT ALSO KEEP MY COURTS, AND I WILL GIVE THEE PLACES TO WALK AMONG THESE THAT STAND BY.

HEBREWS 12:1 - WHEREFORE SEEING WE ALSO ARE COMPASSED ABOUT WITH SO GREAT A CLOUD OF WITNESSES, LET US LAY ASIDE EVERY WEIGHT, AND THE SIN WHICH DOTH SO EASILY BESET [US], AND LET US RUN WITH PATIENCE THE RACE THAT IS SET BEFORE US,

COLOSSIANS 2:6 - AS YE HAVE THEREFORE RECEIVED CHRIST JESUS THE LORD, [SO] WALK YE IN HIM:

1 JOHN 4:8 - HE THAT LOVETH NOT KNOWETH NOT GOD; FOR GOD IS LOVE.

GENESIS 5:22-24 - AND ENOCH WALKED WITH GOD AFTER HE BEGAT METHUSELAH THREE HUNDRED YEARS, AND BEGAT SONS AND DAUGHTERS: *(READ MORE...)*

ROMANS 13:13 - LET US WALK HONESTLY, AS IN THE DAY; NOT IN RIOTING AND DRUNKENNESS, NOT IN CHAMBERING AND WANTONNESS, NOT IN STRIFE AND ENVYING.

JOB 22:21 - ACQUAINT NOW THYSELF WITH HIM, AND BE AT PEACE: THEREBY GOOD SHALL COME UNTO THEE.

GALATIANS 5:16 - [THIS] I SAY THEN, WALK IN THE SPIRIT, AND YE SHALL NOT FULFIL THE LUST OF THE FLESH.

ISAIAH 30:21 - AND THINE EARS SHALL HEAR A WORD BEHIND THEE, SAYING, THIS [IS] THE WAY, WALK YE IN IT, WHEN YE TURN TO THE RIGHT HAND, AND WHEN YE TURN TO THE LEFT.

I AM TO BE CONFIDENT IN CHRIST

PROVERBS 14:26 - IN THE FEAR OF THE LORD [IS] STRONG CONFIDENCE: AND HIS CHILDREN SHALL HAVE A PLACE OF REFUGE.

2 TIMOTHY 1:7 - FOR GOD HATH NOT GIVEN US THE SPIRIT OF FEAR; BUT OF POWER, AND OF LOVE, AND OF A SOUND MIND.

ROMANS 15:13 - NOW THE GOD OF HOPE FILL YOU WITH ALL JOY AND PEACE IN BELIEVING, THAT YE MAY ABOUND IN HOPE, THROUGH THE POWER OF THE HOLY GHOST.

JAMES 4:10 - HUMBLE YOURSELVES IN THE SIGHT OF THE LORD, AND HE SHALL LIFT YOU UP.

1 CORINTHIANS 10:13 - THERE HATH NO TEMPTATION TAKEN YOU BUT SUCH AS IS COMMON TO MAN: BUT GOD [IS] FAITHFUL, WHO WILL NOT SUFFER YOU TO BE TEMPTED ABOVE THAT YE ARE ABLE; BUT WILL WITH THE TEMPTATION ALSO MAKE A

WAY TO ESCAPE, THAT YE MAY BE ABLE TO BEAR [IT].

JOHN 16:23 - AND IN THAT DAY YE SHALL ASK ME NOTHING. VERILY, VERILY, I SAY UNTO YOU, WHATSOEVER YE SHALL ASK THE FATHER IN MY NAME, HE WILL GIVE [IT] YOU.

2 TIMOTHY 3:1 - 4:22 - THIS KNOW ALSO, THAT IN THE LAST DAYS PERILOUS TIMES SHALL COME. *(READ MORE...)*

1 JOHN 1:9 - IF WE CONFESS OUR SINS, HE IS FAITHFUL AND JUST TO FORGIVE US [OUR] SINS, AND TO CLEANSE US FROM ALL UNRIGHTEOUSNESS.

ROMANS 5:1 - THEREFORE BEING JUSTIFIED BY FAITH, WE HAVE PEACE WITH GOD THROUGH OUR LORD JESUS CHRIST:

JOHN 20:19-24 - THEN THE SAME DAY AT EVENING, BEING THE FIRST [DAY] OF THE WEEK, WHEN THE DOORS WERE SHUT WHERE THE DISCIPLES WERE ASSEMBLED FOR FEAR OF THE JEWS, CAME JESUS AND STOOD IN THE MIDST, AND SAITH UNTO THEM, PEACE [BE] UNTO YOU. *(READ MORE...)*

EPHESIANS 5:8 - FOR YE WERE SOMETIMES DARKNESS, BUT NOW [ARE YE] LIGHT IN THE LORD: WALK AS CHILDREN OF LIGHT:

JAMES 1:2 - MY BRETHREN, COUNT IT ALL JOY WHEN YE FALL INTO DIVERS TEMPTATIONS;

PHILIPPIANS 1:6 - BEING CONFIDENT OF THIS VERY THING, THAT HE WHICH HATH BEGUN A GOOD WORK

IN YOU WILL PERFORM [IT] UNTIL THE DAY OF JESUS CHRIST:

GALATIANS 6:9 - AND LET US NOT BE WEARY IN WELL DOING: FOR IN DUE SEASON WE SHALL REAP, IF WE FAINT NOT.

EPHESIANS 2:10 - FOR WE ARE HIS WORKMANSHIP, CREATED IN CHRIST JESUS UNTO GOOD WORKS, WHICH GOD HATH BEFORE ORDAINED THAT WE SHOULD WALK IN THEM.

JEREMIAH 29:11 - FOR I KNOW THE THOUGHTS THAT I THINK TOWARD YOU, SAITH THE LORD, THOUGHTS OF PEACE, AND NOT OF EVIL, TO GIVE YOU AN EXPECTED END.

I AM TO BE A ROYAL DIADEM

Isaiah 62:3 Thou shalt also be a crown of glory in the hand of the LORD, and a royal diadem in the hand of thy God.

I AM TO BE CRUCIFYING THE FLESH

Romans 6:6 Knowing this, that our old man is crucified with him, that the body of sin might be destroyed, that henceforth we should not serve sin.

1 Corinthians 1:23 But we preach Christ crucified, unto the Jews a stumblingblock, and unto the Greeks foolishness;

1 Corinthians 2:2 For I determined not to know any thing among you, save Jesus Christ, and him crucified.

Galatians 2:20 I am crucified with Christ: nevertheless I live; yet not I, but Christ liveth in me: and the life which I now live in the flesh I live by the faith of the Son of God, who loved me, and gave himself for me.

Galatians 5:24 And they that are Christ's have crucified the flesh with the affections and lusts.

Galatians 6:14 But God forbid that I should glory, save in the cross of our Lord Jesus Christ, by whom the world is crucified unto me, and I unto the world.

I AM TO BE STEADFAST

1 CORINTHIANS 15:58 - THEREFORE, MY BELOVED BRETHREN, BE YE STEDFAST, UNMOVEABLE, ALWAYS ABOUNDING IN THE WORK OF THE LORD, FORASMUCH AS YE KNOW THAT YOUR LABOUR IS NOT IN VAIN IN THE LORD.

JAMES 1:12 - BLESSED [IS] THE MAN THAT ENDURETH TEMPTATION: FOR WHEN HE IS TRIED, HE SHALL RECEIVE THE CROWN OF LIFE, WHICH THE LORD HATH PROMISED TO THEM THAT LOVE HIM.

JAMES 1:2-4 - MY BRETHREN, COUNT IT ALL JOY WHEN YE FALL INTO DIVERS TEMPTATIONS; *(READ MORE...)*

PSALMS 112:7 - HE SHALL NOT BE AFRAID OF EVIL

TIDINGS: HIS HEART IS FIXED, TRUSTING IN THE LORD.

TITUS 2:2 - THAT THE AGED MEN BE SOBER, GRAVE, TEMPERATE, SOUND IN FAITH, IN CHARITY, IN PATIENCE.

2 PETER 1:5-8 - AND BESIDE THIS, GIVING ALL DILIGENCE, ADD TO YOUR FAITH VIRTUE; AND TO VIRTUE KNOWLEDGE; *(READ MORE...)*

ISAIAH 40:31 - BUT THEY THAT WAIT UPON THE LORD SHALL RENEW [THEIR] STRENGTH; THEY SHALL MOUNT UP WITH WINGS AS EAGLES; THEY SHALL RUN, AND NOT BE WEARY; [AND] THEY SHALL WALK, AND NOT FAINT.

HEBREWS 6:18 - THAT BY TWO IMMUTABLE THINGS, IN WHICH [IT WAS] IMPOSSIBLE FOR GOD TO LIE, WE MIGHT HAVE A STRONG CONSOLATION, WHO HAVE FLED FOR REFUGE TO LAY HOLD UPON THE HOPE SET BEFORE US:

ROMANS 8:18-25 - FOR I RECKON THAT THE SUFFERINGS OF THIS PRESENT TIME [ARE] NOT WORTHY [TO BE COMPARED] WITH THE GLORY WHICH SHALL BE REVEALED IN US. *(READ MORE...)*

I AM TO BE SET APART

ROMANS 12:2 - AND BE NOT CONFORMED TO THIS WORLD: BUT BE YE TRANSFORMED BY THE RENEWING OF YOUR MIND, THAT YE MAY PROVE WHAT [IS] THAT

GOOD, AND ACCEPTABLE, AND PERFECT, WILL OF GOD.

1 PETER 2:9 - BUT YE [ARE] A CHOSEN GENERATION, A ROYAL PRIESTHOOD, AN HOLY NATION, A PECULIAR PEOPLE; THAT YE SHOULD SHEW FORTH THE PRAISES OF HIM WHO HATH CALLED YOU OUT OF DARKNESS INTO HIS MARVELLOUS LIGHT:

JOHN 17:15-18 - I PRAY NOT THAT THOU SHOULDEST TAKE THEM OUT OF THE WORLD, BUT THAT THOU SHOULDEST KEEP THEM FROM THE EVIL. *(READ MORE...)*

JOHN 15:19 - IF YE WERE OF THE WORLD, THE WORLD WOULD LOVE HIS OWN: BUT BECAUSE YE ARE NOT OF THE WORLD, BUT I HAVE CHOSEN YOU OUT OF THE WORLD, THEREFORE THE WORLD HATETH YOU.

EPHESIANS 2:10 - FOR WE ARE HIS WORKMANSHIP, CREATED IN CHRIST JESUS UNTO GOOD WORKS, WHICH GOD HATH BEFORE ORDAINED THAT WE SHOULD WALK IN THEM.

1 CORINTHIANS 6:19 - WHAT? KNOW YE NOT THAT YOUR BODY IS THE TEMPLE OF THE HOLY GHOST [WHICH IS] IN YOU, WHICH YE HAVE OF GOD, AND YE ARE NOT YOUR OWN?

GALATIANS 2:20 - I AM CRUCIFIED WITH CHRIST: NEVERTHELESS I LIVE; YET NOT I, BUT CHRIST LIVETH IN ME: AND THE LIFE WHICH I NOW LIVE IN THE FLESH I LIVE BY THE FAITH OF THE SON OF GOD, WHO LOVED ME, AND GAVE HIMSELF FOR ME.

ROMANS 12:1 - I BESEECH YOU THEREFORE, BRETHREN, BY THE MERCIES OF GOD, THAT YE PRESENT YOUR BODIES A LIVING SACRIFICE, HOLY, ACCEPTABLE UNTO GOD, [WHICH IS] YOUR REASONABLE SERVICE.

1 PETER 1:16 - BECAUSE IT IS WRITTEN, BE YE HOLY; FOR I AM HOLY.

2 CORINTHIANS 6:14-18 - BE YE NOT UNEQUALLY YOKED TOGETHER WITH UNBELIEVERS: FOR WHAT FELLOWSHIP HATH RIGHTEOUSNESS WITH UNRIGHTEOUSNESS? AND WHAT COMMUNION HATH LIGHT WITH DARKNESS? *(READ MORE...)*

ROMANS 13:14 - BUT PUT YE ON THE LORD JESUS CHRIST, AND MAKE NOT PROVISION FOR THE FLESH, TO [FULFIL] THE LUSTS [THEREOF].

ROMANS 1:1-32 - PAUL, A SERVANT OF JESUS CHRIST, CALLED [TO BE] AN APOSTLE, SEPARATED UNTO THE GOSPEL OF GOD, *(READ MORE...)*

2 CORINTHIANS 7:1 - HAVING THEREFORE THESE PROMISES, DEARLY BELOVED, LET US CLEANSE OURSELVES FROM ALL FILTHINESS OF THE FLESH AND SPIRIT, PERFECTING HOLINESS IN THE FEAR OF GOD.

1 PETER 2:1-25 - WHEREFORE LAYING ASIDE ALL MALICE, AND ALL GUILE, AND HYPOCRISIES, AND ENVIES, AND ALL EVIL SPEAKINGS, *(READ MORE...)*

ROMANS 12:1-2 - I BESEECH YOU THEREFORE, BRETHREN, BY THE MERCIES OF GOD, THAT YE

PRESENT YOUR BODIES A LIVING SACRIFICE, HOLY, ACCEPTABLE UNTO GOD, [WHICH IS] YOUR REASONABLE SERVICE. *(READ MORE...)*

COLOSSIANS 3:10 - AND HAVE PUT ON THE NEW [MAN], WHICH IS RENEWED IN KNOWLEDGE AFTER THE IMAGE OF HIM THAT CREATED HIM:

I AM TO BE FILLED WITH THE SPIRIT

I AM TO BE MEDITATING ON GODS TRUTH

1 Timothy 4:15 Meditate upon these things; give thyself wholly to them; that thy profiting may appear to all.

PSALMS 1:2 - BUT HIS DELIGHT [IS] IN THE LAW OF THE LORD; AND IN HIS LAW DOTH HE MEDITATE DAY AND NIGHT.

PSALMS 19:14 - LET THE WORDS OF MY MOUTH, AND THE MEDITATION OF MY HEART, BE ACCEPTABLE IN THY SIGHT, O LORD, MY STRENGTH, AND MY REDEEMER.

PSALMS 119:15 - I WILL MEDITATE IN THY PRECEPTS, AND HAVE RESPECT UNTO THY WAYS.

PSALMS 104:34 - MY MEDITATION OF HIM SHALL BE SWEET: I WILL BE GLAD IN THE LORD.

PHILIPPIANS 4:8 - FINALLY, BRETHREN, WHATSOEVER THINGS ARE TRUE, WHATSOEVER

THINGS [ARE] HONEST, WHATSOEVER THINGS [ARE] JUST, WHATSOEVER THINGS [ARE] PURE, WHATSOEVER THINGS [ARE] LOVELY, WHATSOEVER THINGS [ARE] OF GOOD REPORT; IF [THERE BE] ANY VIRTUE, AND IF [THERE BE] ANY PRAISE, THINK ON THESE THINGS.

PROVERBS 4:20-22 - MY SON, ATTEND TO MY WORDS; INCLINE THINE EAR UNTO MY SAYINGS. *(READ MORE...)*

PSALMS 119:97 - MEM. O HOW LOVE I THY LAW! IT [IS] MY MEDITATION ALL THE DAY.

PSALMS 49:3 - MY MOUTH SHALL SPEAK OF WISDOM; AND THE MEDITATION OF MY HEART [SHALL BE] OF UNDERSTANDING.

ISAIAH 26:3 - THOU WILT KEEP [HIM] IN PERFECT PEACE, [WHOSE] MIND [IS] STAYED [ON THEE]: BECAUSE HE TRUSTETH IN THEE.

MATTHEW 6:6 - BUT THOU, WHEN THOU PRAYEST, ENTER INTO THY CLOSET, AND WHEN THOU HAST SHUT THY DOOR, PRAY TO THY FATHER WHICH IS IN SECRET; AND THY FATHER WHICH SEETH IN SECRET SHALL REWARD THEE OPENLY.

PSALMS 1:1-6 - BLESSED [IS] THE MAN THAT WALKETH NOT IN THE COUNSEL OF THE UNGODLY, NOR STANDETH IN THE WAY OF SINNERS, NOR SITTETH IN THE SEAT OF THE SCORNFUL. *(READ MORE...)*

PSALMS 119:127 - THEREFORE I LOVE THY

COMMANDMENTS ABOVE GOLD; YEA, ABOVE FINE GOLD.

PSALMS 119:11 - THY WORD HAVE I HID IN MINE HEART, THAT I MIGHT NOT SIN AGAINST THEE.

PSALMS 119:97-99 - MEM. O HOW LOVE I THY LAW! IT [IS] MY MEDITATION ALL THE DAY. *(READ MORE...)*

PSALMS 63:6 - WHEN I REMEMBER THEE UPON MY BED, [AND] MEDITATE ON THEE IN THE [NIGHT] WATCHES.

I AM TO BE PRAYING

Philippians 4:6 - Be careful for nothing; but in every thing by prayer and supplication with thanksgiving let your requests be made known unto God.

John 15:7 - If ye abide in me, and my words abide in you, ye shall ask what ye will, and it shall be done unto you.

Mark 11:24 - Therefore I say unto you, What things soever ye desire, when ye pray, believe that ye receive [them], and ye shall have [them].

1 Thessalonians 5:17 - Pray without ceasing.

Romans 8:26 - Likewise the Spirit also helpeth our infirmities: for we know not what we should pray for as we ought: but the Spirit itself maketh intercession for us with groanings which cannot be uttered.

Matthew 6:6 - But thou, when thou prayest, enter into thy closet, and when thou hast shut thy door, pray to thy Father which is in secret; and thy Father which seeth in secret shall reward thee openly.

Matthew 6:7 - But when ye pray, use not vain repetitions, as the heathen [do]: for they think that they shall be heard for their much speaking.

Luke 11:9 - And I say unto you, Ask, and it shall be given you; seek, and ye shall find; knock, and it shall be opened unto you.

1 Timothy 2:1-4 - I exhort therefore, that, first of all, supplications, prayers, intercessions, [and] giving of thanks, be made for all men; *(Read More...)*

Jeremiah 33:3 - Call unto me, and I will answer thee, and shew thee great and mighty things, which thou knowest not.

Matthew 26:41 - Watch and pray, that ye enter not into temptation: the spirit indeed [is] willing, but the flesh [is] weak.

1 Timothy 2:5 - For [there is] one God, and one mediator between God and men, the man Christ Jesus;

James 5:16 - Confess [your] faults one to another, and pray one for another, that ye may be healed. The effectual fervent prayer of a righteous man availeth much.

Matthew 6:5-8 - And when thou prayest, thou shalt not be as the hypocrites [are]: for they love to pray standing in the synagogues and in the corners of the streets, that they may be seen of men. Verily I say unto you, They have their reward. *(Read More...)*

Ephesians 6:18 - Praying always with all prayer and supplication in the Spirit, and watching thereunto with all perseverance and supplication for all saints;

Psalms 34:17 - [The righteous] cry, and the LORD heareth, and delivereth them out of all their troubles.

Luke 18:1 - And he spake a parable unto them [to this end], that men ought always to pray, and not to faint;

Matthew 6:9-13 - After this manner therefore pray ye: Our Father which art in heaven, Hallowed be thy name. *(Read More...)*

CHAPTER EIGHT

I AM TO BE PUTTING ON ARMOUR

EPHESIANS 6:10-18 - FINALLY, MY BRETHREN, BE STRONG IN THE LORD, AND IN THE POWER OF HIS MIGHT. *(READ MORE...)*

EPHESIANS 6:11 - PUT ON THE WHOLE ARMOUR OF GOD, THAT YE MAY BE ABLE TO STAND AGAINST THE WILES OF THE DEVIL.

EPHESIANS 6:10-20 - FINALLY, MY BRETHREN, BE STRONG IN THE LORD, AND IN THE POWER OF HIS MIGHT. *(READ MORE...)*

EPHESIANS 6:15 - AND YOUR FEET SHOD WITH THE PREPARATION OF THE GOSPEL OF PEACE;

EPHESIANS 6:14 - STAND THEREFORE, HAVING YOUR LOINS GIRT ABOUT WITH TRUTH, AND HAVING ON THE BREASTPLATE OF RIGHTEOUSNESS;

1 THESSALONIANS 5:8 - BUT LET US, WHO ARE OF THE DAY, BE SOBER, PUTTING ON THE BREASTPLATE OF FAITH AND LOVE; AND FOR AN HELMET, THE HOPE OF SALVATION.

EPHESIANS 6:17 - AND TAKE THE HELMET OF SALVATION, AND THE SWORD OF THE SPIRIT, WHICH IS THE WORD OF GOD:

HEBREWS 4:12 - FOR THE WORD OF GOD [IS] QUICK, AND POWERFUL, AND SHARPER THAN ANY TWOEDGED SWORD, PIERCING EVEN TO THE DIVIDING ASUNDER OF SOUL AND SPIRIT, AND OF THE JOINTS AND MARROW, AND [IS] A DISCERNER OF THE THOUGHTS AND INTENTS OF THE HEART.

EPHESIANS 6:10-17 - FINALLY, MY BRETHREN, BE STRONG IN THE LORD, AND IN THE POWER OF HIS MIGHT. *(READ MORE...)*

1 PETER 5:8 - BE SOBER, BE VIGILANT; BECAUSE YOUR ADVERSARY THE DEVIL, AS A ROARING LION, WALKETH ABOUT, SEEKING WHOM HE MAY DEVOUR:

1 PETER 3:15 - BUT SANCTIFY THE LORD GOD IN YOUR HEARTS: AND [BE] READY ALWAYS TO [GIVE] AN ANSWER TO EVERY MAN THAT ASKETH YOU A REASON OF THE HOPE THAT IS IN YOU WITH MEEKNESS AND FEAR:

EPHESIANS 6:10-24 - FINALLY, MY BRETHREN, BE

STRONG IN THE LORD, AND IN THE POWER OF HIS MIGHT. *(READ MORE...)*

EPHESIANS 6:16 - ABOVE ALL, TAKING THE SHIELD OF FAITH, WHEREWITH YE SHALL BE ABLE TO QUENCH ALL THE FIERY DARTS OF THE WICKED.

I AM TO BE CONFESSING MY SINS

1 JOHN 1:9 - IF WE CONFESS OUR SINS, HE IS FAITHFUL AND JUST TO FORGIVE US [OUR] SINS, AND TO CLEANSE US FROM ALL UNRIGHTEOUSNESS.

JAMES 5:16 - CONFESS [YOUR] FAULTS ONE TO ANOTHER, AND PRAY ONE FOR ANOTHER, THAT YE MAY BE HEALED. THE EFFECTUAL FERVENT PRAYER OF A RIGHTEOUS MAN AVAILETH MUCH.

PROVERBS 28:13 - HE THAT COVERETH HIS SINS SHALL NOT PROSPER: BUT WHOSO CONFESSETH AND FORSAKETH [THEM] SHALL HAVE MERCY.

PSALMS 32:5 - I ACKNOWLEDGED MY SIN UNTO THEE, AND MINE INIQUITY HAVE I NOT HID. I SAID, I WILL CONFESS MY TRANSGRESSIONS UNTO THE LORD; AND THOU FORGAVEST THE INIQUITY OF MY SIN. SELAH.

ACTS 19:18 - AND MANY THAT BELIEVED CAME, AND CONFESSED, AND SHEWED THEIR DEEDS.

ROMANS 3:23 - FOR ALL HAVE SINNED, AND COME SHORT OF THE GLORY OF GOD;

PSALMS 51:1-5 - (TO THE CHIEF MUSICIAN, A PSALM

OF DAVID, WHEN NATHAN THE PROPHET CAME UNTO HIM, AFTER HE HAD GONE IN TO BATHSHEBA.) HAVE MERCY UPON ME, O GOD, ACCORDING TO THY LOVINGKINDNESS: ACCORDING UNTO THE MULTITUDE OF THY TENDER MERCIES BLOT OUT MY TRANSGRESSIONS. *(READ MORE...)*

1 CORINTHIANS 10:13 - THERE HATH NO TEMPTATION TAKEN YOU BUT SUCH AS IS COMMON TO MAN: BUT GOD [IS] FAITHFUL, WHO WILL NOT SUFFER YOU TO BE TEMPTED ABOVE THAT YE ARE ABLE; BUT WILL WITH THE TEMPTATION ALSO MAKE A WAY TO ESCAPE, THAT YE MAY BE ABLE TO BEAR [IT].

ROMANS 10:9 - THAT IF THOU SHALT CONFESS WITH THY MOUTH THE LORD JESUS, AND SHALT BELIEVE IN THINE HEART THAT GOD HATH RAISED HIM FROM THE DEAD, THOU SHALT BE SAVED.

ACTS 17:30 - AND THE TIMES OF THIS IGNORANCE GOD WINKED AT; BUT NOW COMMANDETH ALL MEN EVERY WHERE TO REPENT:

I AM TO BE TO GET BACK UP WHEN I FALL DOWN

Proverbs 24:16 For a just man falleth seven times, and riseth up again: but the wicked shall fall into mischief.

PSALMS 31:24 - BE OF GOOD COURAGE, AND HE SHALL STRENGTHEN YOUR HEART, ALL YE THAT HOPE IN THE LORD.

GALATIANS 6:9 - AND LET US NOT BE WEARY IN WELL DOING: FOR IN DUE SEASON WE SHALL REAP, IF WE FAINT NOT.

ROMANS 12:12 - REJOICING IN HOPE; PATIENT IN TRIBULATION; CONTINUING INSTANT IN PRAYER;

1 CORINTHIANS 13:7 - BEARETH ALL THINGS, BELIEVETH ALL THINGS, HOPETH ALL THINGS, ENDURETH ALL THINGS.

EPHESIANS 4:26 - 6:24 - BE YE ANGRY, AND SIN NOT: LET NOT THE SUN GO DOWN UPON YOUR WRATH: *(READ MORE...)*

PHILIPPIANS 1:6 - BEING CONFIDENT OF THIS VERY THING, THAT HE WHICH HATH BEGUN A GOOD WORK IN YOU WILL PERFORM [IT] UNTIL THE DAY OF JESUS CHRIST:

ISAIAH 41:10 - FEAR THOU NOT; FOR I [AM] WITH THEE: BE NOT DISMAYED; FOR I [AM] THY GOD: I WILL STRENGTHEN THEE; YEA, I WILL HELP THEE; YEA, I WILL UPHOLD THEE WITH THE RIGHT HAND OF MY RIGHTEOUSNESS.

MATTHEW 11:28-30 - COME UNTO ME, ALL [YE] THAT LABOUR AND ARE HEAVY LADEN, AND I WILL GIVE YOU REST. *(READ MORE...)*

PSALMS 71:14 - BUT I WILL HOPE CONTINUALLY, AND WILL YET PRAISE THEE MORE AND MORE.

I AM TO BE SPEAKING TO THE MOUNTAIN

Matthew 17:20 And Jesus said unto them, Because of your unbelief: for verily I say unto you, If ye have faith as a grain of mustard seed, ye shall say unto this mountain, Remove hence to yonder place; and it shall remove; and nothing shall be impossible unto you.

Mark 11:23 For verily I say unto you, That whosoever shall say unto this mountain, Be thou removed, and be thou cast into the sea; and shall not doubt in his heart, but shall believe that those things which he saith shall come to pass; he shall have whatsoever he saith.

I AM TO BE BINDING AND LOOSING

MATTHEW 16:19 - AND I WILL GIVE UNTO THEE THE KEYS OF THE KINGDOM OF HEAVEN: AND WHATSOEVER THOU SHALT BIND ON EARTH SHALL BE BOUND IN HEAVEN: AND WHATSOEVER THOU SHALT LOOSE ON EARTH SHALL BE LOOSED IN HEAVEN.

MATTHEW 18:18 - VERILY I SAY UNTO YOU, WHATSOEVER YE SHALL BIND ON EARTH SHALL BE BOUND IN HEAVEN: AND WHATSOEVER YE SHALL LOOSE ON EARTH SHALL BE LOOSED IN HEAVEN.

JOHN 20:23 - WHOSE SOEVER SINS YE REMIT, THEY ARE REMITTED UNTO THEM; [AND] WHOSE SOEVER [SINS] YE RETAIN, THEY ARE RETAINED.

MATTHEW 18:15-20 - MOREOVER IF THY BROTHER SHALL TRESPASS AGAINST THEE, GO AND TELL HIM HIS FAULT BETWEEN THEE AND HIM ALONE: IF HE

SHALL HEAR THEE, THOU HAST GAINED THY BROTHER. *(READ MORE...)*

EPHESIANS 6:10-20 - FINALLY, MY BRETHREN, BE STRONG IN THE LORD, AND IN THE POWER OF HIS MIGHT. *(READ MORE...)*

ACTS 15:1-41 - AND CERTAIN MEN WHICH CAME DOWN FROM JUDAEA TAUGHT THE BRETHREN, [AND SAID], EXCEPT YE BE CIRCUMCISED AFTER THE MANNER OF MOSES, YE CANNOT BE SAVED. *(READ MORE...)*

MATTHEW 12:29 - OR ELSE HOW CAN ONE ENTER INTO A STRONG MAN'S HOUSE, AND SPOIL HIS GOODS, EXCEPT HE FIRST BIND THE STRONG MAN? AND THEN HE WILL SPOIL HIS HOUSE.

MATTHEW 16:1-28 - THE PHARISEES ALSO WITH THE SADDUCEES CAME, AND TEMPTING DESIRED HIM THAT HE WOULD SHEW THEM A SIGN FROM HEAVEN. *(READ MORE...)*

MATTHEW 18:18-20 - VERILY I SAY UNTO YOU, WHATSOEVER YE SHALL BIND ON EARTH SHALL BE BOUND IN HEAVEN: AND WHATSOEVER YE SHALL LOOSE ON EARTH SHALL BE LOOSED IN HEAVEN. *(READ MORE...)*

JAMES 5:16 - CONFESS [YOUR] FAULTS ONE TO ANOTHER, AND PRAY ONE FOR ANOTHER, THAT YE MAY BE HEALED. THE EFFECTUAL FERVENT PRAYER OF A RIGHTEOUS MAN AVAILETH MUCH.

PHILIPPIANS 2:10 - THAT AT THE NAME OF JESUS

EVERY KNEE SHOULD BOW, OF [THINGS] IN HEAVEN, AND [THINGS] IN EARTH, AND [THINGS] UNDER THE EARTH;

PROVERBS 3:3 - LET NOT MERCY AND TRUTH FORSAKE THEE: BIND THEM ABOUT THY NECK; WRITE THEM UPON THE TABLE OF THINE HEART:

I AM TO BE TAKING UP MY CROSS

Matthew 10:38 And he that taketh not his cross, and followeth after me, is not worthy of me.

Luke 9:23 And he said to them all, If any man will come after me, let him deny himself, and take up his cross daily, and follow me.

Matthew 16:24 Then said Jesus unto his disciples, If any man will come after me, let him deny himself, and take up his cross, and follow me.

Luke 14:27 And whosoever doth not bear his cross, and come after me, cannot be my disciple.

I AM TO BE FOLLOWING JESUS

1 CORINTHIANS 11:1-2 - BE YE FOLLOWERS OF ME, EVEN AS I ALSO [AM] OF CHRIST. *(READ MORE...)*

1 PETER 2:21 - FOR EVEN HEREUNTO WERE YE CALLED: BECAUSE CHRIST ALSO SUFFERED FOR US, LEAVING US AN EXAMPLE, THAT YE SHOULD FOLLOW

HIS STEPS:

MATTHEW 16:24 - THEN SAID JESUS UNTO HIS DISCIPLES, IF ANY [MAN] WILL COME AFTER ME, LET HIM DENY HIMSELF, AND TAKE UP HIS CROSS, AND FOLLOW ME.

JOHN 8:12 - THEN SPAKE JESUS AGAIN UNTO THEM, SAYING, I AM THE LIGHT OF THE WORLD: HE THAT FOLLOWETH ME SHALL NOT WALK IN DARKNESS, BUT SHALL HAVE THE LIGHT OF LIFE.

MATTHEW 7:21-23 - NOT EVERY ONE THAT SAITH UNTO ME, LORD, LORD, SHALL ENTER INTO THE KINGDOM OF HEAVEN; BUT HE THAT DOETH THE WILL OF MY FATHER WHICH IS IN HEAVEN. *(READ MORE...)*

1 JOHN 2:3-4 - AND HEREBY WE DO KNOW THAT WE KNOW HIM, IF WE KEEP HIS COMMANDMENTS. *(READ MORE...)*

MARK 8:34 - AND WHEN HE HAD CALLED THE PEOPLE [UNTO HIM] WITH HIS DISCIPLES ALSO, HE SAID UNTO THEM, WHOSOEVER WILL COME AFTER ME, LET HIM DENY HIMSELF, AND TAKE UP HIS CROSS, AND FOLLOW ME.

LUKE 9:23 - AND HE SAID TO [THEM] ALL, IF ANY [MAN] WILL COME AFTER ME, LET HIM DENY HIMSELF, AND TAKE UP HIS CROSS DAILY, AND FOLLOW ME.

JOHN 10:27 - MY SHEEP HEAR MY VOICE, AND I KNOW THEM, AND THEY FOLLOW ME:

1 PETER 1:14-16 - AS OBEDIENT CHILDREN, NOT FASHIONING YOURSELVES ACCORDING TO THE FORMER LUSTS IN YOUR IGNORANCE: *(READ MORE...)*

MATTHEW 4:19-25 - AND HE SAITH UNTO THEM, FOLLOW ME, AND I WILL MAKE YOU FISHERS OF MEN. *(READ MORE...)*

1 CORINTHIANS 11:1 - BE YE FOLLOWERS OF ME, EVEN AS I ALSO [AM] OF CHRIST.

JOHN 15:16-17 - YE HAVE NOT CHOSEN ME, BUT I HAVE CHOSEN YOU, AND ORDAINED YOU, THAT YE SHOULD GO AND BRING FORTH FRUIT, AND [THAT] YOUR FRUIT SHOULD REMAIN: THAT WHATSOEVER YE SHALL ASK OF THE FATHER IN MY NAME, HE MAY GIVE IT YOU. *(READ MORE...)*

MATTHEW 10:22 - AND YE SHALL BE HATED OF ALL [MEN] FOR MY NAME'S SAKE: BUT HE THAT ENDURETH TO THE END SHALL BE SAVED.

JOHN 15:5-8 - I AM THE VINE, YE [ARE] THE BRANCHES: HE THAT ABIDETH IN ME, AND I IN HIM, THE SAME BRINGETH FORTH MUCH FRUIT: FOR WITHOUT ME YE CAN DO NOTHING. *(READ MORE...)*

JOHN 15:14 - YE ARE MY FRIENDS, IF YE DO WHATSOEVER I COMMAND YOU.

LUKE 18:22 - NOW WHEN JESUS HEARD THESE THINGS, HE SAID UNTO HIM, YET LACKEST THOU ONE THING: SELL ALL THAT THOU HAST, AND DISTRIBUTE UNTO THE POOR, AND THOU SHALT HAVE TREASURE

IN HEAVEN: AND COME, FOLLOW ME.

I AM TO BE WALKING IN THE LIGHT

John 8:12 Then spake Jesus again unto them, saying, I am the light of the world: he that followeth me shall not walk in darkness, but shall have the light of life.

1 John 1:7 But if we walk in the light, as he is in the light, we have fellowship one with another, and the blood of Jesus Christ his Son cleanseth us from all sin.

Ephesians 5:8 For ye were sometimes darkness, but now are ye light in the Lord: walk as children of light:

John 12:35 Then Jesus said unto them, Yet a little while is the light with you. Walk while ye have the light, lest darkness come upon you: for he that walketh in darkness knoweth not whither he goeth.

John 11:10 But if a man walk in the night, he stumbleth, because there is no light in him.

John 11:9 Jesus answered, Are there not twelve hours in the day? If any man walk in the day, he stumbleth not, because he seeth the light of this world.

Revelation 21:24 And the nations of them which are saved shall walk in the light of it: and the kings of the earth do bring their glory and honour into it.

I AM TO BE IN AGREEMENT WITH GOD

MATTHEW 18:19 - AGAIN I SAY UNTO YOU, THAT IF TWO OF YOU SHALL AGREE ON EARTH AS TOUCHING ANY THING THAT THEY SHALL ASK, IT SHALL BE DONE FOR THEM OF MY FATHER WHICH IS IN HEAVEN.

AMOS 3:3 - CAN TWO WALK TOGETHER, EXCEPT THEY BE AGREED?

2 CORINTHIANS 6:16 - AND WHAT AGREEMENT HATH THE TEMPLE OF GOD WITH IDOLS? FOR YE ARE THE TEMPLE OF THE LIVING GOD; AS GOD HATH SAID, I WILL DWELL IN THEM, AND WALK IN [THEM]; AND I WILL BE THEIR GOD, AND THEY SHALL BE MY PEOPLE.

ACTS 2:1-47 - AND WHEN THE DAY OF PENTECOST WAS FULLY COME, THEY WERE ALL WITH ONE ACCORD IN ONE PLACE. *(READ MORE...)*

COLOSSIANS 2:8 - BEWARE LEST ANY MAN SPOIL YOU THROUGH PHILOSOPHY AND VAIN DECEIT, AFTER THE TRADITION OF MEN, AFTER THE RUDIMENTS OF THE WORLD, AND NOT AFTER CHRIST.

1 JOHN 5:7-8 - FOR THERE ARE THREE THAT BEAR RECORD IN HEAVEN, THE FATHER, THE WORD, AND THE HOLY GHOST: AND THESE THREE ARE ONE. *(READ MORE...)*

JOHN 14:14 - IF YE SHALL ASK ANY THING IN MY NAME, I WILL DO [IT].

COLOSSIANS 3:17 - AND WHATSOEVER YE DO IN WORD OR DEED, [DO] ALL IN THE NAME OF THE LORD JESUS, GIVING THANKS TO GOD AND THE FATHER BY

HIM.

1 CORINTHIANS 1:10-11 - NOW I BESEECH YOU, BRETHREN, BY THE NAME OF OUR LORD JESUS CHRIST, THAT YE ALL SPEAK THE SAME THING, AND [THAT] THERE BE NO DIVISIONS AMONG YOU; BUT [THAT] YE BE PERFECTLY JOINED TOGETHER IN THE SAME MIND AND IN THE SAME JUDGMENT. *(READ MORE...)*

I AM TO BE LOOKING FOR RETURN OF CHRIST

REVELATION 1:7 - BEHOLD, HE COMETH WITH CLOUDS; AND EVERY EYE SHALL SEE HIM, AND THEY [ALSO] WHICH PIERCED HIM: AND ALL KINDREDS OF THE EARTH SHALL WAIL BECAUSE OF HIM. EVEN SO, AMEN.

HEBREWS 9:28 - SO CHRIST WAS ONCE OFFERED TO BEAR THE SINS OF MANY; AND UNTO THEM THAT LOOK FOR HIM SHALL HE APPEAR THE SECOND TIME WITHOUT SIN UNTO SALVATION.

MATTHEW 25:31-46 - WHEN THE SON OF MAN SHALL COME IN HIS GLORY, AND ALL THE HOLY ANGELS WITH HIM, THEN SHALL HE SIT UPON THE THRONE OF HIS GLORY: *(READ MORE...)*

TITUS 2:13 - LOOKING FOR THAT BLESSED HOPE, AND THE GLORIOUS APPEARING OF THE GREAT GOD AND OUR SAVIOUR JESUS CHRIST;

REVELATION 19:11-16 - AND I SAW HEAVEN

OPENED, AND BEHOLD A WHITE HORSE; AND HE THAT SAT UPON HIM [WAS] CALLED FAITHFUL AND TRUE, AND IN RIGHTEOUSNESS HE DOTH JUDGE AND MAKE WAR. *(READ MORE...)*

1 THESSALONIANS 5:2 - FOR YOURSELVES KNOW PERFECTLY THAT THE DAY OF THE LORD SO COMETH AS A THIEF IN THE NIGHT.

REVELATION 3:7-11 - AND TO THE ANGEL OF THE CHURCH IN PHILADELPHIA WRITE; THESE THINGS SAITH HE THAT IS HOLY, HE THAT IS TRUE, HE THAT HATH THE KEY OF DAVID, HE THAT OPENETH, AND NO MAN SHUTTETH; AND SHUTTETH, AND NO MAN OPENETH; *(READ MORE...)*

1 THESSALONIANS 4:16-17 - FOR THE LORD HIMSELF SHALL DESCEND FROM HEAVEN WITH A SHOUT, WITH THE VOICE OF THE ARCHANGEL, AND WITH THE TRUMP OF GOD: AND THE DEAD IN CHRIST SHALL RISE FIRST: *(READ MORE...)*

MATTHEW 24:1-51 - AND JESUS WENT OUT, AND DEPARTED FROM THE TEMPLE: AND HIS DISCIPLES CAME TO [HIM] FOR TO SHEW HIM THE BUILDINGS OF THE TEMPLE. *(READ MORE...)*

MATTHEW 16:27 - FOR THE SON OF MAN SHALL COME IN THE GLORY OF HIS FATHER WITH HIS ANGELS; AND THEN HE SHALL REWARD EVERY MAN ACCORDING TO HIS WORKS.

MATTHEW 24:36 - BUT OF THAT DAY AND HOUR KNOWETH NO [MAN], NO, NOT THE ANGELS OF HEAVEN, BUT MY FATHER ONLY.

I AM TO BE WORKING IN THE HARVEST FIELD

ATTHEW 9:37 - THEN SAITH HE UNTO HIS DISCIPLES, THE HARVEST TRULY [IS] PLENTEOUS, BUT THE LABOURERS [ARE] FEW;

LUKE 10:2 - THEREFORE SAID HE UNTO THEM, THE HARVEST TRULY [IS] GREAT, BUT THE LABOURERS [ARE] FEW: PRAY YE THEREFORE THE LORD OF THE HARVEST, THAT HE WOULD SEND FORTH LABOURERS INTO HIS HARVEST.

JOHN 4:35 - SAY NOT YE, THERE ARE YET FOUR MONTHS, AND [THEN] COMETH HARVEST? BEHOLD, I SAY UNTO YOU, LIFT UP YOUR EYES, AND LOOK ON THE FIELDS; FOR THEY ARE WHITE ALREADY TO HARVEST.

PROVERBS 10:5 - HE THAT GATHERETH IN SUMMER [IS] A WISE SON: [BUT] HE THAT SLEEPETH IN HARVEST [IS] A SON THAT CAUSETH SHAME.

REVELATION 14:15 - AND ANOTHER ANGEL CAME OUT OF THE TEMPLE, CRYING WITH A LOUD VOICE TO HIM THAT SAT ON THE CLOUD, THRUST IN THY SICKLE, AND REAP: FOR THE TIME IS COME FOR THEE TO REAP; FOR THE HARVEST OF THE EARTH IS RIPE.

LEVITICUS 19:9-10 - AND WHEN YE REAP THE HARVEST OF YOUR LAND, THOU SHALT NOT WHOLLY REAP THE CORNERS OF THY FIELD, NEITHER SHALT THOU GATHER THE GLEANINGS OF THY

HARVEST. *(READ MORE...)*

MATTHEW 13:23 - BUT HE THAT RECEIVED SEED INTO THE GOOD GROUND IS HE THAT HEARETH THE WORD, AND UNDERSTANDETH [IT]; WHICH ALSO BEARETH FRUIT, AND BRINGETH FORTH, SOME AN HUNDREDFOLD, SOME SIXTY, SOME THIRTY.

JOHN 15:1-11 - I AM THE TRUE VINE, AND MY FATHER IS THE HUSBANDMAN. *(READ MORE...)*

EXODUS 34:22 - AND THOU SHALT OBSERVE THE FEAST OF WEEKS, OF THE FIRSTFRUITS OF WHEAT HARVEST, AND THE FEAST OF INGATHERING AT THE YEAR'S END.

GALATIANS 6:9 - AND LET US NOT BE WEARY IN WELL DOING: FOR IN DUE SEASON WE SHALL REAP, IF WE FAINT NOT.

GENESIS 8:22 - WHILE THE EARTH REMAINETH, SEEDTIME AND HARVEST, AND COLD AND HEAT, AND SUMMER AND WINTER, AND DAY AND NIGHT SHALL NOT CEASE.

DEUTERONOMY 16:14-15 - AND THOU SHALT REJOICE IN THY FEAST, THOU, AND THY SON, AND THY DAUGHTER, AND THY MANSERVANT, AND THY MAIDSERVANT, AND THE LEVITE, THE STRANGER, AND THE FATHERLESS, AND THE WIDOW, THAT [ARE] WITHIN THY GATES. *(READ MORE...)*

ROMANS 14:1-23 - HIM THAT IS WEAK IN THE FAITH RECEIVE YE, [BUT] NOT TO DOUBTFUL DISPUTATIONS. *(READ MORE...)*

1 JOHN 4:19 - 5:4 - WE LOVE HIM, BECAUSE HE FIRST LOVED US. *(READ MORE...)*

JOHN 4:36 - AND HE THAT REAPETH RECEIVETH WAGES, AND GATHERETH FRUIT UNTO LIFE ETERNAL: THAT BOTH HE THAT SOWETH AND HE THAT REAPETH MAY REJOICE TOGETHER.

I AM TO BE PRODUCING MUCH FRUIT

GALATIANS 5:22-23 - BUT THE FRUIT OF THE SPIRIT IS LOVE, JOY, PEACE, LONGSUFFERING, GENTLENESS, GOODNESS, FAITH, *(READ MORE...)*

JOHN 15:1-17 - I AM THE TRUE VINE, AND MY FATHER IS THE HUSBANDMAN. *(READ MORE...)*

MATTHEW 7:15-20 - BEWARE OF FALSE PROPHETS, WHICH COME TO YOU IN SHEEP'S CLOTHING, BUT INWARDLY THEY ARE RAVENING WOLVES. *(READ MORE...)*

JAMES 3:17 - BUT THE WISDOM THAT IS FROM ABOVE IS FIRST PURE, THEN PEACEABLE, GENTLE, [AND] EASY TO BE INTREATED, FULL OF MERCY AND GOOD FRUITS, WITHOUT PARTIALITY, AND WITHOUT HYPOCRISY.

PSALMS 1:1-6 - BLESSED [IS] THE MAN THAT WALKETH NOT IN THE COUNSEL OF THE UNGODLY, NOR STANDETH IN THE WAY OF SINNERS, NOR SITTETH IN THE SEAT OF THE SCORNFUL. *(READ MORE...)*

EPHESIANS 5:8-11 - FOR YE WERE SOMETIMES DARKNESS, BUT NOW [ARE YE] LIGHT IN THE LORD: WALK AS CHILDREN OF LIGHT: *(READ MORE...)*

ISAIAH 37:31 - AND THE REMNANT THAT IS ESCAPED OF THE HOUSE OF JUDAH SHALL AGAIN TAKE ROOT DOWNWARD, AND BEAR FRUIT UPWARD:

LEVITICUS 26:4-5 - THEN I WILL GIVE YOU RAIN IN DUE SEASON, AND THE LAND SHALL YIELD HER INCREASE, AND THE TREES OF THE FIELD SHALL YIELD THEIR FRUIT. *(READ MORE...)*

ROMANS 6:22 - BUT NOW BEING MADE FREE FROM SIN, AND BECOME SERVANTS TO GOD, YE HAVE YOUR FRUIT UNTO HOLINESS, AND THE END EVERLASTING LIFE.

I AM TO BE ABIDING IN CHRIST AND HIS WORD

1 JOHN 2:6 - HE THAT SAITH HE ABIDETH IN HIM OUGHT HIMSELF ALSO SO TO WALK, EVEN AS HE WALKED. (VERSES LIKE 1 JOHN 2:6)

JOHN 6:56 - HE THAT EATETH MY FLESH, AND DRINKETH MY BLOOD, DWELLETH IN ME, AND I IN HIM. (VERSES LIKE JOHN 6:56)

JOHN 14:20 - AT THAT DAY YE SHALL KNOW THAT I *AM* IN MY FATHER, AND YE IN ME, AND I IN YOU.

(VERSES LIKE JOHN 14:20)

JOHN 17:23 - I IN THEM, AND THOU IN ME, THAT THEY MAY BE MADE PERFECT IN ONE; AND THAT THE

WORLD MAY KNOW THAT THOU HAST SENT ME, AND HAST LOVED THEM, AS THOU HAST LOVED ME. (VERSES LIKE JOHN 17:23)

PHILIPPIANS 1:11 - BEING FILLED WITH THE FRUITS OF RIGHTEOUSNESS, WHICH ARE BY JESUS CHRIST, UNTO THE GLORY AND PRAISE OF GOD.

(VERSES LIKE PHILIPPIANS 1:11)

COLOSSIANS 1:23 - IF YE CONTINUE IN THE FAITH GROUNDED AND SETTLED, AND *BE* NOT MOVED AWAY FROM THE HOPE OF THE GOSPEL, WHICH YE HAVE HEARD, *AND* WHICH WAS PREACHED TO EVERY CREATURE WHICH IS UNDER HEAVEN; WHEREOF I PAUL AM MADE A MINISTER; (VERSES LIKE COLOSSIANS 1:23)

2 JOHN 1:9 - WHOSOEVER TRANSGRESSETH, AND ABIDETH NOT IN THE DOCTRINE OF CHRIST, HATH NOT GOD. HE THAT ABIDETH IN THE DOCTRINE OF CHRIST, HE HATH BOTH THE FATHER AND THE SON.

(VERSES LIKE 2 JOHN 1:9)

SONG OF SOLOMON 8:5 - WHO *IS* THIS THAT COMETH UP FROM THE WILDERNESS, LEANING UPON HER BELOVED? I RAISED THEE UP UNDER THE APPLE TREE: THERE THY MOTHER BROUGHT THEE FORTH: THERE SHE BROUGHT THEE FORTH *THAT* BARE THEE.

(VERSES LIKE SONG OF SOLOMON 8:5)

ISAIAH 27:10-11 - YET THE DEFENCED CITY *SHALL BE* DESOLATE, *AND* THE HABITATION FORSAKEN, AND LEFT LIKE A WILDERNESS: THERE SHALL THE CALF FEED, AND THERE SHALL HE LIE DOWN, AND CONSUME THE BRANCHES THEREOF.WHEN THE BOUGHS THEREOF ARE WITHERED, THEY SHALL BE BROKEN OFF: THE WOMEN COME, *AND* SET THEM ON

FIRE: FOR IT *IS* A PEOPLE OF NO UNDERSTANDING: THEREFORE HE THAT MADE THEM WILL NOT HAVE MERCY ON THEM, AND HE THAT FORMED THEM WILL SHEW THEM NO FAVOUR. (VERSES LIKE ISAIAH 27:10)

EZEKIEL 15:2-5 - SON OF MAN, WHAT IS THE VINE TREE MORE THAN ANY TREE, *OR THAN* A BRANCH WHICH IS AMONG THE TREES OF THE FOREST?SHALL WOOD BE TAKEN THEREOF TO DO ANY WORK? OR WILL *MEN* TAKE A PIN OF IT TO HANG ANY VESSEL THEREON?BEHOLD, IT IS CAST INTO THE FIRE FOR FUEL; THE FIRE DEVOURETH BOTH THE ENDS OF IT, AND THE MIDST OF IT IS BURNED. IS IT MEET FOR *ANY* WORK?BEHOLD, WHEN IT WAS WHOLE, IT WAS MEET FOR NO WORK: HOW MUCH LESS SHALL IT BE MEET YET FOR *ANY* WORK, WHEN THE FIRE HATH DEVOURED IT, AND IT IS BURNED? (VERSES LIKE EZEKIEL 15:2)

HOSEA 14:8 - EPHRAIM *SHALL SAY*, WHAT HAVE I TO DO ANY MORE WITH IDOLS? I HAVE HEARD *HIM*, AND OBSERVED HIM: I *AM* LIKE A GREEN FIR TREE. FROM ME IS THY FRUIT FOUND. (VERSES LIKE HOSEA 14:8)

LUKE 8:15 - BUT THAT ON THE GOOD GROUND ARE THEY, WHICH IN AN HONEST AND GOOD HEART, HAVING HEARD THE WORD, KEEP *IT*, AND BRING FORTH FRUIT WITH PATIENCE. (VERSES LIKE LUKE 8:15)

JOHN 6:68-69 - THEN SIMON PETER ANSWERED HIM, LORD, TO WHOM SHALL WE GO? THOU HAST THE WORDS OF ETERNAL LIFE.AND WE BELIEVE AND ARE SURE THAT THOU ART THAT CHRIST, THE SON OF THE LIVING GOD. (VERSES LIKE JOHN 6:68)

JOHN 8:31 - THEN SAID JESUS TO THOSE JEWS

WHICH BELIEVED ON HIM, IF YE CONTINUE IN MY WORD, *THEN* ARE YE MY DISCIPLES INDEED; (VERSES LIKE JOHN 8:31)

JOHN 15:5-7 - I AM THE VINE, YE *ARE* THE BRANCHES: HE THAT ABIDETH IN ME, AND I IN HIM, THE SAME BRINGETH FORTH MUCH FRUIT: FOR WITHOUT ME YE CAN DO NOTHING.IF A MAN ABIDE NOT IN ME, HE IS CAST FORTH AS A BRANCH, AND IS WITHERED; AND MEN GATHER THEM, AND CAST *THEM* INTO THE FIRE, AND THEY ARE BURNED.IF YE ABIDE IN ME, AND MY WORDS ABIDE IN YOU, YE SHALL ASK WHAT YE WILL, AND IT SHALL BE DONE UNTO YOU.

I AM TO BE EATING, DRINKING JESUS CHRIST

John 6:51 I am the living bread which came down from heaven: if any man eat of this bread, he shall live for ever: and the bread that I will give is my flesh, which I will give for the life of the world.

John 6:53 Then Jesus said unto them, Verily, verily, I say unto you, Except ye eat the flesh of the Son of man, and drink his blood, ye have no life in you.

John 6:54 Whoso eateth my flesh, and drinketh my blood, hath eternal life; and I will raise him up at the last day.

John 6:55 For my flesh is meat indeed, and my blood is drink indeed.

John 6:56 He that eateth my flesh, and drinketh my blood, dwelleth in me, and I in him.

John 6:63 It is the spirit that quickeneth; the flesh profiteth nothing: the words that I speak unto you, they are spirit, and they are life.

I AM TO BE FILLED WITH THE FULNESS OF GOD

Ephesians 3:19 And to know the love of Christ, which passeth knowledge, that ye might be filled with all the fulness of God.

Ephesians 4:13 Till we all come in the unity of the faith, and of the knowledge of the Son of God, unto a perfect man, unto the measure of the stature of the fulness of Christ:

I AM TO BE CONTINUALLY REPENTING

ACTS 3:19 - REPENT YE THEREFORE, AND BE CONVERTED, THAT YOUR SINS MAY BE BLOTTED OUT, WHEN THE TIMES OF REFRESHING SHALL COME FROM THE PRESENCE OF THE LORD;

2 CHRONICLES 7:14 - IF MY PEOPLE, WHICH ARE CALLED BY MY NAME, SHALL HUMBLE THEMSELVES, AND PRAY, AND SEEK MY FACE, AND TURN FROM THEIR WICKED WAYS; THEN WILL I HEAR FROM HEAVEN, AND WILL FORGIVE THEIR SIN, AND WILL HEAL THEIR LAND.

1 JOHN 1:9 - IF WE CONFESS OUR SINS, HE IS FAITHFUL AND JUST TO FORGIVE US [OUR] SINS, AND TO CLEANSE US FROM ALL UNRIGHTEOUSNESS.

2 PETER 3:9 - THE LORD IS NOT SLACK CONCERNING HIS PROMISE, AS SOME MEN COUNT SLACKNESS; BUT IS LONGSUFFERING TO US-WARD, NOT WILLING THAT ANY SHOULD PERISH, BUT THAT ALL SHOULD COME TO REPENTANCE.

LUKE 13:3 - I TELL YOU, NAY: BUT, EXCEPT YE REPENT, YE SHALL ALL LIKEWISE PERISH.

ACTS 17:30 - AND THE TIMES OF THIS IGNORANCE GOD WINKED AT; BUT NOW COMMANDETH ALL MEN EVERY WHERE TO REPENT:

ACTS 2:38 - THEN PETER SAID UNTO THEM, REPENT, AND BE BAPTIZED EVERY ONE OF YOU IN THE NAME OF JESUS CHRIST FOR THE REMISSION OF SINS, AND YE SHALL RECEIVE THE GIFT OF THE HOLY GHOST.

EZEKIEL 18:21-23 - BUT IF THE WICKED WILL TURN FROM ALL HIS SINS THAT HE HATH COMMITTED, AND KEEP ALL MY STATUTES, AND DO THAT WHICH IS LAWFUL AND RIGHT, HE SHALL SURELY LIVE, HE SHALL NOT DIE. *(READ MORE...)*

REVELATION 2:5 - REMEMBER THEREFORE FROM WHENCE THOU ART FALLEN, AND REPENT, AND DO THE FIRST WORKS; OR ELSE I WILL COME UNTO THEE QUICKLY, AND WILL REMOVE THY CANDLESTICK OUT OF HIS PLACE, EXCEPT THOU REPENT.

PROVERBS 28:13 - HE THAT COVERETH HIS SINS SHALL NOT PROSPER: BUT WHOSO CONFESSETH AND FORSAKETH [THEM] SHALL HAVE MERCY.

MATTHEW 4:17 - FROM THAT TIME JESUS BEGAN TO PREACH, AND TO SAY, REPENT: FOR THE KINGDOM OF HEAVEN IS AT HAND.

ROMANS 2:4 - OR DESPISEST THOU THE RICHES OF HIS GOODNESS AND FORBEARANCE AND LONGSUFFERING; NOT KNOWING THAT THE GOODNESS OF GOD LEADETH THEE TO REPENTANCE?

I AM TO BE PRESSING DEEPER

PHILIPPIANS 3:12-15 - NOT AS THOUGH I HAD ALREADY ATTAINED, EITHER WERE ALREADY PERFECT: BUT I FOLLOW AFTER, IF THAT I MAY APPREHEND THAT FOR WHICH ALSO I AM APPREHENDED OF CHRIST JESUS. I PRESS TOWARD THE MARK FOR THE PRIZE OF THE HIGH CALLING OF GOD IN CHRIST JESUS.
(READ MORE...)

ROMANS 12:2 - AND BE NOT CONFORMED TO THIS WORLD: BUT BE YE TRANSFORMED BY THE RENEWING OF YOUR MIND, THAT YE MAY PROVE WHAT [IS] THAT GOOD, AND ACCEPTABLE, AND PERFECT, WILL OF GOD.

COLOSSIANS 4:2-6 - CONTINUE IN PRAYER, AND WATCH IN THE SAME WITH THANKSGIVING; *(READ MORE...)*

PHILIPPIANS 2:13 - FOR IT IS GOD WHICH WORKETH IN YOU BOTH TO WILL AND TO DO OF [HIS] GOOD PLEASURE.

PHILIPPIANS 2:12-13 - WHEREFORE, MY BELOVED, AS YE HAVE ALWAYS OBEYED, NOT AS IN MY PRESENCE ONLY, BUT NOW MUCH MORE IN MY ABSENCE, WORK OUT YOUR OWN SALVATION WITH FEAR AND TREMBLING. *(READ MORE...)*

ACTS 2:38-39 - THEN PETER SAID UNTO THEM, REPENT, AND BE BAPTIZED EVERY ONE OF YOU IN THE NAME OF JESUS CHRIST FOR THE REMISSION OF SINS, AND YE SHALL RECEIVE THE GIFT OF THE HOLY GHOST. *(READ MORE...)*

HEBREWS 12:1 - WHEREFORE SEEING WE ALSO ARE COMPASSED ABOUT WITH SO GREAT A CLOUD OF WITNESSES, LET US LAY ASIDE EVERY WEIGHT, AND THE SIN WHICH DOTH SO EASILY BESET [US], AND LET US RUN WITH PATIENCE THE RACE THAT IS SET BEFORE US,

CHAPTER NINE

I AM TO BE CONSTANTLY HUNGRY FOR MORE

Matthew 5:6 Blessed are they which do hunger and thirst after righteousness: for they shall be filled.

DEUTERONOMY 28:1-68 - AND IT SHALL COME TO PASS, IF THOU SHALT HEARKEN DILIGENTLY UNTO THE VOICE OF THE LORD THY GOD, TO OBSERVE [AND] TO DO ALL HIS COMMANDMENTS WHICH I COMMAND THEE THIS DAY, THAT THE LORD THY GOD WILL SET THEE ON HIGH ABOVE ALL NATIONS OF THE EARTH: *(READ MORE...)*

PSALMS 22:26 - THE MEEK SHALL EAT AND BE SATISFIED: THEY SHALL PRAISE THE LORD THAT SEEK HIM: YOUR HEART SHALL LIVE FOR EVER.

LEVITICUS 26:1-46 - YE SHALL MAKE YOU NO IDOLS NOR GRAVEN IMAGE, NEITHER REAR YOU UP A STANDING IMAGE, NEITHER SHALL YE SET UP [ANY] IMAGE OF STONE IN YOUR LAND, TO BOW DOWN UNTO IT: FOR I [AM] THE LORD YOUR GOD. *(READ MORE...)*

DEUTERONOMY 28:47-48 - BECAUSE THOU SERVEDST NOT THE LORD THY GOD WITH JOYFULNESS, AND WITH GLADNESS OF HEART, FOR THE ABUNDANCE OF ALL [THINGS]; *(READ MORE...)*

I AM TO BE STRONG IN THE LORD!

PHILIPPIANS 4:13 - I CAN DO ALL THINGS THROUGH CHRIST WHICH STRENGTHENETH ME.

DEUTERONOMY 31:6 - BE STRONG AND OF A GOOD COURAGE, FEAR NOT, NOR BE AFRAID OF THEM: FOR THE LORD THY GOD, HE [IT IS] THAT DOTH GO WITH THEE; HE WILL NOT FAIL THEE, NOR FORSAKE THEE.

ISAIAH 41:10 - FEAR THOU NOT; FOR I [AM] WITH THEE: BE NOT DISMAYED; FOR I [AM] THY GOD: I WILL STRENGTHEN THEE; YEA, I WILL HELP THEE; YEA, I WILL UPHOLD THEE WITH THE RIGHT HAND OF MY RIGHTEOUSNESS.

DEUTERONOMY 20:4 - FOR THE LORD YOUR GOD [IS] HE THAT GOETH WITH YOU, TO FIGHT FOR YOU AGAINST YOUR ENEMIES, TO SAVE YOU.

1 CORINTHIANS 10:13 - THERE HATH NO TEMPTATION TAKEN YOU BUT SUCH AS IS COMMON

TO MAN: BUT GOD [IS] FAITHFUL, WHO WILL NOT SUFFER YOU TO BE TEMPTED ABOVE THAT YE ARE ABLE; BUT WILL WITH THE TEMPTATION ALSO MAKE A WAY TO ESCAPE, THAT YE MAY BE ABLE TO BEAR [IT].

2 CORINTHIANS 12:9-10 - AND HE SAID UNTO ME, MY GRACE IS SUFFICIENT FOR THEE: FOR MY STRENGTH IS MADE PERFECT IN WEAKNESS. MOST GLADLY THEREFORE WILL I RATHER GLORY IN MY INFIRMITIES, THAT THE POWER OF CHRIST MAY REST UPON ME. *(READ MORE...)*

ISAIAH 40:31 - BUT THEY THAT WAIT UPON THE LORD SHALL RENEW [THEIR] STRENGTH; THEY SHALL MOUNT UP WITH WINGS AS EAGLES; THEY SHALL RUN, AND NOT BE WEARY; [AND] THEY SHALL WALK, AND NOT FAINT.

MATTHEW 11:28 - COME UNTO ME, ALL [YE] THAT LABOUR AND ARE HEAVY LADEN, AND I WILL GIVE YOU REST.

PSALMS 31:24 - BE OF GOOD COURAGE, AND HE SHALL STRENGTHEN YOUR HEART, ALL YE THAT HOPE IN THE LORD.

EXODUS 15:2 - THE LORD [IS] MY STRENGTH AND SONG, AND HE IS BECOME MY SALVATION: HE [IS] MY GOD, AND I WILL PREPARE HIM AN HABITATION; MY FATHER'S GOD, AND I WILL EXALT HIM.

1 CORINTHIANS 16:13 - WATCH YE, STAND FAST IN THE FAITH, QUIT YOU LIKE MEN, BE STRONG.

MATTHEW 6:33 - BUT SEEK YE FIRST THE KINGDOM

OF GOD, AND HIS RIGHTEOUSNESS; AND ALL THESE THINGS SHALL BE ADDED UNTO YOU.

I AM TO BE A SERVANT OF GOD.

JOHN 12:26 - IF ANY MAN SERVE ME, LET HIM FOLLOW ME; AND WHERE I AM, THERE SHALL ALSO MY SERVANT BE: IF ANY MAN SERVE ME, HIM WILL [MY] FATHER HONOUR.

GALATIANS 5:13 - FOR, BRETHREN, YE HAVE BEEN CALLED UNTO LIBERTY; ONLY [USE] NOT LIBERTY FOR AN OCCASION TO THE FLESH, BUT BY LOVE SERVE ONE ANOTHER.

MARK 10:42-45 - BUT JESUS CALLED THEM [TO HIM], AND SAITH UNTO THEM, YE KNOW THAT THEY WHICH ARE ACCOUNTED TO RULE OVER THE GENTILES EXERCISE LORDSHIP OVER THEM; AND THEIR GREAT ONES EXERCISE AUTHORITY UPON THEM. *(READ MORE...)*

JOHN 13:16 - VERILY, VERILY, I SAY UNTO YOU, THE SERVANT IS NOT GREATER THAN HIS LORD; NEITHER HE THAT IS SENT GREATER THAN HE THAT SENT HIM.

MARK 10:45 - FOR EVEN THE SON OF MAN CAME NOT TO BE MINISTERED UNTO, BUT TO MINISTER, AND TO GIVE HIS LIFE A RANSOM FOR MANY.

COLOSSIANS 3:12 - PUT ON THEREFORE, AS THE ELECT OF GOD, HOLY AND BELOVED, BOWELS OF MERCIES, KINDNESS, HUMBLENESS OF MIND, MEEKNESS, LONGSUFFERING;

1 CORINTHIANS 4:1-2 - LET A MAN SO ACCOUNT OF US, AS OF THE MINISTERS OF CHRIST, AND STEWARDS OF THE MYSTERIES OF GOD. *(READ MORE...)*

EPHESIANS 2:10 - FOR WE ARE HIS WORKMANSHIP, CREATED IN CHRIST JESUS UNTO GOOD WORKS, WHICH GOD HATH BEFORE ORDAINED THAT WE SHOULD WALK IN THEM.

2 TIMOTHY 2:15 - STUDY TO SHEW THYSELF APPROVED UNTO GOD, A WORKMAN THAT NEEDETH NOT TO BE ASHAMED, RIGHTLY DIVIDING THE WORD OF TRUTH.

MATTHEW 25:21 - HIS LORD SAID UNTO HIM, WELL DONE, [THOU] GOOD AND FAITHFUL SERVANT: THOU HAST BEEN FAITHFUL OVER A FEW THINGS, I WILL MAKE THEE RULER OVER MANY THINGS: ENTER THOU INTO THE JOY OF THY LORD.

PHILIPPIANS 2:5-7 - LET THIS MIND BE IN YOU, WHICH WAS ALSO IN CHRIST JESUS: *(READ MORE...)*

MATTHEW 20:26 - BUT IT SHALL NOT BE SO AMONG YOU: BUT WHOSOEVER WILL BE GREAT AMONG YOU, LET HIM BE YOUR MINISTER;

LUKE 14:23 - AND THE LORD SAID UNTO THE SERVANT, GO OUT INTO THE HIGHWAYS AND HEDGES, AND COMPEL [THEM] TO COME IN, THAT MY HOUSE MAY BE FILLED.

MARK 9:35 - AND HE SAT DOWN, AND CALLED THE TWELVE, AND SAITH UNTO THEM, IF ANY MAN DESIRE

TO BE FIRST, [THE SAME] SHALL BE LAST OF ALL, AND SERVANT OF ALL.

PROVERBS 11:25 - THE LIBERAL SOUL SHALL BE MADE FAT: AND HE THAT WATERETH SHALL BE WATERED ALSO HIMSELF.

I AM TO BE LIVING WORTHY

MATTHEW 22:8 - THEN SAITH HE TO HIS SERVANTS, THE WEDDING IS READY, BUT THEY WHICH WERE BIDDEN WERE NOT WORTHY.

PHILIPPIANS 4:8 - FINALLY, BRETHREN, WHATSOEVER THINGS ARE TRUE, WHATSOEVER THINGS [ARE] HONEST, WHATSOEVER THINGS [ARE] JUST, WHATSOEVER THINGS [ARE] PURE, WHATSOEVER THINGS [ARE] LOVELY, WHATSOEVER THINGS [ARE] OF GOOD REPORT; IF [THERE BE] ANY VIRTUE, AND IF [THERE BE] ANY PRAISE, THINK ON THESE THINGS.

GALATIANS 2:20 - I AM CRUCIFIED WITH CHRIST: NEVERTHELESS I LIVE; YET NOT I, BUT CHRIST LIVETH IN ME: AND THE LIFE WHICH I NOW LIVE IN THE FLESH I LIVE BY THE FAITH OF THE SON OF GOD, WHO LOVED ME, AND GAVE HIMSELF FOR ME.

MATTHEW 6:26 - BEHOLD THE FOWLS OF THE AIR: FOR THEY SOW NOT, NEITHER DO THEY REAP, NOR GATHER INTO BARNS; YET YOUR HEAVENLY FATHER FEEDETH THEM. ARE YE NOT MUCH BETTER THAN THEY?

1 CORINTHIANS 6:11 - AND SUCH WERE SOME OF

YOU: BUT YE ARE WASHED, BUT YE ARE SANCTIFIED, BUT YE ARE JUSTIFIED IN THE NAME OF THE LORD JESUS, AND BY THE SPIRIT OF OUR GOD.

REVELATION 5:12 - SAYING WITH A LOUD VOICE, WORTHY IS THE LAMB THAT WAS SLAIN TO RECEIVE POWER, AND RICHES, AND WISDOM, AND STRENGTH, AND HONOUR, AND GLORY, AND BLESSING.

MATTHEW 10:37 - HE THAT LOVETH FATHER OR MOTHER MORE THAN ME IS NOT WORTHY OF ME: AND HE THAT LOVETH SON OR DAUGHTER MORE THAN ME IS NOT WORTHY OF ME.

JOHN 3:16-17 - FOR GOD SO LOVED THE WORLD, THAT HE GAVE HIS ONLY BEGOTTEN SON, THAT WHOSOEVER BELIEVETH IN HIM SHOULD NOT PERISH, BUT HAVE EVERLASTING LIFE. *(READ MORE...)*

EPHESIANS 4:1 - I THEREFORE, THE PRISONER OF THE LORD, BESEECH YOU THAT YE WALK WORTHY OF THE VOCATION WHEREWITH YE ARE CALLED,

---

I AM TO BE FULFILL FIRST COMMANDMENT

LUKE 10:27 - AND HE ANSWERING SAID, THOU SHALT LOVE THE LORD THY GOD WITH ALL THY HEART, AND WITH ALL THY SOUL, AND WITH ALL THY STRENGTH, AND WITH ALL THY MIND; AND THY NEIGHBOUR AS THYSELF.

DEUTERONOMY 6:5 - AND THOU SHALT LOVE THE LORD THY GOD WITH ALL THINE HEART, AND WITH

ALL THY SOUL, AND WITH ALL THY MIGHT.

JOHN 14:21 - HE THAT HATH MY COMMANDMENTS, AND KEEPETH THEM, HE IT IS THAT LOVETH ME: AND HE THAT LOVETH ME SHALL BE LOVED OF MY FATHER, AND I WILL LOVE HIM, AND WILL MANIFEST MYSELF TO HIM.

DEUTERONOMY 7:9 - KNOW THEREFORE THAT THE LORD THY GOD, HE [IS] GOD, THE FAITHFUL GOD, WHICH KEEPETH COVENANT AND MERCY WITH THEM THAT LOVE HIM AND KEEP HIS COMMANDMENTS TO A THOUSAND GENERATIONS;

JOHN 14:15 - IF YE LOVE ME, KEEP MY COMMANDMENTS.

JOHN 15:12-14 - THIS IS MY COMMANDMENT, THAT YE LOVE ONE ANOTHER, AS I HAVE LOVED YOU. *(READ MORE...)*

1 JOHN 4:19 - WE LOVE HIM, BECAUSE HE FIRST LOVED US.

JOHN 14:23-24 - JESUS ANSWERED AND SAID UNTO HIM, IF A MAN LOVE ME, HE WILL KEEP MY WORDS: AND MY FATHER WILL LOVE HIM, AND WE WILL COME UNTO HIM, AND MAKE OUR ABODE WITH HIM. *(READ MORE...)*

MATTHEW 6:24 - NO MAN CAN SERVE TWO MASTERS: FOR EITHER HE WILL HATE THE ONE, AND LOVE THE OTHER; OR ELSE HE WILL HOLD TO THE ONE, AND DESPISE THE OTHER. YE CANNOT SERVE GOD AND MAMMON.

JOHN 17:24-26 - FATHER, I WILL THAT THEY ALSO, WHOM THOU HAST GIVEN ME, BE WITH ME WHERE I AM; THAT THEY MAY BEHOLD MY GLORY, WHICH THOU HAST GIVEN ME: FOR THOU LOVEDST ME BEFORE THE FOUNDATION OF THE WORLD. *(READ MORE...)*

1 JOHN 5:3 - FOR THIS IS THE LOVE OF GOD, THAT WE KEEP HIS COMMANDMENTS: AND HIS COMMANDMENTS ARE NOT GRIEVOUS.

JOHN 14:23 - JESUS ANSWERED AND SAID UNTO HIM, IF A MAN LOVE ME, HE WILL KEEP MY WORDS: AND MY FATHER WILL LOVE HIM, AND WE WILL COME UNTO HIM, AND MAKE OUR ABODE WITH HIM.

I AM TO BE SALT AND LIGHT

MATTHEW 5:13 - YE ARE THE SALT OF THE EARTH: BUT IF THE SALT HAVE LOST HIS SAVOUR, WHEREWITH SHALL IT BE SALTED? IT IS THENCEFORTH GOOD FOR NOTHING, BUT TO BE CAST OUT, AND TO BE TRODDEN UNDER FOOT OF MEN.

COLOSSIANS 4:6 - LET YOUR SPEECH [BE] ALWAY WITH GRACE, SEASONED WITH SALT, THAT YE MAY KNOW HOW YE OUGHT TO ANSWER EVERY MAN.

MATTHEW 5:13-16 - YE ARE THE SALT OF THE EARTH: BUT IF THE SALT HAVE LOST HIS SAVOUR, WHEREWITH SHALL IT BE SALTED? IT IS THENCEFORTH GOOD FOR NOTHING, BUT TO BE CAST OUT, AND TO BE TRODDEN UNDER FOOT OF

MEN. *(READ MORE...)*

MARK 9:50 - SALT [IS] GOOD: BUT IF THE SALT HAVE LOST HIS SALTNESS, WHEREWITH WILL YE SEASON IT? HAVE SALT IN YOURSELVES, AND HAVE PEACE ONE WITH ANOTHER.

LUKE 14:34-35 - SALT [IS] GOOD: BUT IF THE SALT HAVE LOST HIS SAVOUR, WHEREWITH SHALL IT BE SEASONED? *(READ MORE...)*

NUMBERS 18:19 - ALL THE HEAVE OFFERINGS OF THE HOLY THINGS, WHICH THE CHILDREN OF ISRAEL OFFER UNTO THE LORD, HAVE I GIVEN THEE, AND THY SONS AND THY DAUGHTERS WITH THEE, BY A STATUTE FOR EVER: IT [IS] A COVENANT OF SALT FOR EVER BEFORE THE LORD UNTO THEE AND TO THY SEED WITH THEE.

2 KINGS 2:20-22 - AND HE SAID, BRING ME A NEW CRUSE, AND PUT SALT THEREIN. AND THEY BROUGHT [IT] TO HIM. *(READ MORE...)*

MARK 9:49 - FOR EVERY ONE SHALL BE SALTED WITH FIRE, AND EVERY SACRIFICE SHALL BE SALTED WITH SALT.

LEVITICUS 2:13 - AND EVERY OBLATION OF THY MEAT OFFERING SHALT THOU SEASON WITH SALT; NEITHER SHALT THOU SUFFER THE SALT OF THE COVENANT OF THY GOD TO BE LACKING FROM THY MEAT OFFERING: WITH ALL THINE OFFERINGS THOU SHALT OFFER SALT.

GENESIS 19:26 - BUT HIS WIFE LOOKED BACK FROM

BEHIND HIM, AND SHE BECAME A PILLAR OF SALT.

LUKE 14:34 - SALT [IS] GOOD: BUT IF THE SALT HAVE LOST HIS SAVOUR, WHEREWITH SHALL IT BE SEASONED?

I AM TO BE LAYING HANDS

1 TIMOTHY 5:22 - LAY HANDS SUDDENLY ON NO MAN, NEITHER BE PARTAKER OF OTHER MEN'S SINS: KEEP THYSELF PURE.

ACTS 28:8 - AND IT CAME TO PASS, THAT THE FATHER OF PUBLIUS LAY SICK OF A FEVER AND OF A BLOODY FLUX: TO WHOM PAUL ENTERED IN, AND PRAYED, AND LAID HIS HANDS ON HIM, AND HEALED HIM.

ACTS 13:3 - AND WHEN THEY HAD FASTED AND PRAYED, AND LAID [THEIR] HANDS ON THEM, THEY SENT [THEM] AWAY.

1 TIMOTHY 4:14 - NEGLECT NOT THE GIFT THAT IS IN THEE, WHICH WAS GIVEN THEE BY PROPHECY, WITH THE LAYING ON OF THE HANDS OF THE PRESBYTERY.

MARK 16:17-18 - AND THESE SIGNS SHALL FOLLOW THEM THAT BELIEVE; IN MY NAME SHALL THEY CAST OUT DEVILS; THEY SHALL SPEAK WITH NEW TONGUES; *(READ MORE...)*

ACTS 19:6 - AND WHEN PAUL HAD LAID [HIS] HANDS UPON THEM, THE HOLY GHOST CAME ON THEM; AND THEY SPAKE WITH TONGUES, AND PROPHESIED.

ACTS 9:17 - AND ANANIAS WENT HIS WAY, AND ENTERED INTO THE HOUSE; AND PUTTING HIS HANDS ON HIM SAID, BROTHER SAUL, THE LORD, [EVEN] JESUS, THAT APPEARED UNTO THEE IN THE WAY AS THOU CAMEST, HATH SENT ME, THAT THOU MIGHTEST RECEIVE THY SIGHT, AND BE FILLED WITH THE HOLY GHOST.

ACTS 8:17 - THEN LAID THEY [THEIR] HANDS ON THEM, AND THEY RECEIVED THE HOLY GHOST.

HEBREWS 6:1-3 - THEREFORE LEAVING THE PRINCIPLES OF THE DOCTRINE OF CHRIST, LET US GO ON UNTO PERFECTION; NOT LAYING AGAIN THE FOUNDATION OF REPENTANCE FROM DEAD WORKS, AND OF FAITH TOWARD GOD, *(READ MORE...)*

JAMES 5:14 - IS ANY SICK AMONG YOU? LET HIM CALL FOR THE ELDERS OF THE CHURCH; AND LET THEM PRAY OVER HIM, ANOINTING HIM WITH OIL IN THE NAME OF THE LORD:

LUKE 4:40 - NOW WHEN THE SUN WAS SETTING, ALL THEY THAT HAD ANY SICK WITH DIVERS DISEASES BROUGHT THEM UNTO HIM; AND HE LAID HIS HANDS ON EVERY ONE OF THEM, AND HEALED THEM.

MARK 6:5 - AND HE COULD THERE DO NO MIGHTY WORK, SAVE THAT HE LAID HIS HANDS UPON A FEW SICK FOLK, AND HEALED [THEM].

GENESIS 48:14 - AND ISRAEL STRETCHED OUT HIS RIGHT HAND, AND LAID [IT] UPON EPHRAIM'S HEAD, WHO [WAS] THE YOUNGER, AND HIS LEFT HAND UPON

MANASSEH'S HEAD, GUIDING HIS HANDS WITTINGLY; FOR MANASSEH [WAS] THE FIRSTBORN.

NUMBERS 27:18-23 - AND THE LORD SAID UNTO MOSES, TAKE THEE JOSHUA THE SON OF NUN, A MAN IN WHOM [IS] THE SPIRIT, AND LAY THINE HAND UPON HIM; *(READ MORE...)*

HEBREWS 6:2 - OF THE DOCTRINE OF BAPTISMS, AND OF LAYING ON OF HANDS, AND OF RESURRECTION OF THE DEAD, AND OF ETERNAL JUDGMENT.

ACTS 6:6 - WHOM THEY SET BEFORE THE APOSTLES: AND WHEN THEY HAD PRAYED, THEY LAID [THEIR] HANDS ON THEM.

2 TIMOTHY 1:6 - WHEREFORE I PUT THEE IN REMEMBRANCE THAT THOU STIR UP THE GIFT OF GOD, WHICH IS IN THEE BY THE PUTTING ON OF MY HANDS.

I AM TO BE RULING AND REIGNING WITH CHRIST

1 Corinthians 4:8 Now ye are full, now ye are rich, ye have reigned as kings without us: and I would to God ye did reign, that we also might reign with you.

1 Corinthians 15:25 For he must reign, till he hath put all enemies under his feet.

Revelation 5:10 And hast made us unto our God kings and priests: and we shall reign on the earth.

I AM TO BE EVER WATCHFUL

1 Timothy 3:2 A bishop then must be blameless, the husband of one wife, vigilant, sober, of good behaviour, given to hospitality, apt to teach;

1 Peter 5:8 Be sober, be vigilant; because your adversary the devil, as a roaring lion, walketh about, seeking whom he may devour:

Revelation 3:2 Be watchful, and strengthen the things which remain, that are ready to die: for I have not found thy works perfect before God.

I AM TO BE AS BOLD AS A LION

Proverbs 28:1 The wicked flee when no man pursueth: but the righteous are bold as a lion.

ACTS 28:31 - PREACHING THE KINGDOM OF GOD, AND TEACHING THOSE THINGS WHICH CONCERN THE LORD JESUS CHRIST, WITH ALL CONFIDENCE, NO MAN FORBIDDING HIM.

EPHESIANS 6:19 - AND FOR ME, THAT UTTERANCE MAY BE GIVEN UNTO ME, THAT I MAY OPEN MY MOUTH BOLDLY, TO MAKE KNOWN THE MYSTERY OF THE GOSPEL,

1 THESSALONIANS 5:14 - NOW WE EXHORT YOU,

BRETHREN, WARN THEM THAT ARE UNRULY, COMFORT THE FEEBLEMINDED, SUPPORT THE WEAK, BE PATIENT TOWARD ALL [MEN].

PSALMS 119:105 - NUN. THY WORD [IS] A LAMP UNTO MY FEET, AND A LIGHT UNTO MY PATH.

2 TIMOTHY 3:16 - ALL SCRIPTURE [IS] GIVEN BY INSPIRATION OF GOD, AND [IS] PROFITABLE FOR DOCTRINE, FOR REPROOF, FOR CORRECTION, FOR INSTRUCTION IN RIGHTEOUSNESS:

I AM TO BE CASTING ALL MY CARES ON CHRIST

PHILIPPIANS 4:6 - BE CAREFUL FOR NOTHING; BUT IN EVERY THING BY PRAYER AND SUPPLICATION WITH THANKSGIVING LET YOUR REQUESTS BE MADE KNOWN UNTO GOD.

PROVERBS 3:5 - TRUST IN THE LORD WITH ALL THINE HEART; AND LEAN NOT UNTO THINE OWN UNDERSTANDING.

PHILIPPIANS 4:13 - I CAN DO ALL THINGS THROUGH CHRIST WHICH STRENGTHENETH ME.

MATTHEW 18:15-18 - MOREOVER IF THY BROTHER SHALL TRESPASS AGAINST THEE, GO AND TELL HIM HIS FAULT BETWEEN THEE AND HIM ALONE: IF HE SHALL HEAR THEE, THOU HAST GAINED THY BROTHER. *(READ MORE...)*

PROVERBS 3:6 - IN ALL THY WAYS ACKNOWLEDGE HIM, AND HE SHALL DIRECT THY PATHS.

MATTHEW 7:7 - ASK, AND IT SHALL BE GIVEN YOU; SEEK, AND YE SHALL FIND; KNOCK, AND IT SHALL BE OPENED UNTO YOU:

MARK 11:22-25 - AND JESUS ANSWERING SAITH UNTO THEM, HAVE FAITH IN GOD. *(READ MORE...)*

PSALMS 50:15 - AND CALL UPON ME IN THE DAY OF TROUBLE: I WILL DELIVER THEE, AND THOU SHALT GLORIFY ME.

1 Peter 5:7 Casting all your care upon him; for he careth for you.

1 JOHN 1:9 - IF WE CONFESS OUR SINS, HE IS FAITHFUL AND JUST TO FORGIVE US [OUR] SINS, AND TO CLEANSE US FROM ALL UNRIGHTEOUSNESS.

JOHN 3:16 - FOR GOD SO LOVED THE WORLD, THAT HE GAVE HIS ONLY BEGOTTEN SON, THAT WHOSOEVER BELIEVETH IN HIM SHOULD NOT PERISH, BUT HAVE EVERLASTING LIFE.

2 PETER 3:9 - THE LORD IS NOT SLACK CONCERNING HIS PROMISE, AS SOME MEN COUNT SLACKNESS; BUT IS LONGSUFFERING TO US-WARD, NOT WILLING THAT ANY SHOULD PERISH, BUT THAT ALL SHOULD COME TO REPENTANCE.

ECCLESIASTES 1:2 - VANITY OF VANITIES, SAITH THE PREACHER, VANITY OF VANITIES; ALL [IS] VANITY.

1 JOHN 4:19 - WE LOVE HIM, BECAUSE HE FIRST LOVED US.

LUKE 17:3-4 - TAKE HEED TO YOURSELVES: IF THY BROTHER TRESPASS AGAINST THEE, REBUKE HIM; AND IF HE REPENT, FORGIVE HIM. *(READ MORE...)*

I AM TO BE PUTTING NOTHING EVIL BEFORE EYES

Psalms 101:3 I
will set no wicked thing before mine eyes: I hate the work of them that turn aside; it shall not cleave to me.

I AM TO BE PURE IN HEART

1 THESSALONIANS 4:3-5 - FOR THIS IS THE WILL OF GOD, [EVEN] YOUR SANCTIFICATION, THAT YE SHOULD ABSTAIN FROM FORNICATION: *(READ MORE...)*

MATTHEW 5:8 - BLESSED [ARE] THE PURE IN HEART: FOR THEY SHALL SEE GOD.

2 TIMOTHY 2:22 - FLEE ALSO YOUTHFUL LUSTS: BUT FOLLOW RIGHTEOUSNESS, FAITH, CHARITY, PEACE, WITH THEM THAT CALL ON THE LORD OUT OF A PURE HEART.

HEBREWS 13:4 - MARRIAGE [IS] HONOURABLE IN ALL, AND THE BED UNDEFILED: BUT WHOREMONGERS AND ADULTERERS GOD WILL JUDGE.

1 JOHN 3:3 - AND EVERY MAN THAT HATH THIS HOPE IN HIM PURIFIETH HIMSELF, EVEN AS HE IS PURE.

1 PETER 2:11 - DEARLY BELOVED, I BESEECH [YOU] AS STRANGERS AND PILGRIMS, ABSTAIN FROM FLESHLY LUSTS, WHICH WAR AGAINST THE SOUL;

1 CORINTHIANS 6:18 - FLEE FORNICATION. EVERY SIN THAT A MAN DOETH IS WITHOUT THE BODY; BUT HE THAT COMMITTETH FORNICATION SINNETH AGAINST HIS OWN BODY.

1 TIMOTHY 1:5 - NOW THE END OF THE COMMANDMENT IS CHARITY OUT OF A PURE HEART, AND [OF] A GOOD CONSCIENCE, AND [OF] FAITH UNFEIGNED:

ROMANS 13:13-14 - LET US WALK HONESTLY, AS IN THE DAY; NOT IN RIOTING AND DRUNKENNESS, NOT IN CHAMBERING AND WANTONNESS, NOT IN STRIFE AND ENVYING. *(READ MORE...)*

1 PETER 1:22 - SEEING YE HAVE PURIFIED YOUR SOULS IN OBEYING THE TRUTH THROUGH THE SPIRIT UNTO UNFEIGNED LOVE OF THE BRETHREN, [SEE THAT YE] LOVE ONE ANOTHER WITH A PURE HEART FERVENTLY:

1 CORINTHIANS 6:13 - MEATS FOR THE BELLY, AND THE BELLY FOR MEATS: BUT GOD SHALL DESTROY BOTH IT AND THEM. NOW THE BODY [IS] NOT FOR FORNICATION, BUT FOR THE LORD; AND THE LORD FOR THE BODY.

PSALMS 12:6 - THE WORDS OF THE LORD [ARE]

PURE WORDS: [AS] SILVER TRIED IN A FURNACE OF EARTH, PURIFIED SEVEN TIMES.

GALATIANS 5:19-21 - NOW THE WORKS OF THE FLESH ARE MANIFEST, WHICH ARE [THESE]; ADULTERY, FORNICATION, UNCLEANNESS, LASCIVIOUSNESS, *(READ MORE...)*

TITUS 2:4-5 - THAT THEY MAY TEACH THE YOUNG WOMEN TO BE SOBER, TO LOVE THEIR HUSBANDS, TO LOVE THEIR CHILDREN, *(READ MORE...)*

EPHESIANS 5:3 - BUT FORNICATION, AND ALL UNCLEANNESS, OR COVETOUSNESS, LET IT NOT BE ONCE NAMED AMONG YOU, AS BECOMETH SAINTS;

PSALMS 51:10 - CREATE IN ME A CLEAN HEART, O GOD; AND RENEW A RIGHT SPIRIT WITHIN ME.

I AM TO BE CONTENT

PHILIPPIANS 4:11-13 - NOT THAT I SPEAK IN RESPECT OF WANT: FOR I HAVE LEARNED, IN WHATSOEVER STATE I AM, [THEREWITH] TO BE CONTENT. *(READ MORE...)*

HEBREWS 13:5 - [LET YOUR] CONVERSATION [BE] WITHOUT COVETOUSNESS; [AND BE] CONTENT WITH SUCH THINGS AS YE HAVE: FOR HE HATH SAID, I WILL NEVER LEAVE THEE, NOR FORSAKE THEE.

1 TIMOTHY 6:6-8 - BUT GODLINESS WITH CONTENTMENT IS GREAT GAIN. *(READ MORE...)*

MATTHEW 6:31-33 - THEREFORE TAKE NO

THOUGHT, SAYING, WHAT SHALL WE EAT? OR, WHAT SHALL WE DRINK? OR, WHEREWITHAL SHALL WE BE CLOTHED? *(READ MORE...)*

PSALMS 16:8-11 - I HAVE SET THE LORD ALWAYS BEFORE ME: BECAUSE [HE IS] AT MY RIGHT HAND, I SHALL NOT BE MOVED. *(READ MORE...)*

LUKE 12:22 - AND HE SAID UNTO HIS DISCIPLES, THEREFORE I SAY UNTO YOU, TAKE NO THOUGHT FOR YOUR LIFE, WHAT YE SHALL EAT; NEITHER FOR THE BODY, WHAT YE SHALL PUT ON.

ECCLESIASTES 5:12 - THE SLEEP OF A LABOURING MAN [IS] SWEET, WHETHER HE EAT LITTLE OR MUCH: BUT THE ABUNDANCE OF THE RICH WILL NOT SUFFER HIM TO SLEEP.

MATTHEW 7:7 - ASK, AND IT SHALL BE GIVEN YOU; SEEK, AND YE SHALL FIND; KNOCK, AND IT SHALL BE OPENED UNTO YOU:

1 TIMOTHY 6:6 - BUT GODLINESS WITH CONTENTMENT IS GREAT GAIN.

JAMES 4:1-10 - FROM WHENCE [COME] WARS AND FIGHTINGS AMONG YOU? [COME THEY] NOT HENCE, [EVEN] OF YOUR LUSTS THAT WAR IN YOUR MEMBERS? *(READ MORE...)*

LUKE 6:46-49 - AND WHY CALL YE ME, LORD, LORD, AND DO NOT THE THINGS WHICH I SAY? *(READ MORE...)*

JEREMIAH 1:5 - BEFORE I FORMED THEE IN THE

BELLY I KNEW THEE; AND BEFORE THOU CAMEST FORTH OUT OF THE WOMB I SANCTIFIED THEE, [AND] I ORDAINED THEE A PROPHET UNTO THE NATIONS.

PROVERBS 14:30 - A SOUND HEART [IS] THE LIFE OF THE FLESH: BUT ENVY THE ROTTENNESS OF THE BONES.

DEUTERONOMY 6:5 - AND THOU SHALT LOVE THE LORD THY GOD WITH ALL THINE HEART, AND WITH ALL THY SOUL, AND WITH ALL THY MIGHT.

I AM TO BE DEVOTED

Leviticus 27:21 But the field, when it goeth out in the jubile, shall be holy unto the LORD, as a field devoted; the possession thereof shall be the priest's.

Psalms 119:38 Stablish thy word unto thy servant, who is devoted to thy fear.

I AM TO BE DILIGENT

PROVERBS 13:4 - THE SOUL OF THE SLUGGARD DESIRETH, AND [HATH] NOTHING: BUT THE SOUL OF THE DILIGENT SHALL BE MADE FAT.

PROVERBS 10:4 - HE BECOMETH POOR THAT DEALETH [WITH] A SLACK HAND: BUT THE HAND OF THE DILIGENT MAKETH RICH.

GALATIANS 6:9 - AND LET US NOT BE WEARY IN WELL DOING: FOR IN DUE SEASON WE SHALL REAP, IF

WE FAINT NOT.

1 CORINTHIANS 15:58 - THEREFORE, MY BELOVED BRETHREN, BE YE STEDFAST, UNMOVEABLE, ALWAYS ABOUNDING IN THE WORK OF THE LORD, FORASMUCH AS YE KNOW THAT YOUR LABOUR IS NOT IN VAIN IN THE LORD.

PROVERBS 12:24 - THE HAND OF THE DILIGENT SHALL BEAR RULE: BUT THE SLOTHFUL SHALL BE UNDER TRIBUTE.

PROVERBS 22:29 - SEEST THOU A MAN DILIGENT IN HIS BUSINESS? HE SHALL STAND BEFORE KINGS; HE SHALL NOT STAND BEFORE MEAN [MEN].

2 TIMOTHY 2:15 - STUDY TO SHEW THYSELF APPROVED UNTO GOD, A WORKMAN THAT NEEDETH NOT TO BE ASHAMED, RIGHTLY DIVIDING THE WORD OF TRUTH.

2 PETER 3:14 - WHEREFORE, BELOVED, SEEING THAT YE LOOK FOR SUCH THINGS, BE DILIGENT THAT YE MAY BE FOUND OF HIM IN PEACE, WITHOUT SPOT, AND BLAMELESS.

2 PETER 1:10 - WHEREFORE THE RATHER, BRETHREN, GIVE DILIGENCE TO MAKE YOUR CALLING AND ELECTION SURE: FOR IF YE DO THESE THINGS, YE SHALL NEVER FALL:

ECCLESIASTES 9:10 - WHATSOEVER THY HAND FINDETH TO DO, DO [IT] WITH THY MIGHT; FOR [THERE IS] NO WORK, NOR DEVICE, NOR KNOWLEDGE, NOR WISDOM, IN THE GRAVE, WHITHER

THOU GOEST.

PROVERBS 11:27 - HE THAT DILIGENTLY SEEKETH GOOD PROCURETH FAVOUR: BUT HE THAT SEEKETH MISCHIEF, IT SHALL COME UNTO HIM.

JAMES 1:12 - BLESSED [IS] THE MAN THAT ENDURETH TEMPTATION: FOR WHEN HE IS TRIED, HE SHALL RECEIVE THE CROWN OF LIFE, WHICH THE LORD HATH PROMISED TO THEM THAT LOVE HIM.

PROVERBS 6:6-8 - GO TO THE ANT, THOU SLUGGARD; CONSIDER HER WAYS, AND BE WISE: *(READ MORE...)*

PHILIPPIANS 3:14 - I PRESS TOWARD THE MARK FOR THE PRIZE OF THE HIGH CALLING OF GOD IN CHRIST JESUS.

COLOSSIANS 3:23 - AND WHATSOEVER YE DO, DO [IT] HEARTILY, AS TO THE LORD, AND NOT UNTO MEN;

I AM TO BE GENEROUS

ACTS 20:35 - I HAVE SHEWED YOU ALL THINGS, HOW THAT SO LABOURING YE OUGHT TO SUPPORT THE WEAK, AND TO REMEMBER THE WORDS OF THE LORD JESUS, HOW HE SAID, IT IS MORE BLESSED TO GIVE THAN TO RECEIVE.

LUKE 6:38 - GIVE, AND IT SHALL BE GIVEN UNTO YOU; GOOD MEASURE, PRESSED DOWN, AND SHAKEN

TOGETHER, AND RUNNING OVER, SHALL MEN GIVE INTO YOUR BOSOM. FOR WITH THE SAME MEASURE THAT YE METE WITHAL IT SHALL BE MEASURED TO YOU AGAIN.

PROVERBS 11:24-25 - THERE IS THAT SCATTERETH, AND YET INCREASETH; AND [THERE IS] THAT WITHHOLDETH MORE THAN IS MEET, BUT [IT TENDETH] TO POVERTY. *(READ MORE...)*

LUKE 21:1-4 - AND HE LOOKED UP, AND SAW THE RICH MEN CASTING THEIR GIFTS INTO THE TREASURY. *(READ MORE...)*

MATTHEW 6:21 - FOR WHERE YOUR TREASURE IS, THERE WILL YOUR HEART BE ALSO.

PROVERBS 19:17 - HE THAT HATH PITY UPON THE POOR LENDETH UNTO THE LORD; AND THAT WHICH HE HATH GIVEN WILL HE PAY HIM AGAIN.

1 TIMOTHY 6:17-19 - CHARGE THEM THAT ARE RICH IN THIS WORLD, THAT THEY BE NOT HIGHMINDED, NOR TRUST IN UNCERTAIN RICHES, BUT IN THE LIVING GOD, WHO GIVETH US RICHLY ALL THINGS TO ENJOY; *(READ MORE...)*

1 JOHN 3:17 - BUT WHOSO HATH THIS WORLD'S GOOD, AND SEETH HIS BROTHER HAVE NEED, AND SHUTTETH UP HIS BOWELS [OF COMPASSION] FROM HIM, HOW DWELLETH THE LOVE OF GOD IN HIM?

2 CORINTHIANS 9:6 - BUT THIS [I SAY], HE WHICH SOWETH SPARINGLY SHALL REAP ALSO SPARINGLY; AND HE WHICH SOWETH BOUNTIFULLY SHALL REAP

ALSO BOUNTIFULLY.

MATTHEW 10:42 - AND WHOSOEVER SHALL GIVE TO DRINK UNTO ONE OF THESE LITTLE ONES A CUP OF COLD [WATER] ONLY IN THE NAME OF A DISCIPLE, VERILY I SAY UNTO YOU, HE SHALL IN NO WISE LOSE HIS REWARD.

PROVERBS 21:13 - WHOSO STOPPETH HIS EARS AT THE CRY OF THE POOR, HE ALSO SHALL CRY HIMSELF, BUT SHALL NOT BE HEARD.

2 CORINTHIANS 9:7 - EVERY MAN ACCORDING AS HE PURPOSETH IN HIS HEART, [SO LET HIM GIVE]; NOT GRUDGINGLY, OR OF NECESSITY: FOR GOD LOVETH A CHEERFUL GIVER.

2 CORINTHIANS 9:5-7 - THEREFORE I THOUGHT IT NECESSARY TO EXHORT THE BRETHREN, THAT THEY WOULD GO BEFORE UNTO YOU, AND MAKE UP BEFOREHAND YOUR BOUNTY, WHEREOF YE HAD NOTICE BEFORE, THAT THE SAME MIGHT BE READY, AS [A MATTER OF] BOUNTY, AND NOT AS [OF] COVETOUSNESS. *(READ MORE...)*

LUKE 12:33 - SELL THAT YE HAVE, AND GIVE ALMS; PROVIDE YOURSELVES BAGS WHICH WAX NOT OLD, A TREASURE IN THE HEAVENS THAT FAILETH NOT, WHERE NO THIEF APPROACHETH, NEITHER MOTH CORRUPTETH.

MATTHEW 6:1-4 - TAKE HEED THAT YE DO NOT YOUR ALMS BEFORE MEN, TO BE SEEN OF THEM: OTHERWISE YE HAVE NO REWARD OF YOUR FATHER WHICH IS IN HEAVEN. *(READ MORE...)*

1 TIMOTHY 6:18-19 - THAT THEY DO GOOD, THAT THEY BE RICH IN GOOD WORKS, READY TO DISTRIBUTE, WILLING TO COMMUNICATE; *(READ MORE...)*

CHAPTER TEN

I AM TO BE WALKING IN THE FEAR OF THE LORD

PROVERBS 1:7 - THE FEAR OF THE LORD [IS] THE BEGINNING OF KNOWLEDGE: [BUT] FOOLS DESPISE WISDOM AND INSTRUCTION.

PROVERBS 8:13 - THE FEAR OF THE LORD [IS] TO HATE EVIL: PRIDE, AND ARROGANCY, AND THE EVIL WAY, AND THE FROWARD MOUTH, DO I HATE.

MATTHEW 10:28 - AND FEAR NOT THEM WHICH KILL THE BODY, BUT ARE NOT ABLE TO KILL THE SOUL: BUT RATHER FEAR HIM WHICH IS ABLE TO DESTROY BOTH SOUL AND BODY IN HELL.

ECCLESIASTES 12:13 - LET US HEAR THE CONCLUSION OF THE WHOLE MATTER: FEAR GOD, AND KEEP HIS COMMANDMENTS: FOR THIS [IS] THE WHOLE [DUTY] OF MAN.

JOB 28:28 - AND UNTO MAN HE SAID, BEHOLD, THE FEAR OF THE LORD, THAT [IS] WISDOM; AND TO DEPART FROM EVIL [IS] UNDERSTANDING.

PSALMS 33:8 - LET ALL THE EARTH FEAR THE LORD: LET ALL THE INHABITANTS OF THE WORLD STAND IN AWE OF HIM.

PROVERBS 14:27 - THE FEAR OF THE LORD [IS] A FOUNTAIN OF LIFE, TO DEPART FROM THE SNARES OF DEATH.

PROVERBS 14:26 - IN THE FEAR OF THE LORD [IS] STRONG CONFIDENCE: AND HIS CHILDREN SHALL HAVE A PLACE OF REFUGE.

DEUTERONOMY 10:12 - AND NOW, ISRAEL, WHAT DOTH THE LORD THY GOD REQUIRE OF THEE, BUT TO FEAR THE LORD THY GOD, TO WALK IN ALL HIS WAYS, AND TO LOVE HIM, AND TO SERVE THE LORD THY GOD WITH ALL THY HEART AND WITH ALL THY SOUL,

PSALMS 111:10 - THE FEAR OF THE LORD [IS] THE BEGINNING OF WISDOM: A GOOD UNDERSTANDING HAVE ALL THEY THAT DO [HIS COMMANDMENTS]: HIS PRAISE ENDURETH FOR EVER.

PSALMS 25:14 - THE SECRET OF THE LORD [IS] WITH THEM THAT FEAR HIM; AND HE WILL SHEW THEM HIS COVENANT.

PROVERBS 3:7 - BE NOT WISE IN THINE OWN EYES: FEAR THE LORD, AND DEPART FROM EVIL.

PSALMS 86:11 - TEACH ME THY WAY, O LORD; I WILL

WALK IN THY TRUTH: UNITE MY HEART TO FEAR THY NAME.

LUKE 1:50 - AND HIS MERCY [IS] ON THEM THAT FEAR HIM FROM GENERATION TO GENERATION.

PSALMS 34:9 - O FEAR THE LORD, YE HIS SAINTS: FOR [THERE IS] NO WANT TO THEM THAT FEAR HIM.

ISAIAH 41:10 - FEAR THOU NOT; FOR I [AM] WITH THEE: BE NOT DISMAYED; FOR I [AM] THY GOD: I WILL STRENGTHEN THEE; YEA, I WILL HELP THEE; YEA, I WILL UPHOLD THEE WITH THE RIGHT HAND OF MY RIGHTEOUSNESS.

PROVERBS 19:23 - THE FEAR OF THE LORD [TENDETH] TO LIFE: AND [HE THAT HATH IT] SHALL ABIDE SATISFIED; HE SHALL NOT BE VISITED WITH EVIL.

PHILIPPIANS 2:12-13 - WHEREFORE, MY BELOVED, AS YE HAVE ALWAYS OBEYED, NOT AS IN MY PRESENCE ONLY, BUT NOW MUCH MORE IN MY ABSENCE, WORK OUT YOUR OWN SALVATION WITH FEAR AND TREMBLING. *(READ MORE...)*

2 Corinthians 5:11 Knowing therefore the terror of the Lord, we persuade men; but we are made manifest unto God; and I trust also are made manifest in your consciences.

I AM TO BE LED BY THE SPIRIT

Romans 8:14 For as many as are led by the Spirit of God, they are the sons of God.

I AM TO BE HUMBLE

PHILIPPIANS 2:3-11 - [LET] NOTHING [BE DONE] THROUGH STRIFE OR VAINGLORY; BUT IN LOWLINESS OF MIND LET EACH ESTEEM OTHER BETTER THAN THEMSELVES. *(READ MORE...)*

JAMES 4:6 - BUT HE GIVETH MORE GRACE. WHEREFORE HE SAITH, GOD RESISTETH THE PROUD, BUT GIVETH GRACE UNTO THE HUMBLE.

LUKE 14:11 - FOR WHOSOEVER EXALTETH HIMSELF SHALL BE ABASED; AND HE THAT HUMBLETH HIMSELF SHALL BE EXALTED.

PROVERBS 22:4 - BY HUMILITY [AND] THE FEAR OF THE LORD [ARE] RICHES, AND HONOUR, AND LIFE.

1 PETER 5:6 - HUMBLE YOURSELVES THEREFORE UNDER THE MIGHTY HAND OF GOD, THAT HE MAY EXALT YOU IN DUE TIME:

MATTHEW 23:12 - AND WHOSOEVER SHALL EXALT HIMSELF SHALL BE ABASED; AND HE THAT SHALL HUMBLE HIMSELF SHALL BE EXALTED.

ROMANS 12:3 - FOR I SAY, THROUGH THE GRACE GIVEN UNTO ME, TO EVERY MAN THAT IS AMONG YOU, NOT TO THINK [OF HIMSELF] MORE HIGHLY THAN HE

OUGHT TO THINK; BUT TO THINK SOBERLY, ACCORDING AS GOD HATH DEALT TO EVERY MAN THE MEASURE OF FAITH.

COLOSSIANS 3:12 - PUT ON THEREFORE, AS THE ELECT OF GOD, HOLY AND BELOVED, BOWELS OF MERCIES, KINDNESS, HUMBLENESS OF MIND, MEEKNESS, LONGSUFFERING;

JOHN 3:30 - HE MUST INCREASE, BUT I [MUST] DECREASE.

PROVERBS 11:2 - [WHEN] PRIDE COMETH, THEN COMETH SHAME: BUT WITH THE LOWLY [IS] WISDOM.

1 PETER 5:5 - LIKEWISE, YE YOUNGER, SUBMIT YOURSELVES UNTO THE ELDER. YEA, ALL [OF YOU] BE SUBJECT ONE TO ANOTHER, AND BE CLOTHED WITH HUMILITY: FOR GOD RESISTETH THE PROUD, AND GIVETH GRACE TO THE HUMBLE.

JAMES 4:10 - HUMBLE YOURSELVES IN THE SIGHT OF THE LORD, AND HE SHALL LIFT YOU UP.

EPHESIANS 4:2 - WITH ALL LOWLINESS AND MEEKNESS, WITH LONGSUFFERING, FORBEARING ONE ANOTHER IN LOVE;

JEREMIAH 9:23 - THUS SAITH THE LORD, LET NOT THE WISE [MAN] GLORY IN HIS WISDOM, NEITHER LET THE MIGHTY [MAN] GLORY IN HIS MIGHT, LET NOT THE RICH [MAN] GLORY IN HIS RICHES:

ROMANS 11:18 - BOAST NOT AGAINST THE BRANCHES. BUT IF THOU BOAST, THOU BEAREST NOT

THE ROOT, BUT THE ROOT THEE.

I AM TO STUDY THE WORD OF GOD

2 TIMOTHY 3:16-17 - ALL SCRIPTURE [IS] GIVEN BY INSPIRATION OF GOD, AND [IS] PROFITABLE FOR DOCTRINE, FOR REPROOF, FOR CORRECTION, FOR INSTRUCTION IN RIGHTEOUSNESS: *(READ MORE...)*

2 TIMOTHY 3:14-17 - BUT CONTINUE THOU IN THE THINGS WHICH THOU HAST LEARNED AND HAST BEEN ASSURED OF, KNOWING OF WHOM THOU HAST LEARNED [THEM]; *(READ MORE...)*

PSALMS 119:11 - THY WORD HAVE I HID IN MINE HEART, THAT I MIGHT NOT SIN AGAINST THEE.

PSALMS 119:105 - NUN. THY WORD [IS] A LAMP UNTO MY FEET, AND A LIGHT UNTO MY PATH.

PROVERBS 3:1-2 - MY SON, FORGET NOT MY LAW; BUT LET THINE HEART KEEP MY COMMANDMENTS: *(READ MORE...)*

2 TIMOTHY 2:15 - STUDY TO SHEW THYSELF APPROVED UNTO GOD, A WORKMAN THAT NEEDETH NOT TO BE ASHAMED, RIGHTLY DIVIDING THE WORD OF TRUTH.

1 PETER 3:15 - BUT SANCTIFY THE LORD GOD IN YOUR HEARTS: AND [BE] READY ALWAYS TO [GIVE] AN ANSWER TO EVERY MAN THAT ASKETH YOU A REASON OF THE HOPE THAT IS IN YOU WITH

MEEKNESS AND FEAR:

DEUTERONOMY 11:18-23 - THEREFORE SHALL YE LAY UP THESE MY WORDS IN YOUR HEART AND IN YOUR SOUL, AND BIND THEM FOR A SIGN UPON YOUR HAND, THAT THEY MAY BE AS FRONTLETS BETWEEN YOUR EYES. *(READ MORE...)*

PSALMS 119:18 - OPEN THOU MINE EYES, THAT I MAY BEHOLD WONDROUS THINGS OUT OF THY LAW.

PSALMS 119:9 - BETH. WHEREWITHAL SHALL A YOUNG MAN CLEANSE HIS WAY? BY TAKING HEED [THERETO] ACCORDING TO THY WORD.

ROMANS 12:2 - AND BE NOT CONFORMED TO THIS WORLD: BUT BE YE TRANSFORMED BY THE RENEWING OF YOUR MIND, THAT YE MAY PROVE WHAT [IS] THAT GOOD, AND ACCEPTABLE, AND PERFECT, WILL OF GOD.

ACTS 17:11 - THESE WERE MORE NOBLE THAN THOSE IN THESSALONICA, IN THAT THEY RECEIVED THE WORD WITH ALL READINESS OF MIND, AND SEARCHED THE SCRIPTURES DAILY, WHETHER THOSE THINGS WERE SO.

EPHESIANS 6:11-17 - PUT ON THE WHOLE ARMOUR OF GOD, THAT YE MAY BE ABLE TO STAND AGAINST THE WILES OF THE DEVIL. *(READ MORE...)*

HEBREWS 4:12 - FOR THE WORD OF GOD [IS] QUICK, AND POWERFUL, AND SHARPER THAN ANY TWOEDGED SWORD, PIERCING EVEN TO THE DIVIDING ASUNDER OF SOUL AND SPIRIT, AND OF

THE JOINTS AND MARROW, AND [IS] A DISCERNER OF THE THOUGHTS AND INTENTS OF THE HEART.

ACTS 8:30 - AND PHILIP RAN THITHER TO [HIM], AND HEARD HIM READ THE PROPHET ESAIAS, AND SAID, UNDERSTANDEST THOU WHAT THOU READEST?

JAMES 1:22 - BUT BE YE DOERS OF THE WORD, AND NOT HEARERS ONLY, DECEIVING YOUR OWN SELVES.

JOHN 8:32 - AND YE SHALL KNOW THE TRUTH, AND THE TRUTH SHALL MAKE YOU FREE.

I AM TO BE MERCIFUL

JAMES 2:13 - FOR HE SHALL HAVE JUDGMENT WITHOUT MERCY, THAT HATH SHEWED NO MERCY; AND MERCY REJOICETH AGAINST JUDGMENT.

LUKE 6:36 - BE YE THEREFORE MERCIFUL, AS YOUR FATHER ALSO IS MERCIFUL.

MATTHEW 5:7 - BLESSED [ARE] THE MERCIFUL: FOR THEY SHALL OBTAIN MERCY.

MATTHEW 9:13 - BUT GO YE AND LEARN WHAT [THAT] MEANETH, I WILL HAVE MERCY, AND NOT SACRIFICE: FOR I AM NOT COME TO CALL THE RIGHTEOUS, BUT SINNERS TO REPENTANCE.

HEBREWS 4:16 - LET US THEREFORE COME BOLDLY UNTO THE THRONE OF GRACE, THAT WE MAY OBTAIN MERCY, AND FIND GRACE TO HELP IN TIME OF NEED.

1 JOHN 1:9 - IF WE CONFESS OUR SINS, HE IS FAITHFUL AND JUST TO FORGIVE US [OUR] SINS, AND TO CLEANSE US FROM ALL UNRIGHTEOUSNESS.

PSALMS 103:1-22 - ([A PSALM] OF DAVID.) BLESS THE LORD, O MY SOUL: AND ALL THAT IS WITHIN ME, [BLESS] HIS HOLY NAME. *(READ MORE...)*

1 PETER 1:3 - BLESSED [BE] THE GOD AND FATHER OF OUR LORD JESUS CHRIST, WHICH ACCORDING TO HIS ABUNDANT MERCY HATH BEGOTTEN US AGAIN UNTO A LIVELY HOPE BY THE RESURRECTION OF JESUS CHRIST FROM THE DEAD,

COLOSSIANS 3:12 - PUT ON THEREFORE, AS THE ELECT OF GOD, HOLY AND BELOVED, BOWELS OF MERCIES, KINDNESS, HUMBLENESS OF MIND, MEEKNESS, LONGSUFFERING;

JAMES 2:12-13 - SO SPEAK YE, AND SO DO, AS THEY THAT SHALL BE JUDGED BY THE LAW OF LIBERTY. *(READ MORE...)*

MICAH 6:8 - HE HATH SHEWED THEE, O MAN, WHAT [IS] GOOD; AND WHAT DOTH THE LORD REQUIRE OF THEE, BUT TO DO JUSTLY, AND TO LOVE MERCY, AND TO WALK HUMBLY WITH THY GOD?

LUKE 6:36-37 - BE YE THEREFORE MERCIFUL, AS YOUR FATHER ALSO IS MERCIFUL. *(READ MORE...)*

COLOSSIANS 3:13 - FORBEARING ONE ANOTHER, AND FORGIVING ONE ANOTHER, IF ANY MAN HAVE A QUARREL AGAINST ANY: EVEN AS CHRIST FORGAVE

YOU, SO ALSO [DO] YE.

LUKE 6:37 - JUDGE NOT, AND YE SHALL NOT BE JUDGED: CONDEMN NOT, AND YE SHALL NOT BE CONDEMNED: FORGIVE, AND YE SHALL BE FORGIVEN:

1 CORINTHIANS 10:13 - THERE HATH NO TEMPTATION TAKEN YOU BUT SUCH AS IS COMMON TO MAN: BUT GOD [IS] FAITHFUL, WHO WILL NOT SUFFER YOU TO BE TEMPTED ABOVE THAT YE ARE ABLE; BUT WILL WITH THE TEMPTATION ALSO MAKE A WAY TO ESCAPE, THAT YE MAY BE ABLE TO BEAR [IT].

JUDE 1:23-25 - AND OTHERS SAVE WITH FEAR, PULLING [THEM] OUT OF THE FIRE; HATING EVEN THE GARMENT SPOTTED BY THE FLESH. *(READ MORE...)*

I AM TO BE BUSY TILL JESUS COMES

Luke 19:13 And he called his ten servants, and delivered them ten pounds, and said unto them, Occupy till I come.

I AM TO BE A PEACEMAKER

MATTHEW 5:9 - BLESSED [ARE] THE PEACEMAKERS: FOR THEY SHALL BE CALLED THE CHILDREN OF GOD.

ROMANS 12:18 - IF IT BE POSSIBLE, AS MUCH AS LIETH IN YOU, LIVE PEACEABLY WITH ALL MEN.

MATTHEW 7:12 - THEREFORE ALL THINGS WHATSOEVER YE WOULD THAT MEN SHOULD DO TO

YOU, DO YE EVEN SO TO THEM: FOR THIS IS THE LAW AND THE PROPHETS.

1 THESSALONIANS 5:13 - AND TO ESTEEM THEM VERY HIGHLY IN LOVE FOR THEIR WORK'S SAKE. [AND] BE AT PEACE AMONG YOURSELVES.

PHILIPPIANS 4:6-7 - BE CAREFUL FOR NOTHING; BUT IN EVERY THING BY PRAYER AND SUPPLICATION WITH THANKSGIVING LET YOUR REQUESTS BE MADE KNOWN UNTO GOD. *(READ MORE...)*

MATTHEW 5:22 - BUT I SAY UNTO YOU, THAT WHOSOEVER IS ANGRY WITH HIS BROTHER WITHOUT A CAUSE SHALL BE IN DANGER OF THE JUDGMENT: AND WHOSOEVER SHALL SAY TO HIS BROTHER, RACA, SHALL BE IN DANGER OF THE COUNCIL: BUT WHOSOEVER SHALL SAY, THOU FOOL, SHALL BE IN DANGER OF HELL FIRE.

LUKE 6:31 - AND AS YE WOULD THAT MEN SHOULD DO TO YOU, DO YE ALSO TO THEM LIKEWISE.

NUMBERS 25:12 - WHEREFORE SAY, BEHOLD, I GIVE UNTO HIM MY COVENANT OF PEACE:

MATTHEW 5:3-12 - BLESSED [ARE] THE POOR IN SPIRIT: FOR THEIRS IS THE KINGDOM OF HEAVEN. *(READ MORE...)*

MARK 11:25 - AND WHEN YE STAND PRAYING, FORGIVE, IF YE HAVE OUGHT AGAINST ANY: THAT YOUR FATHER ALSO WHICH IS IN HEAVEN MAY FORGIVE YOU YOUR TRESPASSES.

COLOSSIANS 3:15 - AND LET THE PEACE OF GOD RULE IN YOUR HEARTS, TO THE WHICH ALSO YE ARE CALLED IN ONE BODY; AND BE YE THANKFUL.

MATTHEW 5:24 - LEAVE THERE THY GIFT BEFORE THE ALTAR, AND GO THY WAY; FIRST BE RECONCILED TO THY BROTHER, AND THEN COME AND OFFER THY GIFT.

JAMES 3:17-18 - BUT THE WISDOM THAT IS FROM ABOVE IS FIRST PURE, THEN PEACEABLE, GENTLE, [AND] EASY TO BE INTREATED, FULL OF MERCY AND GOOD FRUITS, WITHOUT PARTIALITY, AND WITHOUT HYPOCRISY. *(READ MORE...)*

PROVERBS 19:17 - HE THAT HATH PITY UPON THE POOR LENDETH UNTO THE LORD; AND THAT WHICH HE HATH GIVEN WILL HE PAY HIM AGAIN.

I AM TO BE PRUDENT

Proverbs 12:16 A fool's wrath is presently known: but a prudent man covereth shame.

Proverbs 12:23 A prudent man concealeth knowledge: but the heart of fools proclaimeth foolishness.

Proverbs 13:16 Every prudent man dealeth with knowledge: but a fool layeth open his folly.

Proverbs 14:8 The wisdom of the prudent is to understand his way: but the folly of fools is deceit.

Proverbs 14:15 The simple believeth every word: but the prudent man looketh well to his going.

Proverbs 14:18 The simple inherit folly: but the prudent are crowned with knowledge.

Proverbs 15:5 A fool despiseth his father's instruction: but he that regardeth reproof is prudent.

Proverbs 16:21 The wise in heart shall be called prudent: and the sweetness of the lips increaseth learning.

Proverbs 18:15 The heart of the prudent getteth knowledge; and the ear of the wise seeketh knowledge.

I AM TO BE RESTING IN GOD

MATTHEW 11:28-30 - COME UNTO ME, ALL [YE] THAT LABOUR AND ARE HEAVY LADEN, AND I WILL GIVE YOU REST. *(READ MORE...)*

EXODUS 33:14 - AND HE SAID, MY PRESENCE SHALL GO [WITH THEE], AND I WILL GIVE THEE REST.

PSALMS 127:2 - [IT IS] VAIN FOR YOU TO RISE UP EARLY, TO SIT UP LATE, TO EAT THE BREAD OF SORROWS: [FOR] SO HE GIVETH HIS BELOVED SLEEP.

MATTHEW 11:29 - TAKE MY YOKE UPON YOU, AND LEARN OF ME; FOR I AM MEEK AND LOWLY IN HEART: AND YE SHALL FIND REST UNTO YOUR SOULS.

MARK 6:31 - AND HE SAID UNTO THEM, COME YE YOURSELVES APART INTO A DESERT PLACE, AND REST A WHILE: FOR THERE WERE MANY COMING AND GOING, AND THEY HAD NO LEISURE SO MUCH AS TO EAT.

EXODUS 34:21 - SIX DAYS THOU SHALT WORK, BUT ON THE SEVENTH DAY THOU SHALT REST: IN EARING TIME AND IN HARVEST THOU SHALT REST.

ISAIAH 30:15 - FOR THUS SAITH THE LORD GOD, THE HOLY ONE OF ISRAEL; IN RETURNING AND REST SHALL YE BE SAVED; IN QUIETNESS AND IN CONFIDENCE SHALL BE YOUR STRENGTH: AND YE WOULD NOT.

PSALMS 37:7 - REST IN THE LORD, AND WAIT PATIENTLY FOR HIM: FRET NOT THYSELF BECAUSE OF HIM WHO PROSPERETH IN HIS WAY, BECAUSE OF THE MAN WHO BRINGETH WICKED DEVICES TO PASS.

PSALMS 46:10 - BE STILL, AND KNOW THAT I [AM] GOD: I WILL BE EXALTED AMONG THE HEATHEN, I WILL BE EXALTED IN THE EARTH.

JEREMIAH 31:25 - FOR I HAVE SATIATED THE WEARY SOUL, AND I HAVE REPLENISHED EVERY SORROWFUL SOUL.

ISAIAH 40:28-31 - HAST THOU NOT KNOWN? HAST THOU NOT HEARD, [THAT] THE EVERLASTING GOD, THE LORD, THE CREATOR OF THE ENDS OF THE EARTH, FAINTETH NOT, NEITHER IS WEARY? [THERE IS] NO SEARCHING OF HIS UNDERSTANDING. *(READ MORE...)*

PSALMS 4:8 - I WILL BOTH LAY ME DOWN IN PEACE, AND SLEEP: FOR THOU, LORD, ONLY MAKEST ME DWELL IN SAFETY.

HEBREWS 4:1-11 - LET US THEREFORE FEAR, LEST, A PROMISE BEING LEFT [US] OF ENTERING INTO HIS REST, ANY OF YOU SHOULD SEEM TO COME SHORT OF IT. *(READ MORE...)*

ROMANS 15:13 - NOW THE GOD OF HOPE FILL YOU WITH ALL JOY AND PEACE IN BELIEVING, THAT YE MAY ABOUND IN HOPE, THROUGH THE POWER OF THE HOLY GHOST.

PSALMS 94:12-14 - BLESSED [IS] THE MAN WHOM THOU CHASTENEST, O LORD, AND TEACHEST HIM OUT OF THY LAW; *(READ MORE...)*

PSALMS 91:1 - HE THAT DWELLETH IN THE SECRET PLACE OF THE MOST HIGH SHALL ABIDE UNDER THE SHADOW OF THE ALMIGHTY.

GENESIS 2:3 - AND GOD BLESSED THE SEVENTH DAY, AND SANCTIFIED IT: BECAUSE THAT IN IT HE HAD RESTED FROM ALL HIS WORK WHICH GOD CREATED AND MADE.

I AM TO BE SEEKING FIRST THE KINGDOM OF GOD

DEUTERONOMY 4:29 - BUT IF FROM THENCE THOU SHALT SEEK THE LORD THY GOD, THOU SHALT FIND [HIM], IF THOU SEEK HIM WITH ALL THY HEART AND WITH ALL THY SOUL.

PROVERBS 8:17 - I LOVE THEM THAT LOVE ME; AND THOSE THAT SEEK ME EARLY SHALL FIND ME.

JEREMIAH 29:12-14 - THEN SHALL YE CALL UPON ME, AND YE SHALL GO AND PRAY UNTO ME, AND I WILL HEARKEN UNTO YOU. *(READ MORE...)*

MATTHEW 7:7-8 - ASK, AND IT SHALL BE GIVEN YOU; SEEK, AND YE SHALL FIND; KNOCK, AND IT SHALL BE OPENED UNTO YOU: *(READ MORE...)*

1 CHRONICLES 16:11 - SEEK THE LORD AND HIS STRENGTH, SEEK HIS FACE CONTINUALLY.

LAMENTATIONS 3:25 - THE LORD [IS] GOOD UNTO THEM THAT WAIT FOR HIM, TO THE SOUL [THAT] SEEKETH HIM.

ISAIAH 55:6-7 - SEEK YE THE LORD WHILE HE MAY BE FOUND, CALL YE UPON HIM WHILE HE IS NEAR: *(READ MORE...)*

PSALMS 119:10 - WITH MY WHOLE HEART HAVE I SOUGHT THEE: O LET ME NOT WANDER FROM THY COMMANDMENTS.

MATTHEW 6:33 - BUT SEEK YE FIRST THE KINGDOM OF GOD, AND HIS RIGHTEOUSNESS; AND ALL THESE THINGS SHALL BE ADDED UNTO YOU.

JEREMIAH 29:13 - AND YE SHALL SEEK ME, AND FIND [ME], WHEN YE SHALL SEARCH FOR ME WITH ALL YOUR HEART.

HEBREWS 11:6 - BUT WITHOUT FAITH [IT IS] IMPOSSIBLE TO PLEASE [HIM]: FOR HE THAT COMETH TO GOD MUST BELIEVE THAT HE IS, AND [THAT] HE IS A REWARDER OF THEM THAT DILIGENTLY SEEK HIM.

PSALMS 34:10 - THE YOUNG LIONS DO LACK, AND SUFFER HUNGER: BUT THEY THAT SEEK THE LORD SHALL NOT WANT ANY GOOD [THING].

PSALMS 63:1 - (A PSALM OF DAVID, WHEN HE WAS IN THE WILDERNESS OF JUDAH.) O GOD, THOU [ART] MY GOD; EARLY WILL I SEEK THEE: MY SOUL THIRSTETH FOR THEE, MY FLESH LONGETH FOR THEE IN A DRY AND THIRSTY LAND, WHERE NO WATER IS;

JOB 5:8-9 - I WOULD SEEK UNTO GOD, AND UNTO GOD WOULD I COMMIT MY CAUSE: *(READ MORE...)*

2 CHRONICLES 7:14 - IF MY PEOPLE, WHICH ARE CALLED BY MY NAME, SHALL HUMBLE THEMSELVES, AND PRAY, AND SEEK MY FACE, AND TURN FROM THEIR WICKED WAYS; THEN WILL I HEAR FROM HEAVEN, AND WILL FORGIVE THEIR SIN, AND WILL HEAL THEIR LAND.

JAMES 4:8 - DRAW NIGH TO GOD, AND HE WILL DRAW NIGH TO YOU. CLEANSE [YOUR] HANDS, [YE] SINNERS; AND PURIFY [YOUR] HEARTS, [YE] DOUBLE MINDED.

PSALMS 40:16 - LET ALL THOSE THAT SEEK THEE REJOICE AND BE GLAD IN THEE: LET SUCH AS LOVE THY SALVATION SAY CONTINUALLY, THE LORD BE MAGNIFIED.

PSALMS 119:2 - BLESSED [ARE] THEY THAT KEEP HIS TESTIMONIES, [AND THAT] SEEK HIM WITH THE WHOLE HEART.

PSALMS 14:2 - THE LORD LOOKED DOWN FROM HEAVEN UPON THE CHILDREN OF MEN, TO SEE IF THERE WERE ANY THAT DID UNDERSTAND, [AND] SEEK GOD.

PSALMS 9:10 - AND THEY THAT KNOW THY NAME WILL PUT THEIR TRUST IN THEE: FOR THOU, LORD, HAST NOT FORSAKEN THEM THAT SEEK THEE.

ACTS 17:26-27 - AND HATH MADE OF ONE BLOOD ALL NATIONS OF MEN FOR TO DWELL ON ALL THE FACE OF THE EARTH, AND HATH DETERMINED THE TIMES BEFORE APPOINTED, AND THE BOUNDS OF THEIR HABITATION; *(READ MORE...)*

I AM TO BE THANKFUL

1 THESSALONIANS 5:18 - IN EVERY THING GIVE THANKS: FOR THIS IS THE WILL OF GOD IN CHRIST JESUS CONCERNING YOU.

PSALMS 107:1 - O GIVE THANKS UNTO THE LORD, FOR [HE IS] GOOD: FOR HIS MERCY [ENDURETH] FOR EVER.

EPHESIANS 5:20 - GIVING THANKS ALWAYS FOR ALL THINGS UNTO GOD AND THE FATHER IN THE NAME OF OUR LORD JESUS CHRIST;

COLOSSIANS 3:15-17 - AND LET THE PEACE OF GOD RULE IN YOUR HEARTS, TO THE WHICH ALSO YE ARE CALLED IN ONE BODY; AND BE YE THANKFUL. *(READ MORE...)*

JAMES 1:17 - EVERY GOOD GIFT AND EVERY PERFECT GIFT IS FROM ABOVE, AND COMETH DOWN FROM THE FATHER OF LIGHTS, WITH WHOM IS NO VARIABLENESS, NEITHER SHADOW OF TURNING.

PHILIPPIANS 4:6 - BE CAREFUL FOR NOTHING; BUT IN EVERY THING BY PRAYER AND SUPPLICATION WITH THANKSGIVING LET YOUR REQUESTS BE MADE KNOWN UNTO GOD.

2 CORINTHIANS 9:15 - THANKS [BE] UNTO GOD FOR HIS UNSPEAKABLE GIFT.

PSALMS 106:1 - PRAISE YE THE LORD. O GIVE THANKS UNTO THE LORD; FOR [HE IS] GOOD: FOR HIS MERCY [ENDURETH] FOR EVER.

PSALMS 105:1 - O GIVE THANKS UNTO THE LORD; CALL UPON HIS NAME: MAKE KNOWN HIS DEEDS AMONG THE PEOPLE.

PSALMS 20:4 - GRANT THEE ACCORDING TO THINE OWN HEART, AND FULFIL ALL THY COUNSEL.

PSALMS 30:12 - TO THE END THAT [MY] GLORY MAY SING PRAISE TO THEE, AND NOT BE SILENT. O LORD MY GOD, I WILL GIVE THANKS UNTO THEE FOR EVER.

PSALMS 118:1-18 - O GIVE THANKS UNTO THE LORD; FOR [HE IS] GOOD: BECAUSE HIS MERCY [ENDURETH] FOR EVER. *(READ MORE...)*

COLOSSIANS 3:15 - AND LET THE PEACE OF GOD RULE IN YOUR HEARTS, TO THE WHICH ALSO YE ARE

CALLED IN ONE BODY; AND BE YE THANKFUL.

COLOSSIANS 4:2 - CONTINUE IN PRAYER, AND WATCH IN THE SAME WITH THANKSGIVING;

COLOSSIANS 3:17 - AND WHATSOEVER YE DO IN WORD OR DEED, [DO] ALL IN THE NAME OF THE LORD JESUS, GIVING THANKS TO GOD AND THE FATHER BY HIM.

PSALMS 100:4 - ENTER INTO HIS GATES WITH THANKSGIVING, [AND] INTO HIS COURTS WITH PRAISE: BE THANKFUL UNTO HIM, [AND] BLESS HIS NAME.

I AM TO BE A WORSHIPER

JOHN 4:24 - GOD [IS] A SPIRIT: AND THEY THAT WORSHIP HIM MUST WORSHIP [HIM] IN SPIRIT AND IN TRUTH.

PSALMS 95:6 - O COME, LET US WORSHIP AND BOW DOWN: LET US KNEEL BEFORE THE LORD OUR MAKER.

ROMANS 12:1 - I BESEECH YOU THEREFORE, BRETHREN, BY THE MERCIES OF GOD, THAT YE PRESENT YOUR BODIES A LIVING SACRIFICE, HOLY, ACCEPTABLE UNTO GOD, [WHICH IS] YOUR REASONABLE SERVICE.

COLOSSIANS 3:14-17 - AND ABOVE ALL THESE THINGS [PUT ON] CHARITY, WHICH IS THE BOND OF PERFECTNESS. *(READ MORE...)*

JOHN 4:23 - BUT THE HOUR COMETH, AND NOW IS, WHEN THE TRUE WORSHIPPERS SHALL WORSHIP THE FATHER IN SPIRIT AND IN TRUTH: FOR THE FATHER SEEKETH SUCH TO WORSHIP HIM.

ISAIAH 12:5 - SING UNTO THE LORD; FOR HE HATH DONE EXCELLENT THINGS: THIS [IS] KNOWN IN ALL THE EARTH.

HEBREWS 13:15 - BY HIM THEREFORE LET US OFFER THE SACRIFICE OF PRAISE TO GOD CONTINUALLY, THAT IS, THE FRUIT OF [OUR] LIPS GIVING THANKS TO HIS NAME.

LUKE 4:8 - AND JESUS ANSWERED AND SAID UNTO HIM, GET THEE BEHIND ME, SATAN: FOR IT IS WRITTEN, THOU SHALT WORSHIP THE LORD THY GOD, AND HIM ONLY SHALT THOU SERVE.

HEBREWS 12:28 - WHEREFORE WE RECEIVING A KINGDOM WHICH CANNOT BE MOVED, LET US HAVE GRACE, WHEREBY WE MAY SERVE GOD ACCEPTABLY WITH REVERENCE AND GODLY FEAR:

PSALMS 95:1-6 - O COME, LET US SING UNTO THE LORD: LET US MAKE A JOYFUL NOISE TO THE ROCK OF OUR SALVATION. *(READ MORE...)*

PSALMS 29:2 - GIVE UNTO THE LORD THE GLORY DUE UNTO HIS NAME; WORSHIP THE LORD IN THE BEAUTY OF HOLINESS.

I AM TO RUN THE RACE

1 CORINTHIANS 9:24-27 - KNOW YE NOT THAT THEY WHICH RUN IN A RACE RUN ALL, BUT ONE RECEIVETH THE PRIZE? SO RUN, THAT YE MAY OBTAIN. *(READ MORE...)*

HEBREWS 12:1 - WHEREFORE SEEING WE ALSO ARE COMPASSED ABOUT WITH SO GREAT A CLOUD OF WITNESSES, LET US LAY ASIDE EVERY WEIGHT, AND THE SIN WHICH DOTH SO EASILY BESET [US], AND LET US RUN WITH PATIENCE THE RACE THAT IS SET BEFORE US,

ISAIAH 40:31 - BUT THEY THAT WAIT UPON THE LORD SHALL RENEW [THEIR] STRENGTH; THEY SHALL MOUNT UP WITH WINGS AS EAGLES; THEY SHALL RUN, AND NOT BE WEARY; [AND] THEY SHALL WALK, AND NOT FAINT.

1 CORINTHIANS 9:24 - KNOW YE NOT THAT THEY WHICH RUN IN A RACE RUN ALL, BUT ONE RECEIVETH THE PRIZE? SO RUN, THAT YE MAY OBTAIN.

PHILIPPIANS 3:13-14 - BRETHREN, I COUNT NOT MYSELF TO HAVE APPREHENDED: BUT [THIS] ONE THING [I DO], FORGETTING THOSE THINGS WHICH ARE BEHIND, AND REACHING FORTH UNTO THOSE THINGS WHICH ARE BEFORE, *(READ MORE...)*

HEBREWS 12:1-29 - WHEREFORE SEEING WE ALSO ARE COMPASSED ABOUT WITH SO GREAT A CLOUD OF WITNESSES, LET US LAY ASIDE EVERY WEIGHT, AND THE SIN WHICH DOTH SO EASILY BESET [US], AND LET US RUN WITH PATIENCE THE RACE THAT IS SET BEFORE US, *(READ MORE...)*

2 TIMOTHY 4:7-9 - I HAVE FOUGHT A GOOD FIGHT, I HAVE FINISHED [MY] COURSE, I HAVE KEPT THE FAITH: *(READ MORE...)*

1 CORINTHIANS 9:26 - I THEREFORE SO RUN, NOT AS UNCERTAINLY; SO FIGHT I, NOT AS ONE THAT BEATETH THE AIR:

HEBREWS 12:1-2 - WHEREFORE SEEING WE ALSO ARE COMPASSED ABOUT WITH SO GREAT A CLOUD OF WITNESSES, LET US LAY ASIDE EVERY WEIGHT, AND THE SIN WHICH DOTH SO EASILY BESET [US], AND LET US RUN WITH PATIENCE THE RACE THAT IS SET BEFORE US, *(READ MORE...)*

MATTHEW 24:13 - BUT HE THAT SHALL ENDURE UNTO THE END, THE SAME SHALL BE SAVED.

I AM TO BE REDEEMING THE TIME

ECCLESIASTES 3:1-8 - TO EVERY [THING THERE IS] A SEASON, AND A TIME TO EVERY PURPOSE UNDER THE HEAVEN: *(READ MORE...)*

2 PETER 3:8 - BUT, BELOVED, BE NOT IGNORANT OF THIS ONE THING, THAT ONE DAY [IS] WITH THE LORD AS A THOUSAND YEARS, AND A THOUSAND YEARS AS ONE DAY.

PSALMS 90:12 - SO TEACH [US] TO NUMBER OUR DAYS, THAT WE MAY APPLY [OUR] HEARTS UNTO

WISDOM.

PROVERBS 16:9 - A MAN'S HEART DEVISETH HIS WAY: BUT THE LORD DIRECTETH HIS STEPS.

JAMES 4:13-15 - GO TO NOW, YE THAT SAY, TO DAY OR TO MORROW WE WILL GO INTO SUCH A CITY, AND CONTINUE THERE A YEAR, AND BUY AND SELL, AND GET GAIN: *(READ MORE...)*

EPHESIANS 5:16 - REDEEMING THE TIME, BECAUSE THE DAYS ARE EVIL.

JEREMIAH 29:11 - FOR I KNOW THE THOUGHTS THAT I THINK TOWARD YOU, SAITH THE LORD, THOUGHTS OF PEACE, AND NOT OF EVIL, TO GIVE YOU AN EXPECTED END.

JAMES 4:14 - WHEREAS YE KNOW NOT WHAT [SHALL BE] ON THE MORROW. FOR WHAT [IS] YOUR LIFE? IT IS EVEN A VAPOUR, THAT APPEARETH FOR A LITTLE TIME, AND THEN VANISHETH AWAY.

EPHESIANS 1:10 - THAT IN THE DISPENSATION OF THE FULNESS OF TIMES HE MIGHT GATHER TOGETHER IN ONE ALL THINGS IN CHRIST, BOTH WHICH ARE IN HEAVEN, AND WHICH ARE ON EARTH; [EVEN] IN HIM:

PROVERBS 16:3 - COMMIT THY WORKS UNTO THE LORD, AND THY THOUGHTS SHALL BE ESTABLISHED.

PSALMS 31:15 - MY TIMES [ARE] IN THY HAND: DELIVER ME FROM THE HAND OF MINE ENEMIES, AND FROM THEM THAT PERSECUTE ME.

2 CORINTHIANS 6:2 - (FOR HE SAITH, I HAVE HEARD THEE IN A TIME ACCEPTED, AND IN THE DAY OF SALVATION HAVE I SUCCOURED THEE: BEHOLD, NOW [IS] THE ACCEPTED TIME; BEHOLD, NOW [IS] THE DAY OF SALVATION.)

MARK 13:32 - BUT OF THAT DAY AND [THAT] HOUR KNOWETH NO MAN, NO, NOT THE ANGELS WHICH ARE IN HEAVEN, NEITHER THE SON, BUT THE FATHER.

1 THESSALONIANS 5:1-3 - BUT OF THE TIMES AND THE SEASONS, BRETHREN, YE HAVE NO NEED THAT I WRITE UNTO YOU. *(READ MORE...)*

I AM TO BE PREACHING THE GOSPEL

MARK 16:15 - AND HE SAID UNTO THEM, GO YE INTO ALL THE WORLD, AND PREACH THE GOSPEL TO EVERY CREATURE.

2 TIMOTHY 2:24-26 - AND THE SERVANT OF THE LORD MUST NOT STRIVE; BUT BE GENTLE UNTO ALL [MEN], APT TO TEACH, PATIENT, *(READ MORE...)*

ROMANS 1:16 - FOR I AM NOT ASHAMED OF THE GOSPEL OF CHRIST: FOR IT IS THE POWER OF GOD UNTO SALVATION TO EVERY ONE THAT BELIEVETH; TO THE JEW FIRST, AND ALSO TO THE GREEK.

ACTS 10:42 - AND HE COMMANDED US TO PREACH UNTO THE PEOPLE, AND TO TESTIFY THAT IT IS HE WHICH WAS ORDAINED OF GOD [TO BE] THE JUDGE OF QUICK AND DEAD.

1 CORINTHIANS 15:1-58 - MOREOVER, BRETHREN, I DECLARE UNTO YOU THE GOSPEL WHICH I PREACHED UNTO YOU, WHICH ALSO YE HAVE RECEIVED, AND WHEREIN YE STAND; *(READ MORE...)*

MATTHEW 10:7 - AND AS YE GO, PREACH, SAYING, THE KINGDOM OF HEAVEN IS AT HAND.

MATTHEW 28:19-20 - GO YE THEREFORE, AND TEACH ALL NATIONS, BAPTIZING THEM IN THE NAME OF THE FATHER, AND OF THE SON, AND OF THE HOLY GHOST: *(READ MORE...)*

DANIEL 12:3 - AND THEY THAT BE WISE SHALL SHINE AS THE BRIGHTNESS OF THE FIRMAMENT; AND THEY THAT TURN MANY TO RIGHTEOUSNESS AS THE STARS FOR EVER AND EVER.

MATTHEW 10:8 - HEAL THE SICK, CLEANSE THE LEPERS, RAISE THE DEAD, CAST OUT DEVILS: FREELY YE HAVE RECEIVED, FREELY GIVE.

MATTHEW 10:27 - WHAT I TELL YOU IN DARKNESS, [THAT] SPEAK YE IN LIGHT: AND WHAT YE HEAR IN THE EAR, [THAT] PREACH YE UPON THE HOUSETOPS.

JOHN 21:15-17 - SO WHEN THEY HAD DINED, JESUS SAITH TO SIMON PETER, SIMON, [SON] OF JONAS, LOVEST THOU ME MORE THAN THESE? HE SAITH UNTO HIM, YEA, LORD; THOU KNOWEST THAT I LOVE THEE. HE SAITH UNTO HIM, FEED MY LAMBS. *(READ MORE...)*

JOHN 3:16 - FOR GOD SO LOVED THE WORLD, THAT HE GAVE HIS ONLY BEGOTTEN SON, THAT

WHOSOEVER BELIEVETH IN HIM SHOULD NOT PERISH, BUT HAVE EVERLASTING LIFE.

JOHN 3:1-36 - THERE WAS A MAN OF THE PHARISEES, NAMED NICODEMUS, A RULER OF THE JEWS: *(READ MORE...)*

ROMANS 10:13 - FOR WHOSOEVER SHALL CALL UPON THE NAME OF THE LORD SHALL BE SAVED.

GALATIANS 3:26 - FOR YE ARE ALL THE CHILDREN OF GOD BY FAITH IN CHRIST JESUS.

MARK 1:15 - AND SAYING, THE TIME IS FULFILLED, AND THE KINGDOM OF GOD IS AT HAND: REPENT YE, AND BELIEVE THE GOSPEL.

1 CORINTHIANS 15:1-4 - MOREOVER, BRETHREN, I DECLARE UNTO YOU THE GOSPEL WHICH I PREACHED UNTO YOU, WHICH ALSO YE HAVE RECEIVED, AND WHEREIN YE STAND; *(READ MORE...)*

Some of the Books Written by Doc Yeager:

"Living in the Realm of the Miraculous #1."
"I need God Cause I'm Stupid."
"The Miracles of Smith Wigglesworth"
"How Faith Comes 28 WAYS"
"Horrors of Hell, Splendors of Heaven"
"The Coming Great Awakening"
"Sinners in The Hands of an Angry GOD,"
"Brain Parasite Epidemic"
"My JOURNEY to HELL" - illustrated for teenagers
"Divine Revelation of Jesus Christ"
"My Daily Meditations"
"Holy Bible of JESUS CHRIST"
"War In The Heavenlies - (Chronicles of Micah)"
"Living in the Realm of the Miraculous #2."
"My Legal Rights to Witness"
"Why We (MUST) Gather! - 30 Biblical Reasons"
"My Incredible, Supernatural, Divine Experiences"
"Living in the Realm of the Miraculous #3."
"How GOD Leads & Guides! - 20 Ways"
"Weapons of Our Warfare"
"How You Can Be Healed"
"Hell Is For Real"
"Heaven Is For Real"
"God Still Heals"
"God Still Provides"
"God Still Protects"
"God Still Gives Dreams & Visions."
"God Still Does Miracles"
"God Still Gives Prophetic Words"
"God Still Confirms His Word With Power"
"Life Changing Quotes of Smith Wigglesworth"
"The Experts Handbook of Exorcism"

ABOUT THE AUTHOR

Dr. Michael and Kathleen Yeager have served as pastors/apostles, missionaries, evangelists, broadcasters, and authors for over four decades. They flow in the gifts of the Holy Spirit, teaching the Word of God with wonderful signs and miracles following in confirmation of God's Word. Up to 2021 Doc has authored over 150 books. In 1983, they began Jesus is Lord Ministries International, Biglerville, PA 17307.

Websites Connected to Doc Yeager

www.docyeager.com

www.jilmi.org

www.wbntv.org

Made in the USA
Middletown, DE
10 November 2022

14336670R00144